T0290758

BRAUN

Fifty Years of Design and Innovation

ABK 30 wall clock. Design: Dietrich Lubs, 1982.

Bernd Polster

BRAUN

Fifty Years of Design
and Innovation

Edition Axel Menges

© 2009 Edition Axel Menges, Stuttgart / London

ISBN 978-3-936681-35-2

German edition: Braun – 50 Jahre Produkt-innovationen, Cologne 2005

Concept: Bernd Polster and Olaf Meyer

Editorial assistance: Marc Mougeotte and Florian Rühmann

Design: Olaf Meyer

Photography: IF Publication Service, Peter Volkmer, et al.

Coordination: Gerlinde Kress (PR-IMAGE-CI)

Braun Archives: Horst Kaupp (CCS)

English translation: Jennifer Taylor

Copy-editing: Michael Dills

Type setting: Björn Schötten

Prepress: Reinhard Truckenmüller

Printing and binding: Graspo CZ, a.s., Zlín, Czech Republic

About this book

A selection of interconnected forms of text allows each reader to map out his own route through the world of Braun Design.

The functional components of the book:

1 The introductory **Picture Gallery** shows close-ups of exemplary products from the eight product groups in the historical and current Braun product range.

2 The **Company History** names the major figures and describes the concept behind Braun Design. It provides an overview of the main lines pursued in the company's design concepts and innovations from the 1950s to today.

3 The main section of the book is divided according to eight **Product Groups**, each of which is introduced by a short portrait describing the chief lines of development.

4 For each of the product groups, key products – **the Milestones** – are described in detail and placed in the context of the history of Braun Design as well as the general product history.

5 In the long **Picture Series** the development of the product groups can be traced visually, with brief commentaries.

6 A **Product List** in the appendix lists all Braun products, indicating the page numbers of those pictured in this book.

7 **Compact Biographies** present the main figures behind Braun Design.

Flex control 4550 universal cc electric razor.
Design: Roland Ullmann, 1991.

Content

CSV 12 amplifier. Design: Dieter Rams, 1966.

A Design Journey

The first Braun product I ever used was a record player. We threw a party at the home of a classmate whose father was an architect and I kept playing *Stand Up*, the latest LP from Jethro Tull, over and over again. It was 1969. That same year, our art teacher gave a slide presentation on the topic of "good design". Naturally, he was a Braun fan. His observations fell on fertile ground in my case, coming as I did from a family of "free thinkers" who had brought me up to reject all frills. My physics teacher in my senior year met with less success in his efforts to explain to us the principles of electronics using the *Lectron* construction kit. I couldn't afford to buy my first Braun appliance until I went to college. The *370 BVC* flash was a major purchase for me at the time.

Although I was never part of the inner circle of Braun enthusiasts, Braun products accompanied me during every phase of my life. Just how firmly they are anchored in our everyday lives became apparent to me recently when I was watching a play. It began with a dark stage and the beeping of an alarm clock. This was unmistakably the typical Braun sound, an acoustic icon that everyone recognizes. Braun-brand alarm clocks have accompanied me on travels through a host of countries. *Voice control* was something I appreciated from the outset as representing a major step toward the humanization of the wake-up process. When my son discovered this technique at four, I suddenly understood that it also had a playful dimension. Oh yes, and then there's the Braun shaver – I'm on my third one by now – which is always ready and waiting for me in the bathroom.

I made my first personal contact with the Braun company in 2002, when I already had a few books on design under my belt. I was doing a radio show on that firebrand of functionalism, Dieter

KMM 2 Aromatic coffee mill.
Design: Dieter Rams, 1969.

1 The accomplishments of Jo Klatt and Günter Staeffler are especially worthy of mention in this context. In their book *Braun + Design Collection*, published in 1990 and reissued in 1995, compiled with the assistance of dedicated Braun employees – chief among them Claus C. Cobarg and Professor Dieter Rams – they systematically traced the development of Braun products in the period from 1955 to 1995. We would like to thank them for their pioneering efforts, which led to the first comprehensive overview of Braun products.

Rams, and had prevailed upon the expert knowledge of Jo Klatt, who knows the historical Braun products better than almost anyone.[1] Even more importantly, I paid a visit to the company's design department during my research, where my meeting with Peter Schneider, the current director, gave birth to the idea for this book. What followed was a fascinating, ultimately two-year-long journey through the galaxy of Braun design.

No, in this oh-so-famous design department there's no cupboard harbouring a book of secret teachings. Modern product design is instead a constant search. A creative process whose results vitally depend on the people involved, the designers with their individual personalities, strengths and the special credentials they bring to the team. Just as important is the exchange with other departments, with those responsible for development, manufacturing and marketing. This interdisciplinary communication flow, the pre-eminence of which Braun recognized at an early stage and with which the designers therefore have a wealth of experience, is perhaps the true secret of success.

What astounded me was the joy, the enthusiasm with which the designers helped me during my interviews. This is surely based in part on the fact that most of them had never been questioned so intensely about what it is they do. The close-ups of Braun Design that resulted are assembled here for the first time to form an historic trajectory. This book therefore also represents an attempt, in an industry that always has its eye on tomorrow and beyond, to achieve a modicum of balance with what went before.

Bernd Polster

The enlightened radio. Sensibly sized controls, sensibly arranged within a sensible shape. Once the Ulm Academy of Design took charge of Braun radios, the spirit of reason prevailed. The new phono devices, based on Ulm principles, were the heralds of modern product design.

exporter 2 portable receiver. Design: Ulm Academy of Design, 1956.

Typecasting. Braun succeeded again and again in giving shape to what the Bauhaus postulated, but seldom implemented. With its cine film cameras, however, the company managed to establish a product type that the entire industry followed. The colour schemes were likewise seminal: black and silver came to signal perfection, high value and elegance.

Nizo S 480 cine film camera. Design: Robert Oberheim, 1970.

The art of the small format. When technical components hardly require any space anymore, and an ever greater array of functions are packed into increasingly compact appliances, the designer is needed more than ever. Braun's first radio-controlled alarm clock is a prime example of successful miniaturization showcased in a striking form.

DB 10 sl alarm clock. Design: Dietrich Lubs, 1991.

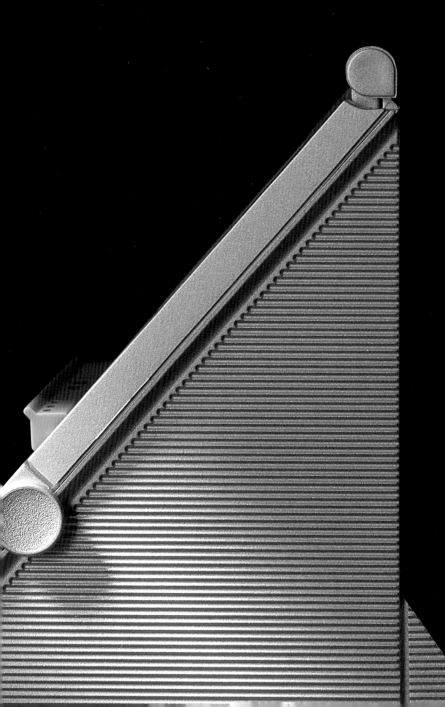

Humane minimalism. In the beginning was the question of what we really need. The answer: a focus on essentials, eliminating superfluous, seldom-used functions, and making keys convex. This is how Braun changed our concept of the pocket calculator.

ET 33 pocket calculator. Design: Dietrich Lubs, Dieter Rams and Ludwig Littmann, 1977.

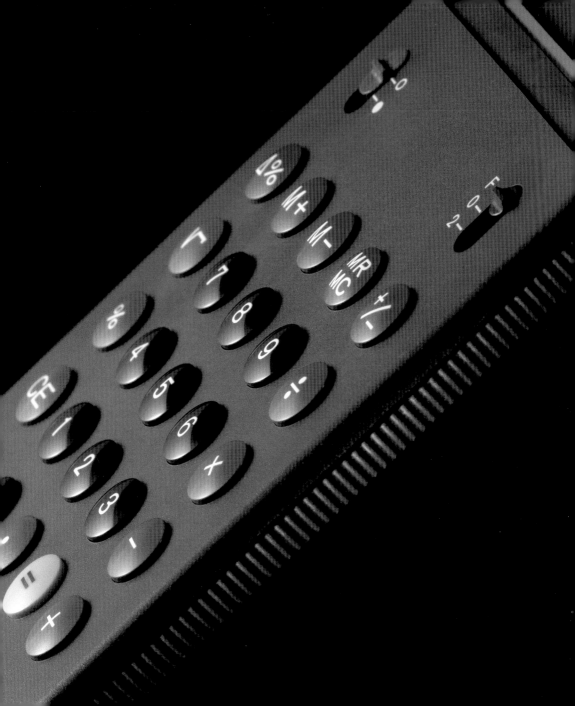

Premiere. The 1960s was an era of upheaval. A dedicated division of the board now took charge of developing new products. The first brainchild produced by this think tank was a table lighter that ignited electromagnetically and took the form of a flat block standing on a narrow edge: tabletop architecture accented with a finely limned grid.

TFG 1 table lighter. Design: Reinhold Weiss, 1966.

Evolution of design. Of all the Braun product groups, the principle of succession can be observed best in the electric razors. Here the design trail leads to continual optimization of the way the device lies in the hand, while adding a variety of extra features, such as a flexible shaver head that hugs every curve. The changing arrangement of grip bumps and ridges is another example of ongoing refinements.

Syncro electric razor. Design: Roland Ullmann, 2001.

Design down to the last millimetre. The effectiveness of rotating bristles is reflected in the new round form of the brush head. This dental innovation was accompanied by others that are less visible: an ergonomically optimized and hence sure-grip handle as well as bristles with rounded ends to protect the gums.

D 17.525 3D Excel electric toothbrush. Design: Peter Hartwein, 2001.

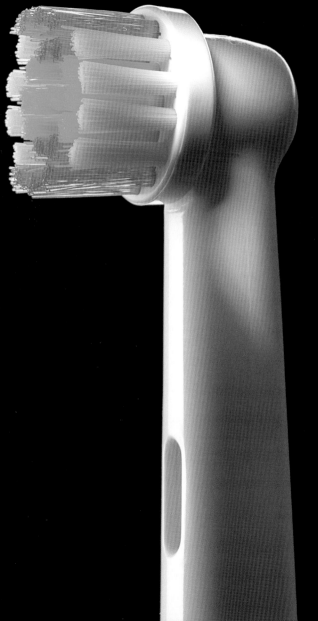

New dimensions. The foot of the hand blender recalls the folds in a skirt, or perhaps a flower. Modern software opens up heretofore unexplored three-dimensional landscapes on the design continent. At the same time, the organically formed body of the product takes on a new coherence while offering some practical advantages: the "skirt" helps keep the blender from tipping when stood on end and prevents splashes.

MR 5000 handblender. Design: Ludwig Littmann, 2001.

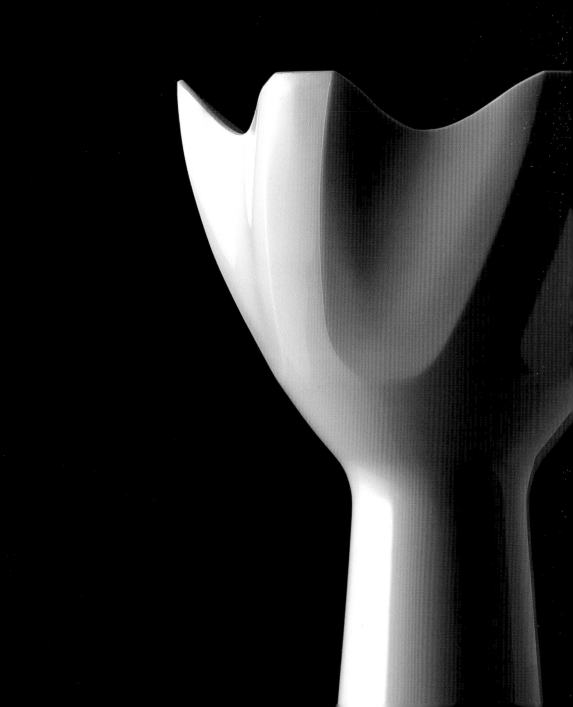

Braun Design History

The rise: 1921–1951

1   Among the forerunners were the British Arts & Crafts movement surrounding William Morris, the Deutscher Werkbund and the Bauhaus, whereby in the latter the English term "design" was not used, just as it was not mentioned in the first two decades of Braun Design. At first the word "Formgestaltung" was used ("the shaping of form") and later "Produktgestaltung" ("the shaping of products"). Cf. here also the author's essay *Design International* in: Bernd Polster (ed.), *Dumont Handbuch Design International,* Cologne 2003, pp. 6-12. Cf. Notes 7 and 59.

Illus: Braun Design Department – in backround Dieter Rams, left Robert Oberheim, right Dietrich Lubs,1965

Braun products have been shown more frequently at exhibitions than those of any other comparable company. Some people find that they reflect basic human values such as authenticity and integrity. For others, they are the very incarnation of German perfectionism. Braun is not merely a trademark; it stands for an all-encompassing concept. For the last five decades, this concept has spawned innovative products with an unprecedented regularity that begs to be explained – especially as the era spanned by the history of Braun design is not exactly one characterized by continuity. The second half of the 20th century witnessed a dramatic change in living conditions. Prosperity and greater ease entered our daily lives, but also widespread disorientation and alienation. It is to the credit of those who set the Braun design project in motion that they were able to counteract this feeling of alienation – which manifested itself to them not least in poorly designed objects of daily use – with a vision of design reform. There had already been attempts made along these lines.[1]

2 The small stapler-like tool, with which workshops and factories could join drive belts, was the company's first sales success.

Illus.:

left above: Erwin Braun with "swing quiff", ca. 1938

right above: Radio-phonograph combination *6740*, precursor of the *SK 4*, 1939

below: Presentation of the first "kitchen machine", product catalogue, 1955

What was new was that a commercial enterprise spearheaded the movement. Also new was the systematic approach, the application of design principles to modern products and the innovative dynamic thus triggered. Finally, the considerable commercial success this design project enjoyed was likewise a revelation. All of this led the company to establish a design department that was not merely an appendage, but rather an active decision-maker in the development of products from the initial idea to realization. This is how Braun and design became synonymous.

At the beginning of the 1950s there was not yet any sign of this striking trajectory. When Max Braun passed away unexpectedly in 1951, it appeared to be not only a personal tragedy but a great misfortune for the business as well. The company founder, who had lived for a long time in Berlin, rising through the ranks from skilled worker to factory owner, was a powerful, charismatic figure and seemed to be virtually irreplaceable. He embodied a type that was not so rare in the Germany of those days – the inventor / entrepreneur. He was a self-made man who, back in the days of the Kaiser, had acquired his electrical engineering and English skills at night school – a restless man of robust stature and Prussian rigour. The company's ascent was founded on his practical product ideas, including an easy-to-handle belt fastener,[2] a mechanical flashlight and, what would later prove a worldwide success, the electric razor with shear blade.

The company's roots go back to the early 1920s, when radios were still, as a rule, homemade and Max Braun finally succeeded in gaining a foothold in the radio industry that was only just emerging at the time, by offering detectors he had developed himself, and other components. Born in East Prussia, he married a woman from Hesse and relocated to that region, first to Wiesbaden and later to Frankfurt. The couple soon had two sons, Erwin and Artur.

Women were now cutting off their old-fashioned braids and sporting chic pageboys instead. In the second half of the 1920s, with the

1921–1951

3 They were labelled "Max Braun, licensed from Carl Sevecke"; the Sevecke company, which Braun ultimately took over, was used for a time as a licensor in order to be permitted to make radios.

4 This is demonstrated by the clean-lined design of his packaging (see e.g. Artur Braun, *Max Brauns Rasierer*, Hamburg 1996, p. 12) as well as by a few sleek early radios. Frankfurt was already a centre of jazz at the time. As early as 1928, the Dr. Hochsche Conservatory was offering a jazz class, probably the world's first formal course of study in that field.

5 The radio-record players, which later became world-famous with the *SK 4*, were still being offered well into the 1980s.

economic engine gradually gearing up, the American Charleston rhythm started bringing the record and radio industries up to speed. The company presented its first radios at the Radio Show in Berlin in 1929.[3] Frankfurt in the meantime had developed into a centre of the "New Building" movement under the architect and City Building Director Ernst May. Similar to the like-minded Bauhaus, it became a magnet for the design avant-garde. This "New Frankfurt" is where Max Braun built his first factory, an angular block with a "functional-ist" flat roof. Industrialist Braun would certainly not have shared the utopian Socialist notions of the municipal reformers, but he did have much in common with their activism and ability to see beyond the provincial pale.[4] Before the Second World War broke out, the medi-um-sized company was already operating foreign subsidiaries in the Netherlands, France, Switzerland and Spain. Braun ultimately also took up production in England and Belgium.

After surviving the world economic crisis largely unscathed, Braun profited, as did others, from the boost given the arms industry by the rise of the Nazis in the 1930s. Only in 1933 did the company begin to sell radios under its own brand name. These included not only a "people's wireless" but also special developments typical of the brand such as portable radios and radio/record player combina-tions[5] that came off the drawing board of the company founder himself. In 1936 the tireless entrepreneur went on a study tour of the USA that would leave a lasting mark on his idea of mass produc-tion. During the war, when the company offered not only radios but also walkie-talkies, both sons – 14 and 18 years old when war broke out – were drafted into the Wehrmacht. Max Braun developed the *manulux*, a hand-driven flashlight. In the blacked-out 1940s the company sold some three million of these, making the flashlight its first true mass-market product. At the end of 1944 the two plants then in operation were bombed and burned nearly to the ground. The city all around had also been transformed into a field of ruins.

Max Braun, now experiencing his second post-war period, didn't doubt that reconstruction would come. Three years after the end of the war, the company was not only able to make radios again, but even to expand its range of products. Electrical household appliances were added, along with a dry shaver – product types that can't belie their American roots, either in concept or appearance.[6] The razor, for which the engineers could draw on their experience manufacturing the manulux, was based on a proprietary invention, the flexible, perforated shear blade. Key cornerstones in the Braun product range had thus been set in place.

Setting the course: 1952–1954

When Erwin Braun brought his friend Fritz Eichler into the company in 1953 as advisor and maker of advertising films, his position didn't even have a name yet. His area of responsibility had to be invented first. An art historian and film director, Eichler had no experience in industry, but did offer the necessary mental distance from the world of merchandise and machines. He now took his place as critical aesthete in the management of a medium-sized factory making electrical devices – with the job of injecting new ideas into the business. This constellation was anything but ordinary in this rock-solid industrial environment, and sent out a powerful message.[7] Some employees didn't know what to make of it.

In 1954 the company signed an agreement with the American firm Ronson, which then introduced Braun's shear blade razors onto the US market.[8] This coup – along with Eichler's creative potential – was one of the major prerequisites for the company's distinctive further development. Artur and Erwin Braun,[9] who had to take on management positions overnight and whose young, slim faces did not at all correspond with the usual image of the entrepreneur, decided to split up the tasks at hand. While Artur was henceforth responsible for engineering and plant improvements, Erwin would take charge of the commercial side of the business and of forward-looking projects. One such project took off in the very first year – the development of a handy electronic camera flash, an

6 This also goes for *Smoothy*, a self-massage device and one of the first products introduced following the death of Max Braun.

7 In chronicles, Eichler is sometimes referred to as "advisor to the company owner" and sometimes as "in charge of all design matters." For a long time, his position was not formally set down. This corresponded in a way to the actual situation; the film director Eichler, who among other things specialized in children's scenes in feature films, and who also painted, had an apartment in the company but maintained his residence in Munich. Perhaps the inner distance expressed therein and the different environments he experienced as a consequence were in fact important prerequisites for his role as the supreme aesthetic authority. Cf. Note 1.

8 The license fee was no less than 10 million dollars. This was the biggest transatlantic deal ever made by a German consumer goods manufacturer.

9 Both sons, who were, so to speak, weaned on the company's problems and triumphs, had business experience. Artur Braun had done an apprenticeship with the company. Erwin Braun founded an instalment payment company after his studies that also worked for Braun. But taking responsibility for the whole company was of course something else again.

10 Hundreds of Frankfurt youth belonged to the "swing youth" scene, which existed in nearly all German cities and met in dance halls. Cf. Bernd Polster, *Swing Heil! Jazz im Nationalsozialismus*, Berlin 1989, p. 143. Cf. illustration p. 31.

11 By the end of the decade the number of radio listeners had swelled to 16 million.

12 While in the post-war period radios still took a variety of forms, the "standard radio" began to dominate the scene after the launch of FM frequencies in 1949; it was naturally part of the Braun product range.

13 In the 1954 issues of the magazine *Die Kunst und das schöne Heim* (Art and the Beautiful Home), which was read by architects and a progressive middle class and in which interiors furnished in the modern style were regularly featured, radios and record players were lacking entirely, as their old-fashioned exteriors simply didn't fit in with the rational Modernist style.

14 Both the Institute for Demoscopy in Allensbach and Emnid did research into "domestic lifestyle sensibilities".

Illus.:

left above: Erwin Braun, ca. 1960

right above: Hobby *Automatic electronic flash*, 1955 product catalogue

left below: *300 de Luxe* electric shaver, 1953

right below: Brochure for *combi DL 5* electric shaver, 1957

innovation that inaugurated the photography division at Braun while bringing in good money.

The company's ambitions went far beyond mere product innovations, however. Erwin, the elder of the two Braun sons, had an artistic temperament and displayed a tendency toward non-conformity even during his school days. As a sixth-former he sported a pompadour hairstyle, the hallmark of "swing youth", who were distinguished by their striving for individualism and their penchant for American Jazz music.[10] The experience of living under a dictatorship during a formative phase of his life may help to explain the origins of the ideals with which Erwin Braun and his comrades-in-arms attempted to fill the gaping moral vacuum of the post-war period. His experiences as an officer in the war and his return to a bombed-out hometown – now the headquarters of the US Army and once again a stronghold of jazz – worked further to put the cherished old values into perspective. Add to this the fact that in the late 1940s Erwin was forced to give up his dream of studying medicine and take up business administration instead at the behest of his father, and we can well understand why the reluctant entrepreneur wanted more than anything to build something new, something meaningful. Thanks to a strict upbringing, he possessed the necessary discipline to make this desire a reality. In photos taken during that era he looks very young, and just as sophisticated and dynamic as contemporaries described him.

The conditions for embarking on a new beginning were excellent. The radio industry was enjoying an unprecedented boom. The new FM radio was the showpiece of parlours everywhere and one of the early status symbols.[11] These dark-brown radios set off with gold ornament all looked amazingly alike.[12] The clunky "music furniture" reflected the spirit of restoration that was washing over Germany.[13] Magazines that preached new forms of living thus usually remained largely radio-free. However, opinion surveys showed that the majority of the population wanted to furnish their homes in the new, modern style.[14] Offering contemporary new appliances matching the modern

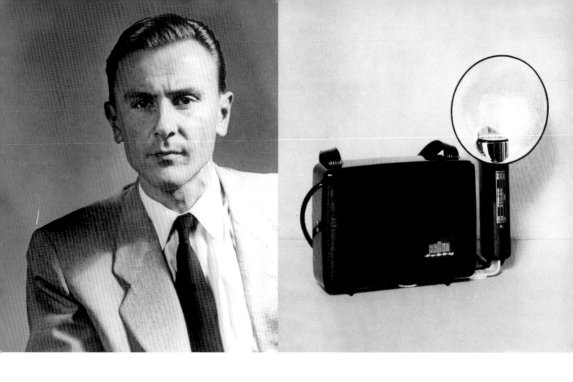

Der Elektro-Trockenrasierer mit kombiniertem Schersystem

15 The company was founded by Hans Knoll, a German, in the USA and managed by Florence Knoll, the daughter of Eliel Saarinen, a Finn by birth and director of the influential Cranbrook Academy of Art. The Scandinavian idiom – which as "Swedish Modern" was moulded in no small part by the Sweden-based Austrian émigré Josef Frank – found its way to Europe via the detour of the USA. In the USA both German and Scandinavian immigrants played a key role in the spread of Scandinavian design. The ties between these two sides ran for example through the Cranbrook Academy and the Knoll company, from which in turn a direct line leads to Charles and Ray Eames.

16 In an interview with the author, Dieter Rams confirmed that Erwin Braun shared this attitude.

17 Erwin Braun also read Never Leave Well Enough Alone – the 1951 bestseller by Franco-American designer Raymond Loewy, which came out in German translation in 1953, promising higher profits through "industrial design".

18 He was made aware of Wagenfeld by his former drawing teacher, with whom he continued to be in contact.

19 The purely utilitarian aesthetic was also a deliberate antithesis to the dramatic emotional symbolism of National Socialism – as it were, a catharsis.

furniture trends and thus claiming for itself a completely unoccupied market niche – this was the basic business plan behind the Braun project. The pragmatic approach of deriving orientation from the latest domestic styles entailed, however, the decision to follow a specific direction in design. Modern styling, at the time defined primarily by the predominant fashions in furniture, was influenced most by the love triangle of Scandinavia, the USA and Germany. This was the force field into which Braun now ventured. The firm's close relationship with the German-American furniture-maker Knoll, which stood for the purist so-called International Style, and whose program likewise betrayed the Scandinavian influence, reflected precisely this constellation.[15] Braun's early collaboration with furniture designers, among them Hans Gugelot, Herbert Hirche and Dieter Rams, showed as well that the cross-fertilization between furniture and the company's own devices was part of the concept.[16]

On the quest for candidates who could design modern devices, the managers at Braun had to leaf through many architecture and furnishing magazines.[17] Finally, Erwin Braun attended a lecture on form held by a certain Wilhelm Wagenfeld in Darmstadt. Wagenfeld had worked at the Bauhaus in Weimar and wanted to see industrial products "purged of individual influence".[18] Erwin Braun was duly impressed and Wagenfeld was awarded the company's first design contract. At the time, Ulm had just launched Germany's first design university. The new institution, conceived as a successor to the Bauhaus, was unusual not only because it would eventually develop into one of the most influential schools of design, but also because it was a "re-education" project, designed to reform Germans who had been blinded by years of dictatorship. Max Bill, the school's first director and, like Wagenfeld, moulded by the Bauhaus, played a major role in spreading the expression "good form". This became the battle call of all those who believed that better, i.e. simpler, products, could lead to a better world.[19]

Ulm and Braun formed a one-of-a-kind conjunction in the history of design, an alliance capable of engendering the kind of radical new ideas that were at the time presumably only imaginable in Germany. The Germans' interrupted links with their own tradition, severed by racial hatred and the traumatic inferno of war, played just as important a part as the opportunity to tie into the tabula rasa mentality inherent in the Bauhaus.[20] The fact that many close collaborators – among them Fritz Eichler – were war comrades speaks for a specifically German convergence of interests.[21] But what was needed to set off the spark was a man from industry capable of weaving together the various strands. Erwin Braun was, one might almost say, the "angry young businessman" who refused to accept the encrusted conditions of the industry, along with stuffy conservatism in general, and apparently also the image of the domineering father, without whose early death the history of the company and of design might have taken quite a different course.

Attempts to put things in a wider context have enjoyed a long tradition in Germany. The Werkbund and Bauhaus already had in common the desire to reconcile art with industry. By way of Ulm, this holism was transferred onto Braun.[22] The efforts to turn the company into a coherent whole ranged from the smallest control button, to the multi-award-winning packaging, all the way to the modern living spaces inhabited by the company's own executives, featuring convenient pass-throughs between rooms – not the only reminiscence of the classical Modernist repertoire with which they surrounded themselves at home.[23] Even the staff health care system, including a canteen serving whole foods, was part of this holistic vision.[24] Rationality, idealism and the courage to experiment were attitudes innate to the Ulm crowd and principles with which Erwin Braun could readily identify. Fritz Eichler provided the contacts, and soon extensive cooperative ventures had been launched. In the following months the company went to work developing new radios and televisions: the Braun and Eichler brothers in Frankfurt, Wilhelm Wagenfeld in Stuttgart, and in Ulm a group orbiting Hans Gugelot, a former assistant to Max Bill. In three places at the same time, people were trying to make the concept of good design a reality.

20 Just how deeply this background influenced the Braun project can be seen in details such as the use of small letters in product names.

21 During the war, Erwin Braun was Fritz Eichler's superior, inspiring him in the course of personal conversations.

22 Several influences complemented and overlapped one another here: the far-reaching cultural background of Fritz Eichler, Erwin Braun's idea of a holistic entrepreneurial philosophy and the grid- and system-steeped Ulm way of doing things.

23 Erwin Braun had Herbert Hirche design a modern home for him; the visionary viewed e.g. a household appliance not merely as machine and product, but also as a tool for promoting good health. Here associations can definitely be found with "life reform", a connection further reinforced by Hirche's later activities in the medical field.

24 The Italian companies Olivetti and ENI took a similarly comprehensive approach. Cf. also the author's remarks in: Bernd Polster, *Super oder Normal? Tankstellen*, Cologne 1996, p. 216.

The Radio-Revolution: 1955–1960

25 Eames, next to Loewy the most famous American designer, was particularly well known for his bent plywood chairs with their three-dimensional curves, key objects of 1950s design that found many emulators in Germany.

26 The arrangements for the visit were facilitated by Ulm.

27 In the October 1955 catalogue, the caption under a picture showing a room outfitted with modern, Scandinavian-looking furniture says: "It is for such rooms that the Ulm Academy of Design has created the housing of the new radios." The text also refers to the "Bauhaus".

28 The various possible combinations were demonstrated in detail in the catalogues of these years; the *SK 1*, too, was to some extent designed as a modular system.

Illus.:

Braun's stand at the Radio Show in Düsseldorf, 1955

1956 the Braun brothers took advantage of an invitation from the Ronson company to take a fact-finding trip through the USA. Erwin Braun, who made the acquaintance of Charles Eames[25] on this occasion, took along Fritz Eichler and Hans Gugelot. The trio – now the core of the design project – roamed through department stores and specialty shops in search of the kind of American design that was so highly prized in Europe in those days – but found little to excite their sensibilities. The return trip via Italy was utilized for a side trip to Olivetti, a glowing example of a successful product and corporate culture.[26] Nonetheless, following their return, the travellers were more than ever convinced that the plans they were hatching were unparalleled anywhere in the world. A few months earlier, a department for "formal design" had been established. In spring 1956 Gerd Alfred Müller, Braun's first full-time designer, the young Dieter Rams and an additional employee moved into their own office. This was the none-too-spacious germ cell of the famed Design Department.

Among industry experts, the name Braun had come to stand for provocative simplicity. With concerted efforts, the company had managed to finish a series of new phonographs in time for the Düsseldorf Radio Show the year before. In addition to the small *SK 1* radio developed in-house and Wagenfeld's portable radio called combi, which stood on their own, a whole series of devices by Hans Gugelot was presented. The world-travelling Porsche driver with a Dutch passport was, like Erwin Braun, an inveterate seeker, and the young entrepreneur felt that he would make a congenial partner. Gugelot's light-coloured maple cases, which matched the "international" style of furnishing and were, like it, influenced in part by Scandinavian design,[27] formed a stark contrast to run-of-the-mill "music furniture". The dimensions of the strictly angular devices were coordinated so that they could be combined, a principle borrowed from the systematic thinking of the Ulm School, and one that would have far-reaching consequences.[28]

38

1955–1960

29 Schmittel had already rationalized the logo in 1952 – the same one that, with slight changes, is still in use today. Under the influence of Otl Aicher and in cooperation with Erwin Braun and Fritz Eichler, his direct superior, he went on to develop Braun's modern corporate identity. In the process – under his management and in parallel with the Design Department – the advertising department responsible for Braun's graphic work emancipated itself more and more.

30 Good examples of this step-by-step method are the progressive variations in the perforated field and in the scale of the pocket radios *T 3* to *T 41* by Dieter Rams.

31 Fritz Eichler, *Die unternehmerische Haltung* (The Entrepreneurial Attitude, lecture 1971), in: *Tatsachen über Braun. Ansichten zum Design* (Facts about Braun. Views on Design), Kronberg 1988, p. 7.

32 Cf. Hans Wichmann, *Mut zum Aufbruch. Erwin Braun 1921–1992* (The Courage to Change), Munich 1998, p. 95.

33 This is demonstrated by its frequent appearance in furnishing how-to guides such as *Die schöne Wohnung* (The Beautiful Home, Munich 1959, p. 6) or *Unsere Wohnung* (Our Home, Gütersloh 1960, p. 199).

Far from incidental to the shockwaves sent by Braun's presentation at the fair – apart from the decision, shortly beforehand, to show only new devices – was the stand designed by Ulm graphic artist Otl Aicher. The airy room made of steel profiles and plywood panels, whose grid system set new standards, stood out sharply from its surroundings. Aicher was the protagonist of a rational and coherent style of communication, an approach that would later be taken up by Wolfgang Schmittel, the company's longstanding Head of Communications.[29] The carefully calibrated, reserved handling of imagery, typography and language – whether in shop windows, advertisements or package and product labelling – became one of the company's key trademarks. In deriving inspiration from Ulm, those involved felt like explorers, like discoverers of a largely unknown continent that would someday be called Design. In the progressive product variations, the gradual process of recognition can sometimes still be traced today.[30] Many an engineer viewed this manner of feeling one's way toward a solution with extreme scepticism. Insisting that Design and Engineering communicate on equal terms – inconceivable without the support of management – was likewise a pioneering achievement. The evolution of this interdisciplinary culture, which also encompassed advertising and marketing, was among the central elements of the Braun project – as Fritz Eichler noted.[31]

The fact that it was possible to "achieve commercial success by withdrawing, by becoming quieter" was something that many found unimaginable, Erwin Braun would later recall.[32] The *SK 4* with its appealing combination of metal, wood and plexiglas, and a brilliantly conceived form that was perceived by some as almost indecent nakedness, delivered proof of this principle, setting off the radio revolution once and for all. This courageous phonographic abstraction, a result of the commuter traffic in the company between Frankfurt and Ulm in which Dieter Rams also had a part, constituted the final departure from the old music furniture.[33] The break with entrenched taboos took place primarily on the aesthetic level. It was a provocative gesture of renunciation that

established a new and ascetic ideal of beauty – as well as representing the antithesis of the style of the German fat cats of the
"economic miracle" era. At the same time, the purism of this
music showcase lent it an aura that no modern device before it
had radiated. The "modular system" already initiated with the *SK 4*
would continue to be pursued until a more recent turning point
arrived with the *studio 2*, the embryo of the modern stereo system.
By 1960 some two dozen new products had been created, a
range that, despite its heterogeneity, represented in Fritz Eichler's
words "design in the spirit of enlightenment".[34] A recurring feature
was the right angle, one of the central symbols of architectural
Modernism. The stacked box thus became the basic form for
phonograph housings. It gave a technical, rational, masculine
impression. But the cube also provided the model for other, in
some cases groundbreaking, designs, such as the pocket radios,
e.g. the *T 41*, the *F 60* electronic flash and the *H 1* heater by
Dieter Rams, or the *HF 1* television by Herbert Hirche, all of them
unprecedented monoliths in programmatic grey.

34 in: Maribel Königer, *Küchengerät des 20. Jahrhunderts* (20th-Century Kitchen Appliances), Munich 1994, p. 51.

The first grey phonograph, the radio-record player combo *studio 1*
by Hans Gugelot and Herbert Lindinger, had a slanted front and
rounded corners. The dominance of the 90-degree angle was
hence not omnipresent, as demonstrated also by Wagenfeld's
combi portable radio and the company's first slide projector, *PA 1*.
This was even more apparent in the food processor *KM 3* and the
SM 3 shaver, two products designed by Gerd Alfred Müller. Both of
these designs – which were among the most enduring and went on
to become the models for their genres – were based on concepts
that still apply today and are notable for their soft silhouettes and
complex proportions. Müller was thus the pioneer of a softer line in
Braun Design. His flowing forms, whose haptic advantages can
readily be grasped, have Scandinavian predecessors. In the 1950s,
"organically" shaped easy chairs by Bruno Mathsson and Finn Juhl,
or an artistic vase by Tapio Wirkkala, were the measure of all things
when it came to stylish furnishings. Their "natural" style often had
ergonomic advantages and evoked expressiveness, emotion, femi-

1955–1960

35 Designers from Scandinavia such as Alvar Aalto, Josef Frank and Bruno Mathsson had already created a sensation before the Second World War with their "organic" designs, i.e. at a time when Germany had veered away from the international discourse. In the early 1950s it was Finnish artists such as Tapio Wirkkala and a whole generation of Danish furniture designers who were responsible for the ascendancy of the naturalist topos, among them Nana Ditzel, Finn Juhl and Arne Jacobsen. The Swede Sigvard Bernadotte was among the first to apply the Nordic style to industrial products, including radios and kitchen appliances. In America, Charles Eames, Ray Eames and Eero Saarinen were famed for their curvy three-dimensionally moulded seating shells. Some Italians were also pioneers of the soft line, such as Carlo Mollino, Flaminio Bertoni, who worked for Citroën, and Olivetti's in-house designer Marcello Nizzoli.

36 The pavilion was designed by Egon Eiermann and Sep Ruf.

37 This was the title of a talk he held in 1959 at the opening of a sales office in Berlin. Published in: Hans Wichmann, *Mut zum Aufbruch. Erwin Braun 1921-1992*, Munich 1998, p. 95.

Illus.:

above: Braun ad with jazz motif (photo and graphic by Wolfgang Schmittel), 1961
below: Interior with *HM 6* music chest and furniture by Herbert Hirche, product catalogue ca. 1960

ninity. This trend rippled out along the transatlantic crosscurrents already mentioned.[35] Next to the stock of forms borrowed from classical Modernism and the dissecting/analytical method courtesy of Ulm, these style elements represented the third, organic line that was in evidence from the very beginning of Braun Design.

Product development was flanked by an advertising campaign that was no less innovative. It would turn Braun into a key player in a cultural sea change. One decisive event during this period was the Interbau trade fair in West Berlin. In 1957 the Hansa Quarter rose up on the fairgrounds, a series of housing blocks made of concrete, glass and steel, designed by architects from 17 countries. The Cold War was on, and this spectacular project launched by the island city was a demonstration of the supremacy of Western culture. Braun was now a part of it, as evidenced by the fact that Fritz Eichler managed to stock the 60 or so model apartments almost exclusively with the company's appliances. This striking demonstration of the international architectural elite's preference for Braun-brand products naturally raised awareness of the company outside Germany, as did the awards that soon followed at the Milan Triennial, at that time a reliable trend barometer. It was almost a foregone conclusion that the company would present an extensive range of products – 16 – at the Brussels World Exhibition in 1958, where, just three decades after Barcelona, the German pavilion demonstrated that sober minimalism had once again become the national style.[36] Braun was one of the messengers for the better Germany.

Erwin Braun did not shy away from reflecting on "art and commerce",[37] those two distinct worlds between which he tried to mediate. He was a rare example of an entrepreneur who gathered around him a motley assortment of intellectuals and artists, almost like a Renaissance prince. His contacts included such disparate figures as the doctor and globetrotter Hans Jenny, philosopher Ludwig Marcuse and artist Arnold Bode, founder of the *documenta* art exhibition, who later organized for Braun the photography

42

BRAUN

Das Mikrofon ist unbestechlich.
Es registriert jeden Ton, jedes Geräusch,
jeden Atemzug. Nichts vom typischen
Klangbild des Jazz geht verloren.

Von Braun-Geräten wiedergegeben, bleibt
dieses Klangbild erhalten - unverfälscht,
wie es Jazzkenner fordern. Die präzise Technik
und die Form dieser Geräte sind
Ausdruck der Gegenwart - wie der Jazz.

38 In German: *Jazz hören – Jazz sehen*.
The photos were the work of Wolfgang
Schmittel, director of the Advertising
Department and a passionate photogra-
pher of the jazz scene.

39 In addition to Braun and Rosenthal,
the Knoll, Rasch and WMF companies
were also members.

exhibition *Hearing Jazz – Seeing Jazz*, a multimedia event at a
Frankfurt gallery.[38] It's hard to imagine anything more avant-garde.
The sounds of the American ghetto, in the 1950s still often demo-
nized as "degenerate", were the chosen music of the Design
Department. The protagonists of jazz represented values the
designers could readily relate to in their own work – perfect per-
formances, dedication and freedom from conventional constraints.

A close friendship united Erwin Braun with another high-profile
manufacturer: Philip Rosenthal, likewise a junior executive, visionary and enthusiast for "good form", naturally also due to its high
added-value quotient. One of the projects undertaken by the two
unorthodox entrepreneurs was the Verbundkreis (Composite Circle),
an initiative launched by design-conscious companies[39] whose
activities the two often discussed, if possible on hikes through the
Taunus hills. These talks may have given rise to the idea for the
exhibition *form, farbe, fertigung* (form, colour, fabrication), which
toured Germany for three years starting in 1956, confronting a
quarter of a million visitors with exemplary design. In the five years
following Braun's spectacular trade fair showing in Düsseldorf, the
number of employees had almost doubled, to more than 3,000.
Revenues were up accordingly – from around 50 to over 100 million
marks. In the course of this expansion the design team also grew.
Gerd Alfred Müller's departure was offset by the arrival of Robert
Oberheim, Richard Fischer and Reinhold Weiss. The two latter men
were the first Ulm graduates to join the department.

Grand Design: 1961–1967

When US President John F. Kennedy held a speech at St. Paul's
Church in Frankfurt during his triumphant tour of Germany in sum-
mer 1963, a small white device was perched before him on the
podium, providing a refreshing breeze. This compact wind machine
was the new *HL 1* desktop fan from Braun, a product type that
hadn't even existed until then. *HL 1* was designed by Reinhold

Weiss, who knew just how to strikingly express the inner workings of an appliance in its structure[40] – in this case in the cylindrically arranged, very effective fan blades and cylindrical motor. The same can be said for the first Braun toaster, *HT 1*, the inaugural black-and-silver appliance, which would be emulated throughout the industry. Ulm-educated Weiss, who along with Richard Fischer introduced the practice of making physical models, supplemented the numerous product innovations of the early 1960s with a whole series of his own designs. As a result, he left his signature on our image of what good design should look like, in particular in the new areas just being developed at the time. His analytical working methods and self-assured handling of spatial geometry predestined him to be a designer of product premieres. From Weiss's drawing board came Braun's first hairdryer, the first electric kettle, the first coffee mill, the first electric grill and the first lighter.

Men now wore their hair in crew-cuts like the astronauts, television went colour and people believed they could control car traffic by computer. This epoch of even more rapid change, in which Europe imported the American model of prosperity along with the requisite appliances, opened up a wide field of endeavour for Braun's design specialists. Whether in the form of a home solarium, electric toothbrush, electric skillet, film camera, dishwasher, freezer or hi-fi system – featuring sound resonating through extremely flat "electrostatic" speakers or via headphones – electric-powered progress, preferably sporting the Braun logo, now penetrated into all spheres of life. By now Erwin Braun was working in tandem with Hans Gugelot on a concept he would later dub "Grand Design".[41] The idea was to improve the technical quality of the products even further, and to tap markets that in some cases had to be created first. The quality of these high-class products would be appealingly expressed in their elegant good looks. A new Executive Board portfolio was set up expressly for "new products". Products were now labelled using modern screen printing. And the models, which now became increasingly important to the development process, took on a more professional profile. But the ascent from the avant-garde

40 Just how forward-looking this device was is demonstrated by the fact that it was re-issued in 1981 as *HL 70*.

41 In order to devote more attention to new developments, Erwin Braun had switched to the Supervisory Board of what was now a publicly traded company. Cf. Hans Wichmann, *Mut zum Aufbruch. Erwin Braun*, Munich 1998, p. 127.

42 Hans Gugelot's early Braun devices and Herbert Lindinger's essay on the "modular system", which he wrote while with the company, formed the basis for these developments. That these ideas were later implemented by Dieter Rams was attributable in part to Fritz Eichler's conviction that design should move closer to engineering; Rams also expressed this interpretation to the author in an interview. Eichler and Rams personally confirmed Lindinger's authorship in a conversation at the time.

43 In particular, amplifiers, record players and speaker "boxes" became prestige objects, the key features being the number of watts and a tone arm that rested as lightly as possible in the grooves.

44 Herbert Lindinger claims that the idea of hanging hi-fi components on the wall was his brainchild.

Illus.:

above: Shop window with products and displays by Braun, 1963

left below: Advertising card with *PCS 4* record player, 1961

right below: Advertising motif with *D 20* slide projector, 1965

underground jazz club to the showy concert hall called for a considerable amount of capital. And despite revenues that were rising in leaps and bounds – in 1965 the 200-million mark was exceeded – regular income was just not sufficient to cover the needed investments. The logical reaction was to go public.

The rapidly evolving phono division played a key role in the innovation plans. *Audio 1* heralded a turning point: the compact system outfitted with exactly 27 transistors ushered in the hi-fi age at Braun. Under the watchful eye of Dieter Rams, who had by then been promoted to Department Head, the emancipation of the stereo system unfolded, to which Braun would lend a technoid face for decades to come. Just as the formal inventors of the 1920s had dissected bourgeois furniture, now audio furniture was systematically pulled apart piece by piece. And just as with the forefathers of Modernism, here too the authorship circumstances behind the liberation movement would sometimes remain blurred.[42] Devices like the *PS 1000* record player or *TG 60* tape player, carefully worked out to the last detail, were small masterpieces in precision engineering and electronics. Details like a bent tone arm or visible pinch roller impressively celebrated this triumph of technology. In iconic elements of this kind it also became clear that form by no means always slavishly followed function. Much of the almost cult-like veneration of Braun, an attitude that still persists today, had its origins in the metamorphosis of the phonograph into an exquisite high-tech object.[43] It is of course not without irony that this process took place in the course of a radical rationalization movement. A technically complex hanging system, with which the devices could be arranged on the wall like artworks, likewise points in this direction.[44]

The mounting frames, adapted to the various device types and designed for stacking, made the "system" even more variable. The perfect, endlessly combinable and self-contained hi-fi universe aimed at here is perhaps the most tangible expression of two basic Braun principles: the systematic approach to design as

Stereo Plattenspieler PCS 4

Viertouren-Plattenspieler für Stereo-
und Normalplatten aller handelsüblichen
Größen. Reibradantrieb mit guter Rumpel-
dämpfung. Geringes, justierbares Auflage-
gewicht. Die halbautomatische Tonarm-
aufsetzhilfe erleichtert die Handhabung
und schont Saphire und Schallplatten.

BRAUN

45 This fan community meets at Braun exchanges organized regularly by Jo Klatt, editor of the Braun collectors' magazine *Design + Design* (formerly *Der Braunsammler*).

46 German title: *Grundregeln für gutes Hören*, published in 1963, written by Dieter Skerutsch. Similar brochures were brought out later, such as *Lebendiger Klang* (Living Sound, autumn 1972).

47 The exhibition *Braun – Das Gesicht einer Firma* (Braun – the Face of a Company) was held starting in 1966 in various German cities, in Japan, in Spain and in Czechoslovakia.

taught in Ulm, and Erwin Braun's vision of the company as a total work of art. In particular the legendary hi-fi division, which still has its own devoted fan club,[45] shows, however, that the utopia-made-real was doomed to remain a compromise. This is evident from the sometimes confusing naming of the products, which is difficult even for insiders to understand. But in many cases the company was simply ahead of its time. Take for example the many attempts, none of which was consistently realized, to incorporate television in the media totality.

Advances in phono and TV technology offered the opportunity for renewed educational activities. Between 1962 and 1966 Braun published six hi-fi brochures with titles like *Basic Rules for Good Hearing*.[46] These usually informed customers and retailers in detail about the benefits of the new sound, and naturally also about the new options for combining the various Braun "building blocks". The company soon set up its own "Information Centres" in four German cities, outfitted with Knoll-brand furniture, where regular "record album concerts" were held. The successful public relations work was stepped up even further, publicizing the activities of the Verbundkreis manufacturers' association and mounting a veritable exhibition marathon, with many shows now taking place abroad.[47] In New York the reopened Museum of Modern Art showed nearly the complete Braun product range in 1964, the first monographic exhibition for the brand. Braun products were also on view at the third *documenta* and the young design team even won the *Berlin Art Award*. These were golden days for Braun's tête-à-tête with the world of culture and museums.

In 1965 a trade fair showcasing the achievements of German industry was held in London under the programmatic title *Gute Form* (Good Form). Braun was of course in strong evidence, but the star of the show was a sports car: the new Porsche *911* by Ferdinand "Butzi" Porsche, also a junior boss and former Ulm student. Ten years after Braun's design about-face, what was commonly known as functionalism had become widespread, albeit not always on the highest aesthetic level.[48] Braun had lost its unique standing. In order to create a new profile for itself, innovations were of the essence. That same year, Braun AG presented its products at the Stuttgart Radio Show, with the biggest stand in the company's history. Among the most popular attractions were two products of "Grand Design": *studio 1000*, by far the best hi-fi system developed up until then, which was presented in a soundproof room, and the portable multifrequency radio *T 1000*, a world first for whose technical development no expense had been spared. With its black-and-silver contrast, this refined portable radio imitated a much smaller product to which the company's future would belong: the *sixtant* electric razor launched the year before, one of the first mass products of the Braun design age. Matte black and matte silver, a highly significant colour combination inaugurated by Hans Gugelot, spelled a departure from the principle of emotional neutrality. The secret model for the *sixtant* was the *Leica*, the miniature camera that set a world standard, promoting the black-and-silver colour scheme and nurturing Germany's legendary reputation for precision.[49] All of this now succeeded as well with the *sixtant*, whose super-fine shear blade took dry shaving to a new level. This was a device that made innovation visible on the outside, while solving one of the most knotty design problems: setting a new price point. The new shaver could be sold for much more than all competing products.

Another milestone of "Grand Design" was the *Nizo S 8* Super 8 camera, designed by Robert Oberheim. Here the black-and-silver colour scheme appeared again, now lending an elegant touch while also signalling perfection and high value. The acquisition of the Niezoldi & Krämer company in Munich, a leading camera-maker, was part of Erwin Braun's expansion plans, just like the introduction of a further product type: lighters. Modern, assertive advertising methods were another element of the forward-looking strategy. Prominent figures from the worlds of sports, politics and the aristocracy were increasingly depicted using Braun products. The product placement with President Kennedy for example was of course no

48 In 1965, the year of the exhibition, *Die Unwirtlichkeit unserer Städte* (The Inhospitality of the Modern City) by Alexander Mitscherlich came out, in which the "monotony of high-rises" and the principle of the "rigid addition" were also lamented. "Functionalism" was being re-examined.

49 The parallels between the two legendary products can be seen in additional aspects as well. In both cases it's a matter of an image that is being created and whose chief criterion is sharpness.

50 Management was aware of this. The discontinuation of the first product lines, such as pocket radios and "world receivers" were early warning signs.

51 These included Bosch, Siemens, Canon in Japan and Gillette in the USA.

Illus.:

above: Hi-fi brochures, 1963 and 1972

below: Hi-fi wall system *TS 45* with *Bertoia* wire armchair, 1964 advertising motif

accident. Within just a few years, Braun had grown to become a global corporation with a far-flung network of activities and holdings. But this high-flying ascendancy harboured certain risks. The dramatically growing costs of the investments required for diversification and innovation once again exceeded the available resources. This was joined by the threatening rise of Japanese industry, which with one of its key strengths, electronics, created direct competition for Braun.[50] Faced with a choice of either giving up cost-intensive product lines such as phonographs or finding deep-pocketed investors for the business, the Braun brothers initiated contacts with various major corporate groups.[51] At the end of 1967 the news that the Gillette Company in America had become majority shareholder hit like a bomb. And when the Braun brothers also left the company, the break with the past was complete.

Upheaval: 1968–1974

With the company's relocation to the idyllic Taunus village of Kronberg in 1967, the traditional Frankfurt location was ceded bit by bit. This was not the only sign that made the takeover by Gillette appear to be a major caesura. The closure of the Ulm Academy of Design just one year later was another seemingly bleak omen. The end of the working relationship between Erwin Braun and Hans Gugelot, who had passed away two years earlier, made way for a completely new set of circumstances. The most important communication pathway now ran between Kronberg and Gillette headquarters in Boston. There, no particularly remarkable design achievements had been forthcoming thus far. Some Braun employees, seeing an era drawing to an end, left the company. At the time of the takeover Braun had 5,700 staff members, and Gillette about three times as many. Although Braun was now reaping revenues to the tune of 280 million marks, sales by the American parent company were six times that high. Just half a decade later, the Braun Group was already up to 700 million marks, a result in part of stepping up advertising and giving it a more international scope.

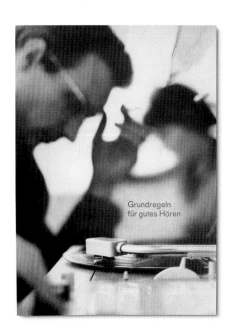

Grundregeln
für gutes Hören

HiFi Stereo Brevier

Informationen und Ratschläge zur
originalgetreuen Musikwiedergabe

1968–1974

52 *Lebendiger Klang. Braun High-Fidelity*, autumn 1972, p. 12.

Despite all misgivings, life under the wing of Gillette turned out to be better than expected. Chairman Vincent Ziegler kept his promise of not thinning out the product range, and even expanded it further. The man from Boston wanted to learn something from the Germans. Moreover, not only Fritz Eichler – who was still in charge of design – but the entire Executive Board remained in office.

Dieter Rams' deputy, Reinhold Weiss, departed from the company, leaving Rams as the contact for the Americans in design matters. The Design Department was likewise undergoing changes. The Braun Prize set up by Erwin Braun turned out to be an effective recruiting tool, even though that was not the original intention. The very first winners, Masanori Umeda and Florian Seiffert, would later rise to international fame. Seiffert was hired on the spot. In the five years following the takeover, seven new designers joined the team. Four of them – Peter Hartwein, Roland Ullmann, Ludwig Littman and Peter Schneider, today's Head of Design – were still active over three decades later, when Braun Design celebrated its 50th anniversary. This unusually longstanding staff, representing an unparalleled accumulation of specialized expertise, is one of the main reasons for the company's success over such an incredibly long period.

At the end of the 1960s the first slight dip in the economy put an end to the naive notion of eternal boom. Signs of change were in evidence everywhere – the kind of change that swept along everything– in its wake. The "1968" generation brought together not only Vietnam demonstrations and the sexual revolution, Karl Marx and Coca-Cola, but also shag rugs and the hi-fi cult under its floppy-brimmed hat. Echoing out of Braun speakers were the tunes of the times, the songs of the Beatles and the other "mop-tops". In the Design Department heads sported hair longer than ever before. With all this individualism afoot, it was clear that design could no longer be addressed to a specific, minority clientele. Instead, the emphasis was placed on creating "Braun appliances to fit every domestic lifestyle".[52] New possibilities were offered by the changeover from duroplast to thermoplast, new higher-quality but less expensive plastics. Pop and plastics began a love affair. The general intoxication with freedom was manifested in this endlessly malleable material. Scandinavian and Italian designers in particular created sculptured plastic chairs – usually in the preferred "neon colours" of the time. These not only looked unconventional; the sitter could also assume a variety of unorthodox positions. Pop design, which was already seeping into Germany daily life – for instance with Helmut Bätzner's *Bofinger Chair* or the *Bulb* table lamp by Ingo Maurer – also found its way to Braun's door. An early example is the *stab B* shaver by Richard Fischer, and also the *domino* lighter by Dieter Rams, whose *audio 308* compact stereo system represented the attempt to satisfy the taste of the young, music-crazed generation through the medium of plastic. Signal colours were used for the keys. The principles dictating their arrangement, familiar ever since the days of the *SK 4*, now took off in utterly new directions, forming a powerful symbol of the broad range of functionality offered by the new devices.

Luigi Colani's spherical kitchen caused a sensation at the Cologne Furniture Fair of 1968. But a real revolution in cooking was launched just a few years later by Florian Seiffert's *Aromaster KF 20* coffee maker – a completely new type of appliance that combined an impressive structural stringency with an elegant look. Seiffert, who was also responsible for some unusual electric razors and all their practical accessories, conceived a design that melded two lines of Braun Design: the analytical Ulm school and the gentle organic idiom. Both tendencies found expression in the *KF 20*, whose resemblance to Gerd Alfred Müller's *KM 3* food processor is surely not incidental, and which was manufactured in a series of bright and cheerful colours typical of the times.[53] The same year as the *KF 20*, the *F 022 vario* flash also came on the market, a utilitarian sculpture by Robert Oberheim that evinced very similar qualities. It's no wonder that even today's flash attachments still orient themselves on this device with its matte black colour. Two years earlier, Oberheim had already presented a virtuoso, definitive

53 These colours could also be found in e.g. the stab *B 1* and stab *B 2* shavers (1965 and 1966, both by Richard Fischer), cassette, ladyshaver and under-armshaver (1970, 1971 and 1972, all by Florian Seiffert), in the diskus flashlight (1970, Hans Gugelot) as well as the *HLD 4* hair dryer and *domino* lighter (both 1970, both Dieter Rams).

1968–1974

54 The transparent, inflatable *Blow* easy chair was produced by Zanotto from 1967; Braun's excursion into pneumatics began in 1971.

55 In 1963 Philips had introduced the "Compact-Cassette", which went into industrial production two years later. The first Braun cassette recorder was made in 1975 (five years after the new system had attained hi-fi quality). The market for professional reel-to-reel players that still existed for some time was served largely by other manufacturers, among them Revox and Teac.

56 Following the *Ela* phonograph system and the Studio flash units, Braun thus once again had to abort an attempt to establish itself in the professional segment; marketing proved difficult for this type of complex system.

57 Phono equipment makers such as Bang&Olufsen, Brionvega and Wega established themselves in Braun's slipstream as design-oriented high-end brands. In 1970 Sony set up shop in Germany, another rival that in many cases followed in Braun's footsteps.

58 Canton was created in 1970 as a result of the ultimately successful idea of offering high-quality speakers as a stand-alone product for use with systems from other manufacturers.

Illus.:

Ad for *regie 510* receiver, 1972

design in the *D 300* projector, a further example of the space-dominating, analytical line in Braun design. It was the first completely black device, setting off more than one wave of imitators. At Braun, products in almost all areas now became "black boxes" – a homemade alternative program to the fashionable pop colours that turned out to be here for good. Two years later, with the *regie 510* receiver, the first phono devices also donned the new and respectable evening dress. Numerous others followed. Following grey, silver and black-and-silver, Braun once again set a colour trend that still reverberates today.

New product genres were conquered, including the first clock, the *phase 1* alarm clock, the first hairstyling set, *HLD 5*, and the first hairdryer with blow-up hood, *Astronette*, a highly practical application of the same principle upon with the much more famous *Blow* armchair was based, and a segment in which Braun was market leader.[54] At design competitions, the company continued to enjoy the accustomed success. At the premiere of the Federal Award for Good Form in 1968, four of the seven award-winning products bore the Braun logo. In 1974 the *TG 1000* reel-to-reel tape player and the *Tandem* slide projector were presented, two extremely ambitious products, but both the last of their kind. Ever since the introduction of the cassette recorder, the *TG 1000* was a member of a dying breed.[55] And the *Tandem* projector system was unable to make a place for itself on the market although, or perhaps because, it represented the ultimate in "multivision" technology.[56] On markets in which one technical advance was following hot on the heels of the last one, it was impossible for the company to continue living by its own maxim of being a pioneer on all fronts. This was even more the case now that other manufacturers were scaling the walls of former Braun strongholds, even on the company's very own terrain of felicitous design.[57]

Just how directly the original continued to exert its influence on this subsequent generation can be seen in the example of speaker manufacturer Canton, founded by former Braun employees.[58]

54

Wiedergabequalität an den Grenzen absoluter Perfektion.

Der neue Receiver von Braun.

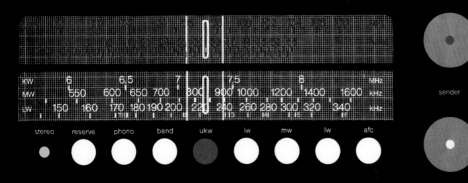

59 The term had been much discussed at the Academy of Design in Ulm. In the body text of Braun catalogues the word "design" was now used side by side with the German term "Gestaltung", occasionally also in the combination "Braun Design" (see e.g. *Lebendiger Klang. Braun High Fidelity*, 1972, p.12).

60 Even when the so-called "8-degree system" was introduced, the word "design" was still not in evidence.

61 There followed a paper in which ten of the principles underlying Braun Design were explained, which was publicized to such an extent that it took on the quality almost of a manifesto. At around the same time there was a series of advertisements called "Überlegungen zum Design" (Thoughts on Design), each of which explained the design of a particular device (published in the magazine *Form*). Cf. Note 71.

62 In "author design", or "designer branding", the name of the designer becomes part of the sales pitch. Memphis, a team of international top designers, was one example of this trend.

63 François Burkhardt and Inez Franksen, Design: *Dieter Rams &*, Berlin 1981; the book was the catalogue for an exhibition at the International Design Centre (IDZ) in Berlin.

64 Reinhold Weiss managed to persuade the publisher to paste his name over false attributions in about half a dozen captions.

Developments like this made it seem all the more urgent for the company to concentrate on its own strengths. Around 1970 the English word "design" began to appear now and again in Braun catalogues – a term that was familiar in expert circles but had not yet come into common usage.[59] In a company where Germans and Americans had to communicate with each other, the use of this Anglicism is hardly surprising. But back then it was not part of the general German vocabulary, which is why the English word was not used for advertising purposes.[60] In the 1972/73 Annual Report, "Braun Design" appeared as a headline for the first time.[61] Thus did this evocative concept, so familiar to us today, enter everyday parlance at the company, where – coupled with the brand name to create a catch phrase – it developed into a crystallization of the corporate identity.

Correcting the course: 1975–1984

In 1981 Dieter Rams took up a post as professor at the Hamburg University of Fine Arts. Recruiting someone with an industry background for an art department was unusual at that time, especially as the anti-capitalist agitation of the late 1960s was still very much in evidence in the ivory tower. That same year, a group called Memphis in Milan called for an end to all design conventions. This was the next revolt, and one that was also linked to the emergence of the high-profile designer.[62] Up until that time, the question as to who conceived the various Braun products had hardly been of interest. Shortly before he began teaching, a book had been published about Dieter Rams,[63] an early designer biography, which was far more than a mere chronicle of his work. In the book, products – only some of which were authored by Rams – were attributed to individual designers. This provoked objections in some cases.[64] All of this can be viewed as part of a process of self-reassurance, since with the departure of Fritz Eichler the last of the firm's pioneering generation was now no longer active.

With the two oil crises of the 1970s, a pessimistic mood set in. Environmental and nuclear anxieties were becoming widespread. Plastic, just yesterday the material of the future, was suddenly a symbol of waste. Braun's reaction was to reduce its range of colours, but since asceticism had always been a key principle there anyway, the new savings mentality fell on fertile ground. In the second half of the decade, the various product lines were given a different weighting. Small products came to the fore, including the conceptually appealing designs of the *PGC 1000* compact hairdryer by Heinz Ulrich Haase and the first oral hygiene centre, *OC 3* by Peter Hartwein, which once again sowed the seed for an entire new product genre. The introduction of the first curling iron and the first clothes iron also took place in this phase. The range of products that still prevails today was taking shape. The area that saw the most growth was clocks. Dietrich Lubs had demonstrated his talent with an alarm clock called *functional*, part of the product pool representing the expressive lineage in Braun design.[65] A whole series of Lubs alarm clocks followed, along with wall clocks and watches that were reduced to the essentials and yet unmistakably Braun, conferring a high-profile image on the brand. Black as a dominant colour contributed to this success. This can also be said of the pocket calculator, a novelty that Lubs developed with Dieter Rams and Ludwig Littmann. In this masterpiece of visual understatement, Braun qualities were reduced to jacket-pocket size.

Among the more ambitious developments in this period was the *micron plus* shaver, with which Roland Ullmann quite literally brought an important innovation into high relief. The field of bumps that ensures a secure grip was a rousing prelude to the new field of hard-and-soft technology, i.e. the permanent fusing of soft plastics onto hard surfaces. This technique, which Ullmann would play a number of variations on in the next generation of shavers, marked the entry into new and as yet unimaginable dimensions of design. This is when individual designers began to focus their attention on specific product lines: Ullmann for shavers, Haase for hair care, Lubs for clocks, Oberheim for flash units, Schneider for film cameras and external

65 This can also be said of the *KM 3* food processor, the *Aromaster KF 20* coffee maker and the *F 022* flash.

57

1975–1984

66 The ads emphasized that this neutral-looking system harmonized with a wide variety of furnishing styles (which is why it was presented in various furniture stores, including IKEA), a statement reflecting not only the change in Braun's target groups, but also the increasing individualization and segmentation of society.

67 Bosch, the company that had once refused Erwin Braun's offer, now seized the opportunity.

68 Braun's erstwhile core business was carried on until 1990 by the Gillette subsidiary Analog & Digital Systems (ads).

69 The only companies that still maintain relative independence today are German manufacturers Metz and Loewe.

Illus.:

above: Steps in the development of the hard/soft technology – *micron plus* universal electric razor, 1978

left below: Catalogue for Braun's last hi-fi system, 1990

right below: Catalogue for *TV 3* television, 1986

contracts, Hartwein for electric toothbrushes, Kahlcke and Littmann for household appliances, Hartwein and Rams for hi-fi systems, Rams for lighters. This division of responsibilities – one that was not always strictly observed – was geared to the promotion of specialized skills. Another strength was the area of model building, which developed further under the leadership of Klaus Zimmermann and was at the time still the only way to visualize complex objects.

Under the newly installed structures, the early 1980s witnessed an incredible sequence of technical and design milestones. In the conception of the new products, the virtue of reserve once again played a role that should not be underestimated, such as in the sound film camera *Nizo Integral* by Peter Schneider or the *atelier* hi-fi system by Peter Hartwein. These were both the non-plus-ultra in their respective segments and exceptional examples of abstraction. While the *Integral* compressed all controls concisely in a single line, *atelier* overcame the era of rows of buttons by banning all less-important functions along with their cables from the device surface.[66] A bestseller in the early 1980s was the *KF 40* coffee maker, with which Hartwig Kahlcke created a type that would endure for two decades. Braun had now grown to become one of the leading manufacturers of small electronics, especially shavers, which replaced the hi-fi sector as the company's core business. "Successfully carrying on this expansion in devices for daily use means that we must concentrate our resources", was how the company's new focus was phrased in a 1981 press release. What sounds like a sober appraisal of the state of affairs was also an announcement of sorts. Soon to follow was the sale of the film and photography division.[67] Thereafter came the spin-off of the hi-fi segment,[68] a measure that in retrospect revealed itself to be the beginning of the end of this erstwhile Braun forte. The double retreat, with which Gillette once again shifted focuses, reflected the priorities of the Americans, but also the growing pressure coming from the Far East, where technology was rushing on ahead, ultimately causing the demise of the German photography and phonograph industry.[69] Dieter Rams fought hard to protect the jobs in his department from the effects of the painful loss of what were once the

Die atelier Anlage.
Letzte Edition.

Die Braun atelier Anlage

CD 5

BRAUN

89.30

CC 4 volume

BRAUN

C 4 record level

BRAUN

PA 4

BRAUN

Braun TV 3.

BRAUN

70 The 1982 exhibition *Möbel perdu – Schöneres Wohnen* (Furniture Perdu – More Gracious Living) in Hamburg sparked a rebellion against what at the time was the widespread doctrine that paradise should be furnished "functionally".

71 In 1962 in the magazine *Industrial Design*, American author Richard Moss had traced the Braun Design of the day to three "laws": order, harmony and frugality. The company itself first invoked its principles in its 1972/73 Annual Report (cf. Note 61). A catalogue of "10 Criteria for Good Industrial Form" had been compiled in 1980 by Herbert Lindinger for the IF Design Award jury in Hanover, borrowing from similar catalogues by Max Bill, Edgar Kaufmann Jr. and Mia Seeger (cf. IF International Forum Design [ed.], *50 Jahre IF*, Hanover 2003, p. 160). The lecture held in 1985 by Dieter Rams was called *Was ist gutes Design?* (What Is Good Design?) and can be found, along with the Moss article, in: *Ansichten zum Design* (Views on Design, internal paper, Kronberg 1988). The wording used – primarily "good" and "bad" – is of course not very selective. The tenth, concluding, thesis is a paradox ("Good design is as little design as possible"), which, problematically, operates with the ambiguity of the term "design" – as process and as result. The same ambiguity is inherent in the word "function". This problem is referred to, among other places, in: Andreas Dorschel, *Gestaltung. Ästhetik des Brauchbaren* (Design. Aesthetics of the Usable), Heidelberg 2002.

company's flagship products. It is thanks to him that the direct connection between the Design Department and the Executive Board remained in place for such a long time, a singular feature that sets Braun apart from all its rivals. Rams worked closely with the CEO at the time, Lorne R. Waxlax, and with Alfred M. Zeien, the Chairman in Boston. This alone showed the great importance the company placed on design. With Waxlax's support and what were now good flight connections, Rams managed to keep the department together and win contracts from the Group. This led to, among other things, collaborations with toothbrush manufacturer Oral-B and with Jafra Cosmetics. In this period Peter Schneider was also charged with procuring and fulfilling outside contracts. Deals were signed with Siemens, Hoechst AG, Lufthansa, Deutsche Bank and others. These contacts called for a rethinking of priorities – toward a more open, more entrepreneurial attitude on the part of the designers – a process that still resonates today.

Rams's teaching activities, which began back when the insurgents of "New German Design" were deliberately running roughshod over all of the hallowed principles of good design, ultimately caused him to compile a canon based on his working doctrine.[70] In a lecture, he presented a thesis-like list of ten criteria by which "good design" could be distinguished from bad. Rams gained considerable recognition for his ideas, which stemmed from long years of experience and which were probably also conceived as guidelines at Braun.[71] The ten design commandments reinforced his reputation as an upholder of fundamental design values, remote from all passing fads.

New markets and technologies: 1985–1994

The fact that in the design-enamoured 1980s the dazzling word was on everyone's lips gave even the Braun Design compositum created a decade earlier a new lease on life. The unwavering adherence to rational form seemed to be a convincing counter-program to the anti-aesthetic tendencies of Punk and Postmodernism.

In 1986 the first issue of the magazine Der Braun-Sammler (The Braun Collector) came out.[72] The enterprising undertaking of historically documenting the company's production might be wholeheartedly embraced, were it not a case of "invented tradition",[73] because here a specific view of the past was to be set down for posterity. One of the journal's latent messages is that in the good old days of Braun the company proceeded according to fixed principles – as if, rather than always feeling its way along, it had at some point laid down some golden rules.[74] Just how rapidly Braun's development actually took place is demonstrated by a surprising figure: in 1986 half of the company's revenues, which had quickly skyrocketed to 1.3 billion marks, came from products that were less than three years old. Only one in four products was still sold in Germany, and only every second one in Western Europe. Important events of that year were the launch of a new computing centre and the replacement of longstanding CEO Lorne Waxlax by Robert J. Murray, who was followed in the early 1990s, in a rapid succession never before experienced at the company, by Jacques Lagarde and then Archibald Livis.

Innovations in the second half of the 1980s included the "listening" alarm clock *voice control* by Dietrich Lubs and the slim shaver *micron vario* by Roland Ullmann. The *Oral-B Plus* toothbrush by Peter Schneider brought a mass-market product largely ignored by designers up until then out of its humble corner, establishing a lasting cooperation with the California partner. With sales of well over one billion toothbrushes, it became one of the most-sold consumer products. With the model called *linear*, a shaver was introduced for the first time that was designed to appeal to a more youthful target group. New markets were opened up.

Most noticeable during this period was the disproportionate growth in sales to the United States, which had already become the third-largest market by 1986. In subsequent years jumps in sales to Japan further underscored this trend toward overseas markets, which did not fail to have its effect on the company's

72 Edited by Jo Klatt and Günter Staeffler, this magazine – later renamed *Braun + Design* and then *Design+ Design* – functions as a forum for Braun collectors.

73 This phrase was coined by British historian Eric Hobsbawm to refer to intellectual or real constructions suggesting that something has "always" been part of history. Hobsbawm thinks that the continuity inferred is actually "artificial" and that "answers to new types of situation ... take the form of a reference to old situations." In this way a "self-made past is created", in particular "through almost obligatory repetition." For Hobsbawm it is the "contrast between the constant changes of the modern world and the attempt ... to structure parts of social life in it as unchanging ... that makes the invention of tradition so interesting for historians." Discovered in: http://www.holme-speare.de/tradition/hobsbawm.html.

74 In a 1971 lecture – in which the word "design" was not uttered – Fritz Eichler did not cite a canon of rules or similar as the core of the Braun project. He defined it instead as a business idea whose aim was "to gain long-term trust." In order to achieve this, a communicative culture first had to be created that ensured the optimal interplay of "marketing, technological development and design" (here the German word for "design" was used). Eichler thus saw design as part of an interdisciplinary process that was open-ended, as it was always geared toward the future (Fritz Eichler, "Die unternehmerische Haltung" ["The Entrepreneurial Attitude"], in: *Ansichten zum Design*, internal paper, Kronberg 1988).

75 Uta Brandes, *Die leise Ordnung der Dinge* (The Quiet Order of Things), Göttingen 1990; the author is a lecturer in the Design Department at the Cologne University of Applied Sciences (today KISD – Cologne International School of Design).

Illus.:

left above: Model construction: development of the design of the *Syncro* electric razor, 1998/1999

right above: CAD/CAM milling pattern for highly complex form

below: Design development of Oral-B *Advantage* toothbrush, 1993

design strategy. In 1988, as the 100-millionth Braun shaver left the factory, a product was feted that had long since become the mainstay in the company's sales and image. Dieter Rams, now endowed with the weight of "fully authorized representative" of the Executive Board, became president of the Council on Design and was now an, if not *the* authority on German design. Another biography[75] of the much-in-demand designer was published in 1990, the year in which the "last edition" of the *atelier* stereo system came out, closing the chapter on phono design with an audible fanfare. The loss of the sector that had given birth to Braun Design, and on which Rams had left an indelible mark, was, in hindsight, the harbinger of Rams' own departure. This would take place incrementally five years later, following 40 years of Braun Design. In 1991 Fritz Eichler passed away, one of the ranks of pioneers who had authored Braun's breakthrough in the early 1950s. He was a member of the Supervisory Board to the end, even at 80 years old. Just one year later Erwin Braun followed him.

The early 1990s saw the end of the Cold War, followed by the opening of the markets of Eastern Europe. The company once again broke into a technological gallop. The third industrial revolution, set off by the advent of electronic and digital technologies, reached the drafting boards of the engineers and designers, and more and more electronics were integrated into small devices. In the same years, hard-and-soft technology as well as the deployment of varying materials in the same product opened up new solutions and more subtle formal vocabularies. The *Plak Control* electric toothbrush by Peter Hartwein, a best-seller with its simultaneously rotating and oscillating bristles and subtle hard-and-soft look, is one outstanding example of the trend of combining conciseness with growing complexity. A product that expressed its high-tech status in a classic triangular form is the multi-award-winning *DB 10 fsl* radio alarm clock by Dietrich Lubs. Another example of the combination of innovation and self-assured design was the *Flex Integral* by Roland Ullmann. This new top-of-the-line shaver, whose grey colour quoted the company's own tradition,

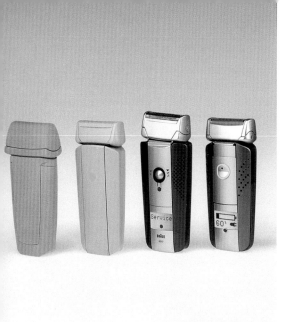

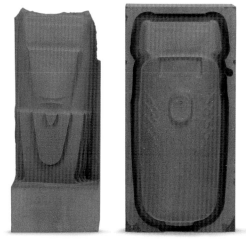

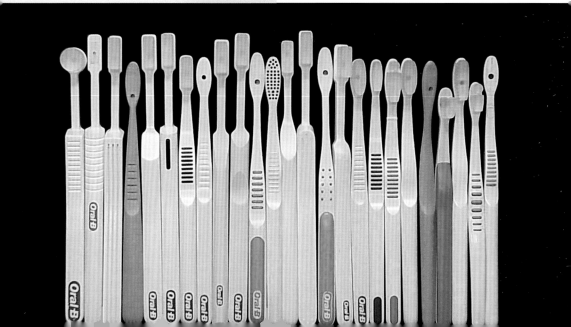

was likewise a popular success, in particular in Germany, Scandinavia and Japan. The growing fragmentation of markets was becoming a challenge for the interplay between marketing and design. Exports now exceeded one billion marks, accounting for almost 70 percent of revenue.

Global design: 1995–2005

When Dieter Rams reached retirement age and Peter Schneider was appointed new head of the Design Department, it was more than just a normal changing of the guard – but not only because yet another father figure was leaving the fold and the industry and media were naturally curious to see what would happen to Braun. The fact was that the company and the conditions in which it worked had changed dramatically. What was once an avant-garde project venturing a foray into the Modernist niche had finally evolved into a mass-market supplier: with plants in France, Ireland, Spain, Mexico, the USA and China. The prime indicator of the soundness of the firm's business strategy was, and still is, its success at cash registers on all continents. Revenues in 2002 totalled one-and-a-half billion euros, having risen by almost one-third since the mid-1990s. Today Braun is the No. 1 manufacturer worldwide of shear-blade razors, electric oral hygiene devices and scan thermometers. In the late 1990s, yet another series of products were introduced that set standards in their respective fields. The hand blender *MR 500*, designed by Ludwig Littmann, took hard-and-soft technology to a whole new level and enhanced the functionality of the appliance with touches such as housing that was more watertight than ever before. The *ThermoScan* infrared scan thermometer, which eliminated one of life's little discomforts while perfecting the measurement of body temperature, was brought, step by step, into a Braun-amenable form by Dietrich Lubs and Björn Kling, who joined the company in the 1990s. Finally, in the midst of the perennial digital revolution, one of the smallest objects ever designed by Braun led to a kind of quantum leap for the company: *Cross Action*, the first toothbrush conceived by Jürgen Greubel and Peter Schneider, which consists entirely of free-form surfaces and can only be illustrated using software. In this utilitarian sculpture in miniature format, the spatial configuration was captured completely by means of computer. And thanks to advanced software, the results could also be transmitted directly to the manufacturing tools. The result was a new, much-copied type of toothbrush, along with a model of how the organic and analytical lines in Braun Design would in future meet and converge. The design opened up completely new, unexplored landscapes on the continent of Design, which were just waiting to be discovered.

But the occupation of designer had now also changed radically. In an era in which the concept of design threatens to be downgraded into a commonplace quality, when the top-earning designers are touted like opera tenors, and similarly positioned corporate groups, such as Panasonic or Philips, manage to afford much larger design departments, it has become even more important to highlight what is special about Braun Design. It's true that product design is no longer subsumed under a universal vision like it was back in the pioneer days. But for that matter, the company works on a professional level today that it could only have dreamt of in those early years. For example, the quality of the models has been continually improved, and they are now manufactured with peerless precision by digitally controlled milling machines. Even though the parent company, Gillette, understandably tailors the product range to its own core areas for economic reasons,[76] Braun's design team, younger these days and also more international,[77] continues to play in the top ranks of the Champions League of the industry. Otherwise, it would be hard to explain the undiminished appeal of the Braun Design Prize.[78]

In order to bring innovation into the spotlight, Design Head Peter Schneider has not hesitated to break some taboos. A new colour scheme, for example, including some unusual pastel hues with

76 The implications of Procter & Gamble's purchase of a majority stake in Gillette in 2005 remain to be seen.

77 The next generation of Braun designers includes Markus Orthey, Till Winkler and Vietnam-born Duy Phong Vu, as well as the Canadian Rory McGarry and Ben Wilson from Australia.

78 In 2005 Braun Design not only celebrates its 50th anniversary – the Braun Award will also be presented for the fifteenth time.

BRAUN

PremioBraunPreisBraunPrize

PromotingDesign
DesignFörderung
PatrocinioDiseño

1995–2005

technically elaborate, mottled surfaces, caused purists to mount
the barricades. A decisive criterion for successful product design
today is global acceptance, an aspect that overlays all formal
decisions. To make sure the Braun brand doesn't turn grey, the
MTV and ebay generation has to be addressed as well. For a
designer working in the global market, the trick is to assess the
profiles of the different sub-markets and intelligently and elegantly
boil them down to a common denominator. That it is possible to
succeed in this effort is demonstrated by products such as the
PRSC 1800 Professional hairdryer. In this daily balancing act, communication with the Marketing Department plays an increasingly
significant role, assisted by business software that ensures, for
instance, that any downward sales trends in sub-markets are registered immediately. This, too, has long been an important
requirement for product development. Where designers once had
to fly based on visuals alone, and sometimes even by the seat of
their pants, today they sit in a fully computerized cockpit.

But the fact that, even in the digital age, decisions still have to be
made is demonstrated by the *Clean&Charge*, a self-cleaning razor
and a completely new kind of product that at first not even everyone at the company really fully believed in. On the other hand, the
designers do not hesitate one bit to quote the company's own
past, as is amply evident in *Impression Line*, a product line consisting of a toaster, electric kettle and coffee maker in what could
almost be called the history-making colour duo of black and silver.
The marriage of plastic and metal – in this case stainless steel –
is still wonderfully well suited to conveying lasting value. And the
flowing lines of these appliances are designed to appeal to the
emotions. Good examples of design that conjoins the tradition of
analytical rationality with a new feeling for form are, apart from the
Cross Action toothbrush, the *FreeStyle* iron, the *MR 5000* hand
blender and the *ThermoScan Pro 3000* thermometer. The *Activator*
as well, in terms of function the nonpareil of all Braun shavers to
date, has a soft silhouette and alludes at the same time to the
third, biomorphic dimension of Braun Design. The reduction of the

anti-slip elements to the essential areas only, and the control rail framed by two parallels, can by all means be read as echoes of the classical Modernism that Braun's pioneers invoked.

"The dogmatic is out today", says Peter Schneider, who nevertheless certainly is still committed to the old values. After all, hasn't the attempt to find the optimal balance between constant renewal and an enduring identity been a basic tenet of the Braun designers from the very beginning? Schneider, no fan of static guidelines, insists on realism with respect to the conditions governing his own work, as well as on professional methodology. Behind these demands is the virtue that we refer to today by the somewhat old-fashioned-sounding concept of thoroughness – something that all who have ever held a Braun product in their hands will have learned to appreciate. Braun today develops innovative mass-market products, paying more attention than ever to customers' wide range of needs and desires – for which marketing delivers increasingly precise indicators. This is one of the reasons why the emotional component of design, which is usually expressed in complex forms, is becoming more and more important. Even though combining design quality with a technical edge is still the same formula that held sway in the early days of Braun Design, the aspect of multi-dimensionality is taking on increasing significance. "The optimal synthesis of function and emotion", postulates Peter Schneider, "is the key to future-ready product design."

Entertainment Electronics

1   Not to mention the downfall of worlds, such as the nearly complete disappearance of the German audio industry, which – Braun included – was not able to stand its ground against the ever-increasing competition from the Far East.

2   Stylistic devices: straighter contours, simplified control buttons and lighter-coloured woods. The console designs were consistent with the then-popular Scandinavian style in which functionality was given a "human" interpretation. This style dominated the work of contemporary architects as well as the interior decorating magazines of the time. But prior to the turning point in design that Braun initiated, there were no phonographic appliances that complemented this style of room.

3   Other, more organic approaches, such as that used in the radio-turntable combination *combi* (1955), were not pursued further in the audio sector.

4   For example, in the tabletop *TS-G* model (with speaker on top).

5   This breakthrough consisted in the renunciation of symbolism, which itself became a powerful symbol: for technology.

6   Over the course of two decades, Braun introduced numerous such record player-radio or record player-receiver combinations. The *PC 4000* audio system (1977) was the last of these.

7   A principle first formulated by Herbert Lindinger, professor at the Ulm Academy of Design, which dominated the audio sector until the 1990s, when it was pushed aside by integrated mini-tower systems and portable "ghetto blasters".

8   His designs shaped the industry for a quarter-century.

9   A configuration whose functional industrial aesthetics are reminiscent of another design innovation that introduced technology into the living space: the tubular furniture of the 1920s.

Illus.: *audio 308* compact system; detail

From the minimalist SK 1 radio to the monumental *atelier* hi-fi system: there is a world of difference between the first and the last of the myriad classics that emerged from Braun's audio sector.[1] Yet there are also similarities to be found between the two extremes – for example, the box-like shape as well as the organizational principles that made Braun appliances so simple to use and which made the brand world famous. The popular radios of the 1950s, which varied only in terms of small nuances, transformed people's living rooms into concert halls, complete with curtains (the large fabric-covered expanses of the speakers), keyboard (rows of ivory-coloured control keys) and gold-coloured baroque ornamentation. Braun can be credited with bringing about the demise of great-grandpa's bourgeois "music furniture". Here, Herbert Hirche and Hans Gugelot were initially entrusted with the rather thankless task of designing contemporary wooden housings for the existing radios and radio-phonographs.[2]

The box became the basic shape for audio equipment, and the battle against kitsch became its common denominator.[3] We can already recognize systematic thinking at this stage – for example, when the position of the speakers was varied.[4] Parallel rows of grooves for ventilation and for speakers became a distinguishing characteristic. Even the legendary *SK 4*, which Hans Gugelot and Dieter Rams designed together, features this type of facade. This flat-roofed architecture, was a manifesto against the stuffiness of the post-war years and marked a breakthrough for the Braun Design project.[5] The *SK 4* also established the line of compact systems with the controls on top.[6] The next milestone – a stereo system made up of individual components[7] – was even more epoch-making. Rams[8] endowed the *studio 2*, the archetype of this innovation, with its technoid face. The principle of stacking almost inevitably resulted in the development of the block shape with a vertical front panel,[9] which soon prevailed worldwide. Braun, which was known for its asceticism as far as colours were concerned, had often been a trendsetter in this regard.

70

10 Certain manufacturers, such as Wega, based their designs very closely on Braun's. Others, such as Dual, took advantage of external similarities to siphon off the mass market.

11 Here, Braun sometimes adopted its technology from other manufacturers: for example, in the case of television sets, VCRs and CD players.

12 Other design-oriented audio companies, such as Bang & Olufsen or Brionvega, were never able to achieve this position.

Illus.: *atelier* hi-fi system; detail

The earliest systems established cool silver as the "in" colour. Later, in the 1970s, deep black set off another fashion wave. Both variations are still current today (at Braun as well as throughout the entire consumer electronics industry) and their associative horizons would be worthy of an in-depth examination.

In the case of static audio appliances, whose purpose is contemplative and whose operation consists primarily of switching and adjusting, the organization of the control elements is the most significant formative step. Braun's organizational systems are legendary. In the early years of the audio industry, the company produced a few special radio models which likewise set fashion standards, even as they remained intermezzi – for example, the portable and transistor radios and the globetrotting *T 1000*. *Studio*, *audio*, *regie*, *atelier*: the names of these hi-fi systems – now the core element in entertainment electronics – can still make connoisseurs' hearts beat faster today. These were perfectly developed ensembles which often served as blueprints for the entire industry. In the 1960s, once the gap between good design and high-performance appliances had been closed, Braun established itself as the top-of-the-line brand. By this time, neutral aesthetics had already become the generally accepted standard.[10] The all-inclusive programme remained an anomaly.[11] Behind the invitation to consumers to fully equip their homes with audio appliances from Braun, in which all the individual components in a single product line complemented one another, lay the company's design standard of delivering ideal product types. The appliances were part of an overall design. This conceptual approach helped Braun achieve its exceptional status.[12] Unfortunately, however, the brand's outstanding characteristics were not reflected in sufficiently high sales figures. With *atelier*, Braun's last hi-fi system, Peter Hartwein underscored this moment of smooth-surfaced sleekness. His monolithic creation, available in black or grey, was one of the most completely successful designs in phonographic history.

din / line ———— recording level ———— micro

C 1

4 5 6   4 5 6
3   7   3   7
2   8 2   8
1   9 1   9
0   10   0   10

R
micro
L   mono

BRAUN

record ———— selector ———— input

A 1

volume

phono 1   tuner •   phono 1   tuner •
phono 2 •   phono 2 •
tape 1·2 •   tape 1 •
tape 2·1 •   tape 2 •
aux •   aux •

BRAUN

fm ● MHz
mw ● kHz
lw ● kHz

106.30

T 1

tuning

fm   mw   lw

BRAUN

SK 1

Tabletop radio
1955
Design: Artur Braun / Fritz Eichler
Kleinsuper, FM
light blue, pale green, light beige,
graphite

1   Braun had also built the small-format
Piccolo 50 and *Piccolino 51* radios (preceded by the *Piccolo BSK 441*, released
in 1941), whose appearance was modelled after American designs.

2   One example of this was the *Philetta*
from Philips, the best-selling model in
this sector. All the details were included,
from the ivory-coloured control buttons
to the obligatory gold edging.

3   This feature was modified several
times in subsequent models, making it the
most crucial detail for dating purposes.

4   In 2002, a new small-format radio,
the *Tivoli Model One*, became a worldwide success. Its format and interplay of
shapes echo those of the SK 1.

5   Initially, the radio was also available
in light yellow, pale green, beige and
blue – colours typical of the era. Later,
only white and graphite were produced.

6   Braun and Eichler had been soldiers
in the Second World War; thus, the *SK 1*
was jokingly known as "Kommissbrot"
("non-coms' bread rations").

7   In the cause of "good form", Braun
entered an alliance with the Rasch wall-
paper company, which produced artistic
wallpapers.

8   The *SK 1* had two jacks and could
also be used as an extra speaker. With
dimensions of 23.4 x 15.2 x 13.0 cm, it
was only half the size of the *Philetta*
(price: 129 DM). Up until 1961, a number
of subsequent versions of the radio were
produced which, in addition to FM, could
also receive MW (*SK 2*) and LW signals
(*SK 3*). They cost 145 and 165 DM,
respectively.

At the Design Triennale in Milan in 1957, two versions of the *SK 1* radio were displayed in the "Showcase of Nations" as examples of German industrial design. However, the effect was anything but impressive. After all, it belonged to the category of small-format radios typical of that time. In a pinch, these "Goggomobils" of the radio world could even be placed on a windowsill.[1] Such addition-al or starter models generally imitated the theatrical gestures of the larger radios.[2]

Braun's *Kleinsuper* was something completely different. This design by Artur Braun and Fritz Eichler is a lesson in the art of frugality. It is a radio in paperback-book format; an exercise in restraint, which it achieves through its simple, self-contained shape, framed by a plastic case, and by abandoning every feature that is not absolutely necessary – including the otherwise obligatory keys. The radio was operated by means of two simple, unlabelled buttons and the large dial.[3] With the *SK 1*, the small-format radio took on a form all its own. Round dials had been seen before this, but never with such unadorned numerals and never as part of a front panel whose graphic structure was so clearly articulated – with the geometric interplay of a circle and a rectangle[4] reiterated in the structure of the perforated panel. Here the design refers back to its origins: the factory floor.[5] At the same time, the dot pattern vaguely recalled the spartan severity of military equipment[6] as well as reminding the observer of the "abstract" art that was inundating German living rooms at the time.[7] Braun's most inexpensive floor-mounted appli-ance still carried the stylistic aura of the 1950s. Ultimately, the *SK 1* was actually a rudimentary building block for a not-yet-existent "system".[8]

74

SK 4

Radio-phonograph combination

1956
Design: Hans Gugelot / Dieter Rams / Herbert Lindinger
white / elmwood
Shown here: SK 5

1   They had been part of Braun's product line since 1929 (with the *Mozart* model); after the Second World War, they usually took the form of "chests" or "cabinets". *Phonosupers*, later called "compact systems with record players", were produced until the late 1970s.

2   From the Braun brochure, 1956.

3   "Unbreakable" was also the magical adjective applied to the new record discs made out of vinyl. Plexiglas is the trade name for polymethyl methacrylate (acrylic glass), a material that has been in use since 1928. Since the 1930s, it has been used as a non-splintering glass substitute in such products as protective goggles and automobile taillights. Used here on a record player for the first time, the transparent plexiglas cover (here, too, the authorship is disputed) subsequently became a standard feature for decades to come. Plexiglas was soon put to use in other Braun products – for example, for the cover glass for the *HF 1*. In the 1990s, the principle of transparency experienced a second boom, in such products as Apple computers.

If today one were to take a survey about the best-known products from Braun, this appliance from the early years would most certainly be near the top. According to Fritz Eichler, the *SK 4* became the virtual "embodiment of Braun Design." In the 1950s, radio-phonograph combinations[1] were the top-of-the-line product for radio manufacturers – usually in the form of corpulent Musiktruhen ("music chest" radiograms). The *SK 4* was an alternative design that "consciously rejected the form of 'music furniture'."[2] Thus, the company used materials here that had no place in a bourgeois sitting room: a metal case and transparent plexiglas cover – an invention attributed to Dieter Rams. This was the show-stopping feature of this design milestone. The wondrous object proved so unsettling to people's accustomed visual aesthetic that it acquired the nickname "Snow White's coffin".

This lightweight artificial glass – as "unbreakable" as the vinyl of the record discs – was the kind of technological promise that set off waves of euphoria.[3] The *SK 4* was one of the first audio appliances whose design emphasized its functional character rather than concealing it. Further breaks with tradition were the compact box shape as well as a degree of minimalism that bordered on culture shock. The appliance appeared naked, almost obscene: a white hexahedron, defined by right angles. The resemblance to Bauhaus-style "functionalism" was no coincidence. Here, the application of ascetic architecture to modern industrial products celebrated its premiere. There were also other principles whose origins could be traced to classical Modernism: whereas the design pioneers of the early 20th century reduced their furniture creations to their component parts, the same principle was now applied to an audio appliance. Behind this concept lay the soon-to-be executed option of developing the product into a hi-fi system, as well as that of transposing the design onto other products. In contrast, as far as sound was concerned,

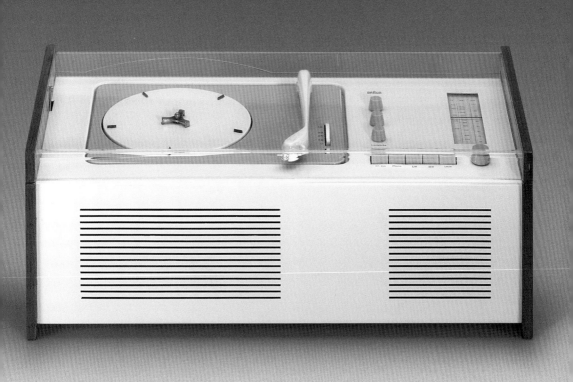

SK 4

4 The same arrangement, with controls on the top surface of the appliance, had already been implemented in 1939, with the model *6740*. The geometry of the surface and the controls represented a dramatic contrast to the "everyman's radio" which prevailed at the time. They evolved from graphic as well as ergonomic considerations: rectangular, concave buttons for the radio, round buttons for the volume controls. The light, monochrome grey seems to anticipate the computer aesthetic of the years to come.

5 The *PC 3* was a further development of the record player in the combi portable appliance released in 1955 (Wagenfeld staffer Ralph Michel was responsible for this project).

6 Also called red elm; Fritz Eichler is credited with selecting the colour.

7 The steel plate was mounted into the wooden side panels; Gugelot's *M 125* systemized furniture was also constructed using this technique, which we find frequently in his work. Originally conceived of as an inexpensive solution, the uniform bending of the steel plate proved to be an additional problem in production.

8 These grooves had already been seen in the *PK-G* radio, designed one year earlier, and on the *L 1* external speaker (which could also be connected to the *SK 4*). Dieter Rams later developed them further (the *SK 6*, for example, had larger, divided speaker grooves).

9 A characteristic of nearly every Braun radio during the thermionic era.

10 Up until that time, architects didn't really know what kind of radios they should place in their stylishly decorated living spaces. Up until the mid-1950s, they frequently dispensed with them altogether.

Braun's most famous Phonosuper with its four (!) watts of power output provided a rather ordinary level of listening enjoyment. This product, in which Braun's new design concept materialized for the first time, was a joint effort. Eichler and Rams were responsible for the practical yet still novel placement of the controls on top of the appliance as well as for the revolutionary stripped-down design.[4] A special chassis was created for the L-shaped arrangement of the control buttons. The typography of the dial was based on Otl Aicher's specifications, and the design of the record player – with its somewhat softer contours – came from the office of Wilhelm Wagenfeld.[5] In other words, the individual components were not simply ordered from a supplier, but rather – and this was also a seminal approach – the vast majority were produced according to the designers' specifications. Hans Gugelot had the idea of using a U-shaped steel plate for the housing; his younger colleague, Herbert Lindinger, also worked on developing it. The contrast between the white appliance block and its side panels further emphasized the construction principle. At the time, the reddish elmwood[6] was interpreted as a Scandinavian and therefore highly contemporary element. The warm colour of the material adds a certain tension to the *SK 4*'s appearance, and with it, a special, almost "timeless" charm.[7] The window-like ventilation grooves[8] are also a product of Gugelot's repertoire – even though the cutting process did not always function perfectly.[9] Since they are nearly identical on both the front and rear panels of the appliance, there was no longer any such thing as an unsightly back side. As an object in the room, the *SK 4* thus fulfilled another requirement of modern decorating philosophies. It comes as no surprise that it quickly became a favourite accessory among architects[10]. After all, with its matter-of-fact, rectilinear form, the cuboid phonograph corresponded perfectly to the blocks of stone, steel and glass that the master builders of the "economic miracle" were constructing on the bombed-out lots of German cities.

HF 1

Television set

1958
Design: Herbert Hirche
Tabletop appliance
(tubular steel stand available as an accessory)
dark grey / light grey

1   In this way, Braun put one of the fundamental objectives of the Bauhaus into practice.

2   The technology for the appliance was developed by Telefunken.

3   In 1969, Marco Zanuso and Richard Sapper designed the rectangular Black ST 201 (for Brionvega), a model that was far ahead of its time. The box shape became standard in the 1990s.

4   The matte dark-grey housing was fitted with a lighter-coloured front panel made of plastic.

5   At the time, Germany had only one television channel, the ARD (German Association of Public Broadcasters).

6   Braun picked up on this same principle in its atelier appliances.

Braun achieved the goal that the Bauhaus had professed but had scarcely been able to implement: that of developing product types that serve as representatives of an entire genre.[1] An excellent yet nearly forgotten example of this achievement is the *HF 1*[2] television set, produced in the late 1950s. Herbert Hirche's dramatically clear-cut design signalled a break with the original forms taken by this category of appliances. Whereas two years earlier the *SK 4* had represented a departure from "music furniture", this new design succeeded in breaking away from the concept of "television furniture". The most striking characteristic of the *HF 1* is its box-like shape, which proved to be seminal, albeit over a protracted period of time.[3] Its monochrome colour scheme further emphasized the appliance's formal coherency.

The apparatus – which looks as foreign as an alien in a science fiction film – seems surprisingly modern even half a century later. Hirche's grey TV cube was the first set to be produced using no visible wood.[4] The severity of its colours and form gave it a neutral appearance that aided viewers' concentration on the screen – principles that have long since become the norm, but which were established only gradually. The thin-legged steel stand provided as an accessory completed the look of the *HF 1* as a solitary object in space. Another important characteristic is its consistent symmetry, further underscored by the conspicuous line pattern of the speaker grooves. Centred between them is a single on-off button[5]; the brand logo appears directly below. The controls that are not constantly in use are concealed under a flap on the top surface. Through this separation of the less essential functions[6] – a standard feature in today's television sets – the central on-off switch became the only visible control element. This was the ultimate in minimalism.

TP 1

**Transistor
radio-phonograph**
1959
Design: Dieter Rams / Ulm Academy
of Design
combines the *T 4* and *P 1*
light grey

1   The *exporter 1* still had a shimmering
gold housing typical of the period (it was
sold primarily outside of Germany until
1960); the *exporter 2* (designed at the
Ulm Academy of Design) was reworked
in white, and the graphics were greatly
simplified.

2   This was first seen in the *SK 1*.

3   As an inset disc (*T 3* and *T 31*), as a
rectangular window with a numbered dial
(*T 4*) and as a window with an inset sector
of a circle specifying the frequencies
(*T 41*).

4   Grey appeared early on, in the studio
1 compact audio system and in the *HF 1*
television set. Fritz Eichler maintained
sovereignty over the selection of colours.

5   The same principle employed in the
Transistor 1 portable radio.

6   Thus, the red of the station control
knob corresponds to that of the markings
on the dial below. This type of informative
colour coding was later used in other
areas as well – for example in clocks.

7   The Metz company had already produced a portable tandem appliance of
this kind. Dieter Rams came up with the
idea for personal reasons: for his new
position, he needed to learn English, and
he wanted to be able to listen to recorded
lessons even when he was on the road.

8   This is especially evident in combination with the *T 4* and *T 41* radios, whose
circular perforated field corresponds with
the radius of the turntable.

9   Transistor radios were the first line of
products to be discontinued.

From the time that transistors made miniaturization possible, the sound of the pocket-sized radio was part of the background music of the rock'n'roll era. Braun entered the market early with the *exporter* model, which, thanks to the vivisections carried out by the Ulm School ascetics, was transformed into a pure slab shape, characterized by the geometric simplicity of its front panel.[1] Dieter Rams perfected this spartan approach by elongating the format to a manageable size (made possible by the use of transistors), repositioning the sunk-in control buttons onto the top surface, using a perforated panel for the speaker[2] and embedding the dial into the body of the appliance.[3] A silk-screening department was established to produce the high-quality typography; it would later play a significant role in the development of Braun's shavers. The special grey colour[4] of the housing – which was composed of two polystyrene shells[5] that provided a fitting cover for the messianic austerity of the design – simultaneously served as the template for a precise system of colours which facilitated easy comprehension of the controls.[6]

The idea of developing a portable appliance for the new 17 cm record discs had been in the works for some time.[7] But it was Braun's by now deep-seated practice of systematic thinking which allowed it to be produced as a single, harmonious unit.[8] The *P 1* portable record player, whose pick-up arm emerges like a cuckoo from a clock by means of a slide control, adopted the format of a transistor radio. Some of the most intricate details can be found in the metal parts: the turntable with its pneumatic rubber ring and the aluminium bars which hold the two elements together in the simplest possible way. A small set of headphones completed this multifunctional combination and anticipated the mobility of the *Walkman*, if not its sales success[9]: It was simply too far ahead of its time.

studio 2

Modular system

1959
Design: Dieter Rams
CS 11 control module/record player
CE 11 receiver
CV 11 power amplifier
light grey/aluminium-coloured

1 From the August 1959 Braun product catalogue. The first stereo records had been introduced onto the market one year earlier.

2 The first signs could already be seen in the *SK 1* (1955) and the *SK 4* (1956). The compact system *atelier 1* (1957), which contained no integrated speaker and could be operated with two separate speakers, is considered to be the first true stereo system.

3 They measured 11 cm high and either 40 or 20 cm wide; compatibility was a goal that was not always achieved in the years to come.

4 In the years that followed, many manufacturers specialized in certain individual components. By contrast, Braun typically continued to develop complete stereo systems.

5 A format used in inexpensive systems that remained popular into the 1970s.

6 With the *CSV 13* amplifier, developed in 1961.

7 As a two-fold sensual metaphor for both technology and luxury, silver is a standard colour for hi-fi components even today. In the case of the *studio 2*, it matched the aluminium meshwork of the new speakers (the housing itself was made of light grey painted steel plate). Without speakers, the *studio 2* cost 1,350 DM – approximately the monthly salary of a high-ranking white-collar worker.

"Stereo reproduction requires two speaker units."[1] The *studio 2* audio combination, introduced in 1959, was so new that the catalogue had to explain the ABCs of stereophonics. *studio 2*, created by Dieter Rams, marked the final departure from the classic radio apparatus that Rams had already heralded in some of his earlier models.[2] This was the birth of what soon came to be known as an audio "system".

From an historical point of view, the transition from "music furniture" to audio system came about through the detachment of the radio. The *CE 11* "receiver" – the tuner – was the first component, or "building block", as they were called at the time. This principle of separation was groundbreaking, and the rationale behind it was revelatory: the compatible components[3] could be developed separately in accordance with the specific demands of each particular appliance,[4] and consumers could place them on top of or beside each other as they pleased. In addition, this approach allowed users the option of assembling their own individual hi-fi systems. The amplifier – which in the *CS 11* was still integrated into the record player[5] – was emancipated two years later.[6] In its appearance, the *studio 2* anticipated today's hi-fi systems – for example, with its format and its silver colour.[7] Shallow steel shoeboxes whose aluminium front panels served as the kind of vertical dashboard previously associated only with technical gadgetry became the cult objects of the Beatles generation. Nowadays we take this configuration completely for granted, and yet it was once as revolutionary as the introduction of tubular steel in the furniture designs of the 1920s. The control elements were also defined by an industrial coolness; their rational arrangement gave the impression of scientific precision. Such a clean, unemotional design could surely produce only pure sounds.

T 1000

Short-wave receiver

1963
Design: Dieter Rams
aluminium-coloured / black, white dial

1 "T" stands for "tragbar" (portable) radio.

2 It was introduced in 1959 along with the studio 2 stereo system. One year prior to the *T 1000*, the black and silver sixtant electric shaver had come onto the market – a strongly masculine colour combination.

3 In every area, the margin of positioning error was below 1 percent; a "short-wave bandspread magnifier" allows the user to "sample" sections of the dial. The appliance, which can even be operated on rough seas, was ordered by the German embassies. Accessory instruments such as direction-finding adapters, direction-finding antennas and direction-finding compasses are highly sought-after collectors' items today.

4 This had first been seen in the *SK 1* tabletop radio.

5 This was made possible through the use of new silk-screening technology.

Never before had so much radio taken up so little space. And high performance had rarely been so clearly legible in the look of an appliance. These unique qualities ensured the *T 1000* a regular place in the great design collections. The mobile radio,[1] one of Dieter Rams' seminal designs, is a multi-purpose appliance which, with its 13 wavebands, was the first radio capable of receiving almost any frequency being broadcast. It could also function as a component in a hi-fi system and it established a new category of appliance: the "world receiver". In the same era when the first manned spaceships were flying into the stratosphere, Braun was conquering the airwaves. With the cover closed, this über-radio was transformed into an elegant, high-tech box with a silver-coloured outer shell.[2] For many of its owners, this all-round appliance was also a status symbol – just as it was for the Braun company.

Never before had so much effort been put into the development of a single product. Once again, Braun had succeeded in creating a new category of appliance. Nevertheless, it was not the only appliance for which no successor models were produced – although designs for such models existed. The all-round radio was a masterpiece of German engineering,[3] comparable to the *Leica* camera in its versatility and its unique initial position – but at a weight of 8.5 kg. On top of all this, the *T 1000* represented a summation of the new, rational style of design. Many of the elements employed here had already been seen in the products of the previous eight years. In the open position, the appliance's overall appearance is shaped by the spatial layout of the speaker, dial and control panel. These three approximately equal-sized areas are placed in a ratio approaching a "golden mean", which ushered in a new formula for radio design. Each of the fields is intricately subdivided within itself: the speaker as a regular arrangement of holes,[4] the unusually large dial with a previously unseen degree of complexity,[5] and

T 1000

the control knobs in a sequential array that both continued an established system of order and anticipated control hierarchies to come. Colourful accents such as the red FM button, the red dot on the lower adjusting knob for frequency settings and – directly adjacent – the red lettering on the lower edge of the dial place special visual emphasis on an important function: FM reception. This too, was an informative system that had already been put to use and would later be developed further.[6] The heart and soul of the *T 1000* is the 12-zone tuner drum that corresponds to the frequency control on the right side. The palm-sized metal lever is powerful and elegant at the same time. A cut-away area signals that the appliance can be opened; the recess indicates the direction and the comparatively large format illustrates the amount of effort involved.

An appliance of this degree of complexity required an equally extensive instruction manual, the likes of which had not been seen before. It was located in a compartment inside the metal cover. This was just one of the numerous extra features included with the radio, such as the flywheel drive for the frequency control buttons and the threaded holes on the bottom which allowed the appliance to be secured in place so that it could be operated even on an unsteady ship's deck.

6 The systematic use of colour coding had begun even earlier – for example, in the *T 41* transistor radio. Later, the approach was developed further in audio appliances such as the *audio 308* compact system, as well as in such products as clocks, pocket calculators and electric shavers.

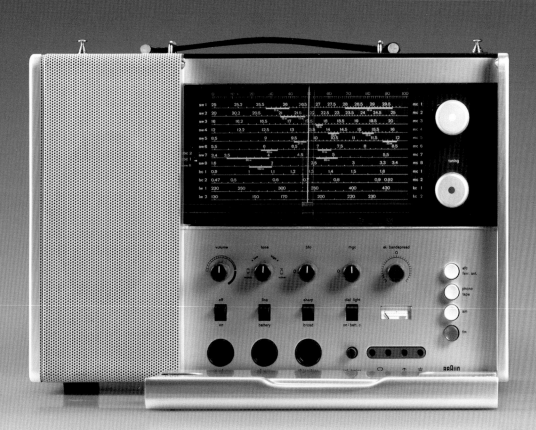

PS 1000

Record player

1965
Design: Dieter Rams
anthracite

1 In the early years, Braun consciously linked its modern image with that of "cool" American jazz music.

2 The first Braun record player was the *G 12*, released in 1955, followed one year later by the *PC 3*; the first stereo records appeared in 1958.

3 Braun made a decisive contribution to this breakthrough with its *studio 2* system (1959). The placement of the record player at the top of the ensemble – for purely practical reasons – further underscored its symbolic importance.

4 This element, which was introduced with the *SK 4*, was first seen in its modern form – as a plexiglas box set atop the appliance – in the *PC 5* model (1962).

5 The first metal pick-up arm (its configuration – including Rams' characteristic curve – was preceded, as usual, by heated discussions with the technicians) appeared in the *audio 1* system (1962); the record player was also available separately as model *PCS 45*.

6 The colour chosen for this legendary component of the *studio 1000* system was anthracite.

7 Thus, the record player could still be used to play shellac records with 78 or 16 rpm.

8 The arm was configured for a minimum weight of 0.4 ponds – an outstanding value for the time and one of the decisive criteria among record lovers.

The record player was one of the everyday icons of the 20th century, and is now becoming an extinct species. Once the crown jewel of every good stereo system, it was also a lifestyle vehicle[1] – as much a cult object as the black discs that rotated upon it. Its emancipation as a pure playback device began in the 1950s,[2] largely brought about by the development of the stereo system,[3] which necessitated the standardization of its dimensions. The image of the modern record player – which Braun played a major role in shaping – included the following elements: a box-shaped underbody, a plexiglas cover[4] and a turntable in long-playing record format. Last but not least was the constructive element of the ensemble: the pick-up arm which, balanced out by a counterweight, brought a touch of precision engineering into people's living rooms. Its character was defined by the use of a steel tube,[5] a choice based on stability, light weight and cost, which simultaneously evokes an association with the tubular steel furniture of the 1920s. The shape of the counterweight was also cylindrical.

With its formal, dark-coloured underbody and elegant silver finish, the *PS 1000*[6] – a Dieter Rams design with which Braun carried the record player generation forward – displayed all of the above-mentioned characteristics and was equipped with a number of convenient extra features. The propulsion of the turntable by means of a friction wheel, an intermediate roll and a rubber belt ensured a constant velocity without the dreaded grinding sound. A continuous optical display regulated the four speeds needed to accommodate all of the record types available at that time.[7] Finally, the tone arm on the typically uncluttered surface of the appliance could be operated at the touch of a button via relay control.[8]

TG 60

Reel-to-reel tape recorder
1965
Design: Dieter Rams
white / aluminium-coloured, graphite /
aluminium-coloured

1   The low height requirement led to a
tightly compressed inner structure. The
subsequent model, the technically outstanding TG 1000, was compatible with
the TS 45 and the L 45.

2   A reel-to-reel tape recorder cannot be
stacked.

3   Wall-mounted systems, an idea for
which Herbert Lindinger obtained a
copyright and which was attempted
again later with the audio 308 system,
were quite difficult to put into practice in
the home and were rejected by retailers.
Furthermore, it was impossible to operate a record player in the vertical position.
Nevertheless, wall-mounted systems are
now experiencing a renaissance (e.g. at
Bang & Olufsen).

4   Compatible stands were also available.

5   The magnetic tape era at Braun
remained a brief interlude that lasted
barely a decade – the last model, the
TG 1020, was released in 1974.

The creative possibilities seemed endless. Magnetic tape allowed
people to copy records, edit radio programmes and record the
voices of children and adults through a microphone. There was
nothing to prevent you from assembling your own private sound
archive. In the middle of the ever-wilder 1960s, when Braun released a home tape recorder onto the market, this already quite
popular technology was intended to round off the home hi-fi system. As far as its dimensions were concerned, the TG 60 model
fit the requirements, albeit imperfectly.[1]

In stark contrast to competing products, designer Dieter Rams
endowed the appliance with a sparse, industrial aesthetic. The
numerous open screw connections contributed to this effect, as did
the unusually long, bent pressure arm. This imposing lever, fitted
with a spring and a rubber roller, was not hidden under the control
panel as was usually the case; rather, it served as an emblem for
the tape recorder's productive character. The symbolism was
acoustic as well as visual: every time the "record" or "play" button
was pushed, a magnet set the lever into operation with an audible
click. The linear arrangement of the control buttons hearkens back
to the repertoire of earlier audio appliances, as does the plexiglas cover – an unusual feature for a tape recorder. Designers
approached the problem of combining the appliance[2] with other
components in two different ways: the first, highly original, solution
of hanging the appliance on the wall remained a brief episode.[3] A
horizontal combination with the audio 2 compact system[4] seemed
to make more practical sense. Whatever the case, the dilemma
quickly became irrelevant: The reel-to-reel tape recorder was soon
supplanted in hi-fi systems and living rooms by the much simpler-
to-operate cassette recorder.[5]

L 710

Studio speaker

1969
Design: Dieter Rams
white/aluminium-coloured, walnut/
aluminium-coloured, white/black

1 For example in the early music cabinets.

2 For example with the *SK 4*, produced
in 1956, and the *atelier 1* "control module" (receiver), which was intended to be
placed directly adjacent to it. The *L 1*'s
successor, the *L 2*, released in 1958, for
which a tubular steel stand was available, was the first truly freestanding "speaker box". Here, Rams clearly offset the
speaker opening – a black disc of perforated steel – from the white rectangle of
the front panel. Braun retained this graphic approach for several years; in 1959,
it produced the ultra-flat *LE 1*, a black
rectangle that brings to mind today's
LCD screens, particularly when combined with its pedestal stand.

3 The aluminium was nevertheless
rolled and anodized.

4 This was similar to the breakthrough
achieved by the German lighting manufacturer Bega with its "Lichtbaustein"
("light building block") lamps.

5 Both in common parlance and in
Braun's own production halls, the new
speakers were soon known as "rabbit
hutches".

6 For example, the model *GSL 1030*
(1977).

7 The Canton company, founded by
former Braun employees, finally accom-
plished this goal.

"A good speaker should not be heard." This advertising slogan
from the early 1960s got right to the paradoxical point. The imper-
ative of categorical restraint was carried over into the area of
acoustics. The first speaker to meet this requirement in terms of
both technology and design was the *L 80*, which appeared in the
early 1960s. It was followed soon afterward by the *L 700* or *L 710*,
Braun's first true hi-fi speaker, which included a groundbreaking
extra feature in the form of its adjustable stand. Up until that time,
radio speakers were generally covered with thick fabric that complemented people's plush sofas. The result was a muffled sound.
Braun developed alternative covers that greatly increased the
sound output: first in the form of slatted wooden panels,[1] and later
in perforated metal and rolled aluminium mesh.

These materials from the factory floor radically rationalized the
look of hi-fi speakers. Single speakers had originally been seen
only onstage. Braun's first separate "additional speaker" for home
use was the *L 1*, designed in 1957 by Dieter Rams, a horizontal
wooden block whose length and height were designed to make it
combinable with various other appliances.[2] Finally, one of the new
products introduced at the 1961 Consumer Electronics Show was
the *L 40* – the forerunner to the *L 80* and the first speaker in which
an exposed aluminium meshwork was used,[3] and whose white
housing was visible from the front only as a thin line. This was a
speaker in pure block form, a point of sound in a room, so to
speak – a material abstraction[4] that was just as style-defining as
it was difficult to get used to.[5] Although Braun repeatedly came
up with new innovations – such as the tripod-mounted tweeter or
"active" speaker columns[6] – the overriding goal of producing
speakers for use with other companies' systems was ultimately
never achieved.[7]

audio 308

Compact system
with record player
1973
Design: Dieter Rams
black

1 The Bayer chemical company introduced an automobile body made of
plastic. There was a veritable flood of
spectacular plastic products coming onto the market – particularly in the area of
seating furniture.

2 With Braun's *regie 308* receiver.

3 With its thermoplastic housings,
Braun approached the limits of technical feasibility; in terms of sales, the low-
priced system was highly profitable.

4 The plexiglas cover reciprocated the
angle so that the appliance as a whole
assumed the familiar block shape.
However, attempts to incorporate this
slope into the record player proved
unsuccessful. The relatively low height of
the housing (17 cm including the lid) was
determined by the dimensions of the
transformer. The receiver and speakers
could also be operated vertically, as a
wall-mounted system – which was most
likely the exception. The accompanying
L 308 speakers incorporated the same
angle.

5 The attempts to tilt the record player
forward illustrate how highly prized the
incline concept was. Nevertheless, this
project proved to be too technically
complex.

6 The category of appliance was virtually the same.

7 Designers of the era were experimenting with "pop colours", even in such
product categories as hairdryers and
cigarette lighters.

8 The most popular artist was Victor
Vasarély.

Around 1970, as the world's youth succumbed to rock 'n' roll fever
and scoffed at conventions, Braun also hoped to attract younger
customers to its showcase product segment – not only via pricing,
but also by appealing to a generation that was eager to experiment
with the new. Plastic seemed to be the ideal means to achieve both
of these goals.[1] The radio-record player combination *audio 308*,[2]
designed by Dieter Rams, was one of the first systems whose
housing came out of an injection moulding machine.[3] The system
consisted of a cover panel and a hull beneath, which contained the
power units. The surprise effect came with the fact that the upper
surface of the system was inclined forward by a moderate eight
degrees.[4] When seen from the side, this slope resulted in a wedge
shape, a dynamic form with which automobile designers were also
experimenting at the time.[5]

If we place this sleek low-rider side by side with the orange-crate-
size *SK 4*[6] of 13 years earlier, we can clearly see what a long way
Dieter Rams had come in that time. From the user's point of view,
the *audio 308* is a keyboard with equipment reminiscent of a DJ's
mixing board. The rows of control knobs vaulted the art of opera-
tional geometry and colour symbolism to new heights – although
the intense stoplight colours can also be interpreted simply as a
mod style element.[7] By now, the black housing had become
classy everyday attire for hi-fi systems. But ever since Op Art
posters[8] had become available in every stationery store, black and
white graphics had also assumed a new associative status. On the
machine's surface, futuristic-looking details such as the large tuning dial with two finger indentations accompanied members of the
hi-fi society on their trip into musical orbit.

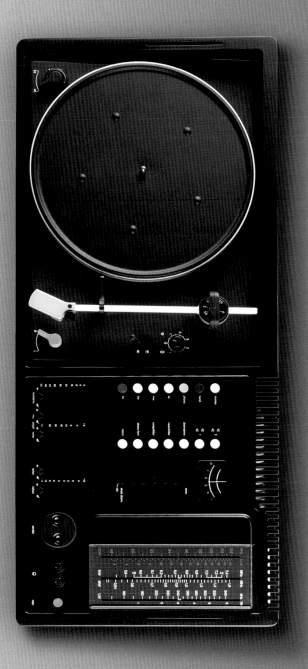

atelier

Hi-fi system
1980–1987
Design: Peter Hartwein (atelier
system) / Dieter Rams (pedestal
stand)
black, crystal grey

1   Four components cost less than
2,000 DM.

2   The system was expanded several
times before the "final edition" was successfully sold in 1989.

3   In 1979, the first CD player was introduced, and the *Walkman* ushered in a
boom in the music cassette industry.

4   The system was so well thought-out
that it could be assembled either vertically or horizontally. Despite their homo-
geneity, the individual components were
clearly distinguishable from one another.

Illus.:
P 4 record player
T 2 receiver
A 2 amplifier
C 2 cassette recorder
AF 1 pedestal stand

Can a product advance into the "S Class" through design? *atelier* is a perfect example of how this is possible. Conceived as an inexpensive starter system[1] in the late 1970s, the later versions of this hi-fi system, designed by Peter Hartwein, became Braun's flagship entertainment electronics product. It was a holistic approach in the best tradition of the Ulm Academy; the final versions even included a television set. This was the closest anyone had ever come to producing a hi-fi video system.[2] In this era of technological breakthroughs,[3] it was essential to create a universal framework that would also be compatible with future categories of appliances. Hartwein developed an open, additive concept that could function vertically as well as horizontally. Subtle tapering on the upper and lower edges of the individual elements made them narrower and separated them optically from one another even as it emphasized their external congruence. At the same time, this artful touch provided a distinctive look for the system as a whole. Matching roll-front cabinets were also available.

This was a lesson in the dialectic of the whole as a sum of its parts,[4] achieved through a comprehensive grid of compatibly designed control elements and delicate seams, as well as unusually uncluttered surfaces. Hartwein achieved the latter by drastically reducing the number of visible control buttons. Infrequently used functions were hidden under flaps or in "drawers". Since the same technique was applied to the cables, the system had no unsightly back panel. All of these factors culminated in a blackbox effect, reinforced by the appliances' black – or crystal grey – housing. The stereo system became a total work of art. The stacking of the elements led to the ideal concept of an integrated hi-fi tower, whose neutrality in relation to the most diverse lifestyles and decorating schemes was stressed in the advertising. A special pedestal stand provided the fitting platform for this audio monument.

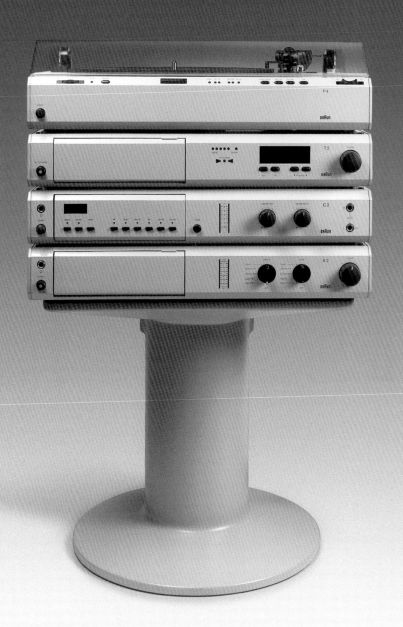

TS-G

1955 | Design: Hans Gugelot / Helmut Müller-Kühn
Tischsuper, RC 60
maple, walnut

Tabletop radios
1955

The speaker grooves (here, located below the dial), the simple grey control knobs and the horizontal and vertical elements were all defining characteristics of the early Braun radios.

G 11
1955 | Design: Hans Gugelot
Tischsuper, RC 60
maple

Gugelot had already used the technique of enclosing the body
between outer panels in his furniture designs. These appliances
could be placed either side-by-side or on top of one another. The
G 11 was identical in width and depth to the *G 12* record player.

SK 25

1961 | Design: Artur Braun / Fritz Eichler
Kleinsuper, FM and MW
graphite, light grey

Tabletop radios
1961

The perforated steel panel, which served as a front surface for the
appliance and a speaker cover in one, reappeared in many other
designs (e.g. the *TP 1* transistor radio). This small-format radio
could also be connected to the *PC 3 SV* record player.

RT 20

1961 | Design: Dieter Rams
Tischsuper, RC 31
beech / white, pearwood / graphite

The apotheosis as well as the swan song. With its austere geometry, Braun's last large-format tabletop radio represented a complete departure from the "standard radio" of the 1950s. The
arrangement of the control knobs was adopted from the *SK 4*.

T 22
1960 | Design: Dieter Rams
portable radio F/S/M/L
light grey

**Transistor
and portable radios**
1960–1961

Right angles, neutral colour, clear typography: the frugal principles employed here were borrowed from classical Modernism. This was the birth of the portable radio genre.

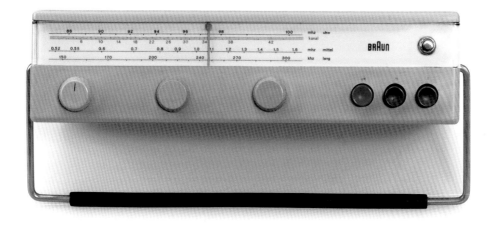

T 52
1961 | Design: Dieter Rams
portable radio F/M/L
light grey, blue-grey

The Braun designers thought of themselves as researchers, and
they varied their designs constantly. This portable appliance with
the dial on top could also be used as a car radio.

exporter 2

1956 | Design: Ulm Academy of Design (re-
design) portable radio with *NA 2* power base
grey-blue / white, English red / white

**Transistor
and portable radios**
1956–1962

The Ulm School approach: to strip an already existing model of
every type of stylish ornamentation. The speaker grooves correspond to those of the floor-mounted models, and the dial is reminiscent of the *Leica* miniature camera.

T 41
1962 | Design: Dieter Rams
transistor radio
light grey

Attention to detail is a Braunian virtue. The control knob is transposed
to the top of the appliance here, the dial is integrated into the housing,
and its radius is repeated in the perforated speaker field. All of these
elements combine to lend the design a sense of completeness.

TP 1

1959 | Design: Dieter Rams / Ulm Academy of Design
transistor radio-phonograph consisting of models *T 4* and *P 1*
light grey

**Transistor
and portable radios**
1959–1963

This set not only combined two portable audio appliances for the first time; it also combined formal brilliance with technical resourcefulness. The result was a category of appliance that was far – perhaps too far – ahead of its time.

108

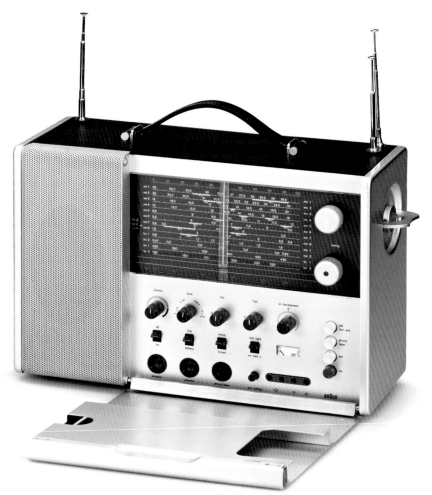

T 1000
1963 | Design: Dieter Rams
shortwave receiver
aluminium-coloured / black, white dial

This multiwave radio – a sensation at the time – was the embodiment
of Erwin Braun's idea of "Grand Design". Since the appliance was
sold out on the very first day, even customers who could afford it had
to go on a waiting list.

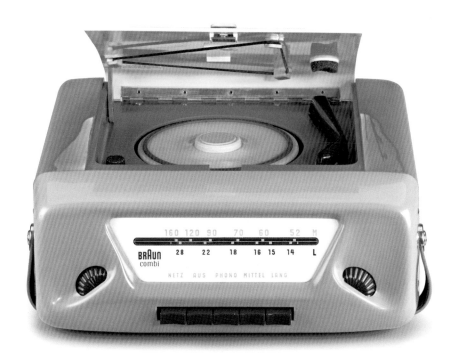

combi

1955 | Design: Wilhelm Wagenfeld
radio-phonograph combination / portable radio
light grey

Radio-phonograph combinations

1955–1956

Wagenfeld, who worked with glass, allowed softer lines to flow into his design. This is a second, less frequently noted idiom in Braun Design. Braun released a record single with a gymnastics course simultaneously with this appliance.

110

PK 1
1956 | Design: Thun Workshops
radio-phonograph combination, RC 61
walnut

The radio-record player unit had been a typical combination for
Braun since the 1930s. The right angles, light colour and simple
control knobs all reflect the influence of the Ulm School.

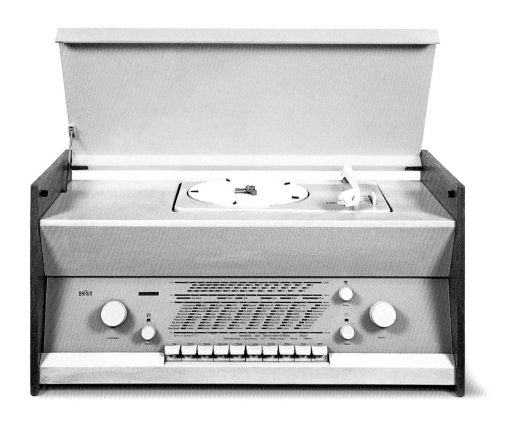

atelier 1
1957 | Design: Dieter Rams
compact system, RC 62
white / red elm

**Compact systems
with record players**
1957

As far as price was concerned (540 DM) this successful receiver was somewhere between the *studio 1* and the *SK 4* (295 DM). In performance and design, it was also an intermediate model. Its dimensions were identical to those of the *L 1* speaker.

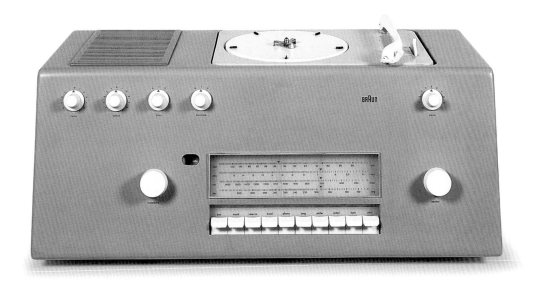

studio 1
1957 | Design: Hans Gugelot / Herbert Lindinger
compact system, RC 62-5
grey

According to the catalogue, the first large audio appliance produced in grey offered hi-fi sound quality. The design was almost
military in its austerity; the 1-metre-wide and 70-cm-high speaker
had a "low-noise" housing. The price: over 1,000 DM.

L 1
1957 | Design: Dieter Rams
compatible speaker for the *atelier* and *SK 4*
white / red elm

**Speakers,
compact systems
with record players**
1957–1963

With this separate speaker, conceived in the true spirit of Ulm School systemization and compatible with the *atelier 1* in both form and dimensions, the principle of the stereo system was already established.

SK 55
1963 | Design: Hans Gugelot / Dieter Rams
Phonosuper, FM, MW, LW, record player
white / ash

This successor to the *SK 4* had a modified front panel (the grooves were divided for technical reasons). The jacks for a tape recorder and additional speakers were located on the back panel.

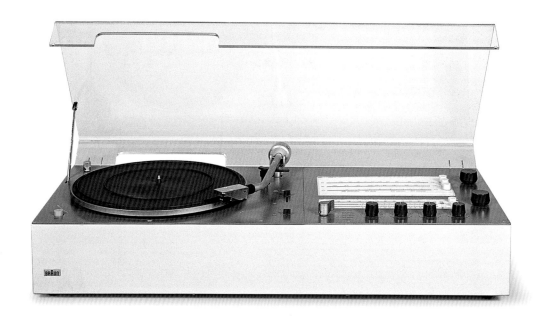

audio 2

1964 | Design: Dieter Rams
TC 45, compact system
white / aluminium-coloured, graphite / aluminium-coloured

**Compact systems
with record players**
1964–1970

This successor model to the *audio 1*, one of the first hi-fi appliances (later the *audio 300*), also had a metal housing. However, it was more powerful (at 40 watts) and had an improved record player. Matching pedestal stands were available.

116

cockpit
1970 | Design: Dieter Rams
250 S, compact system
black / light grey

Thanks to the slanted position of the dials, this particularly compact
system was "unconventional in shape" (catalogue), and the sharply
contrasting colours of its plastic housing made it stand out. The
coloured dots on the tuning knobs were typical for the period.

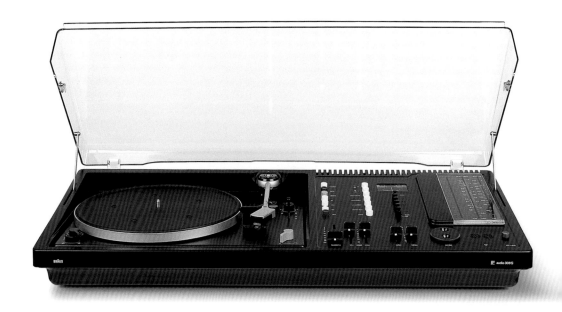

audio 308

1973 | Design: Dieter Rams
compact system (8° Series)
black

**Compact systems
with record players**
1973

The triumph of plastic: the "8° Series" – so called because of the
slant of the top panel – was a new design approach featuring details typical of the time, from the high-contrast colour scheme to
the ventilation ribs.

audio 400
1973 | Design: Dieter Rams
compact system
black

This compact system was one of Braun's top-of-the-line models.
The slide controls for the most important and frequently used
functions were placed on a raked surface, which facilitated their
operation.

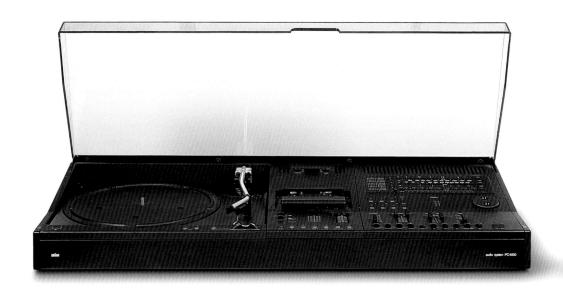

PC 4000

1977 | Design: Dieter Rams
audio system
anthracite / black

**Compact systems
with record players**
1977

This appliance, which included the high-quality *PS 500* record
player as well as a receiver and cassette recorder, was Braun's
last compact system. The angled rear section of the cover panel is
another variation on the lectern design.

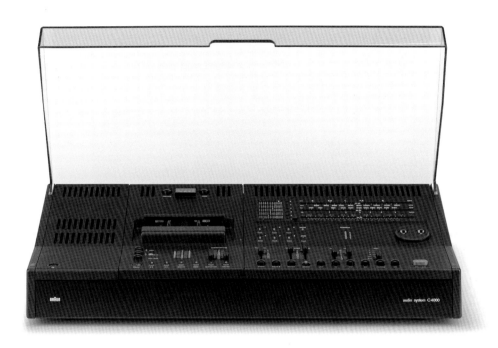

C 4000
1977 | Design: Dieter Rams
audio system
anthracite / black

The only compact system designed as a two-part combination of receiver and cassette recorder was a shorter variation of the *PC 4000* with otherwise nearly identical features.

**Compact systems
with cassette recorders**
1977

PK-G 4
1956 | Design: Hans Gugelot
radio-phonograph combination, RC 61, 10-disc record
changer | maple stand, maple (illus. bottom)

MM 4
1957 | Design: Werkstätten Thun
music cabinet, RC 61-1, 10-disc record
changer | red elm, walnut (illus. top)

Music cabinets
1956–1957

Music cabinets were top-of-the-line appliances. Removed from its
stand, Gugelot's dismountable model could be placed on a table
or shelf. The record player was protected by a sliding glass panel.

HM 1

1956 | Design: Herbert Hirche
music cabinet, RC 61
red elm, walnut

With its smooth front panel, this box complemented Hirche's sectional
cabinets, which likewise exuded the spirit of classical Modernism.
With a red elm or walnut finish, it also fit with the Scandinavian style.
The speaker was covered with a "special mesh fabric".

RB 10 / R 10 / RL 10

1958/1959 | Design: Herbert Hirche
R 10: stereo music cabinet, RC 81 | red elm, teak / RL 10: box speaker | red elm, teak
RB 10: storage cabinet (tape recorder cabinet) | red elm, teak | (illus. bottom)

L 3

1957 | Design: Gerhard Lander
speaker for *studio 1*
walnut / white / anthracite | (illus. top)

Music cabinets
Speaker units
1957–1960

"This music cabinet makes use of the sectional principle familiar to us from the furniture industry", the catalogue explained. The cabinet as well as the *L 3* speaker – which was originally released without a cover – were mounted on steel legs.

HM 6

1958 | Design: Herbert Hirche
stereo music cabinet, RC 7 / RC 8, 10-disc record changer
teak, walnut | (illus. bottom

R 22

1960 | Design: Herbert Hirche
stereo music cabinet, RC 82-C, 10-disc record changer
teak, walnut | (illus. top)

This stereo system, with five speakers located behind the parallel grooves typical of the time, belonged to the luxury class of music cabinets. It provided plenty of storage space for records and included a space for a tape recorder.

L 2
1958 | Design: Dieter Rams
speaker mounted on runners
white / white beech, white / walnut

Speaker units
1958

This eight-watt speaker box combined a tweeter and a woofer. It accentuates the circular shape of the speaker through contrasting colours and rests on nickel-plated tubular steel runners: Marcel Breuer would have approved.

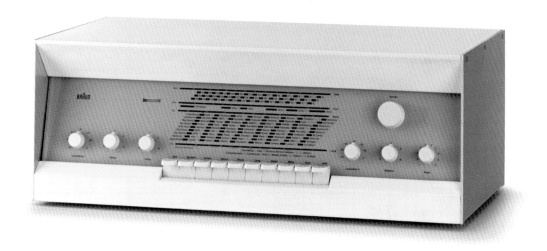

RCS 9

1961 | Design: Dieter Rams
Control unit
light grey / aluminium-coloured

As with the *L 2*, the housing of this stereo receiver was made of wood with a white plastic coating. The side panels are aluminium. It still has the look of an older-generation radio, even though the dials now have a linear format.

Control unit
1961

LE 1

1959 | Design: Dieter Rams
electrostatic speaker with stand
light grey / graphite

L 01

1959 | Design: Dieter Rams
additional speaker with stand
white / aluminium-coloured, graphite grey chrome

**Hi-fi systems
and components**
1959

The *LE 1* speaker, manufactured under licence, rests on a tubular steel stand, and as it is extremely flat, takes up very little space. As a freestanding, tilted surface in a room, it is somewhat reminiscent of a solar module. The *L 01* tweeter can be positioned in a variety of ways.

studio 2
1959 | Design: Dieter Rams
CE 11 receiver | *CV 11* power amplifier | *CS 11* record player control unit
light grey / aluminium-coloured

"Building blocks": the first stereo system to be made completely
out of metal and structured according to the stacking principle
emphasized the technical functions of the control units and ushered in the "silver age" in the hi-fi industry.

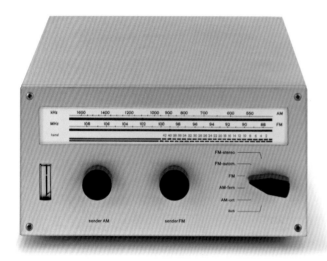

CET 15

1963 | Design: Dieter Rams
receiver
light grey / aluminium-coloured

L 02

1959 | Design: Dieter Rams
additional speaker
light grey / anthracite

**Hi-fi systems
and components**

1959–1966

The tuner could be set to stereo mode even before there were any stereo radio broadcasts. Later, a small light indicated flawless reception. The geometric minimalism of the *L 02* tweeter could scarcely be taken further.

CSV 12

1966 | Design: Dieter Rams
amplifier
light grey / aluminium-coloured

A shorter version of the amplifier (previously the *CSV 10*). The heart
of the stereo system, whose wattage (in this case, 28 watts) soon
took on a symbolic meaning similar to that of automobile horsepow-
er, contained eight control elements for different functions.

131

L 40
1961 | Design: Dieter Rams
bookshelf speaker
white, graphite or walnut / aluminium-coloured

L 1000
1965 | Design: Dieter Rams
floor-standing speaker
white / aluminium-coloured

**Hi-fi systems
and components**
1961–1965

The *L 40* definitely earned the title of "box". Its radically minimized design fit with the style of the new hi-fi "building blocks". The *L 1000*, a component of the *studio 1000* system, could also be used in large halls and discotheques.

132

Hi-fi system
1961/1962 | Design: Dieter Rams
PCS 5 record player | *CSV 13 / CSV 60* amplifier
light grey / aluminium-coloured

With the emancipation of the record player, which became an independent product type, and the amplifier – this one already had four input jacks (for record player, receiver, tape recorder and microphone) and 60 watts of power – the "hi-fi tower" began to take shape.

L 810
1969 | Design: Dieter Rams
studio speaker
white / aluminium-coloured, walnut / aluminium-coloured, white / black

---

**Hi-fi systems
and components**
1967–1969

Even the front panel, made of perforated, sheer aluminium sheeting (in this case, painted black), was a trend-setting element. The corners of the housing were slightly rounded and the stand allowed users to vary the angle at which sound was emitted.

studio 1000
1967/1968 | Design: Dieter Rams
CSV 500 amplifier | *PS 500* record player
light grey / aluminium-coloured, black / aluminium-coloured

The *studio 1000* system was intended to be a product "without prototypes or precedents" – except, perhaps, its own: a typical "Grand Design" project. One small, but not insignificant detail: the screw joints on the front panel were no longer visible.

CE 251
1969 | Design: Dieter Rams
receiver
anthracite / aluminium-coloured

**Hi-fi systems
and components**
1969–1970

This tuner in a compatible narrow format is impressive for its maximum degree of minimalism. Its appearance is modern even today, as further evidenced by such details as the silver-coloured tuning knob.

CSV 300

1970 | Design: Dieter Rams
amplifier
anthracite / aluminium-coloured

In addition to such details as the coloured on-off button and the absence of visible screws on the front panel, this appliance features such high-tech functions as magnetic or relay controls in the switching operations.

L 710
1969 | Design: Dieter Rams
studio speaker
white / aluminium-coloured, walnut / aluminium-coloured

**Hi-fi systems
and components**
1968–1969

Thanks perhaps to its neutral and unassuming appearance, this box – with its anodized aluminium mesh cover and white housing – was widely imitated.

regie 500
1968 | Design: Dieter Rams
control unit
anthracite / aluminium-coloured

This compact amplifier, whose appearance mirrors that of the
studio 1000, may be the very first miniature hi-fi system. By this
time, the elegant anthracite-and-silver colour combination was
already part of Braun's "Corporate Design".

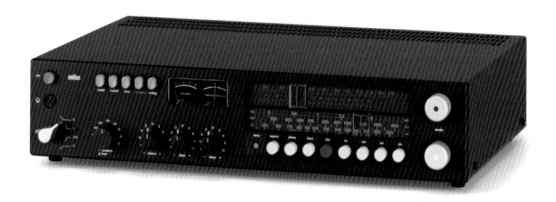

regie 510
1972 | Design: Dieter Rams
control unit
anthracite / aluminium-coloured, anthracite / black

Control units
1972–1976

This receiver was the first hi-fi module to be produced in black, a colour scheme that was already in use at the company and which would soon become typical for Braun. Black quickly became a standard colour, both inside and outside the audio industry.

140

regie 350
1976 | Design: Dieter Rams
control unit
anthracite / black

The sober black body also became an invitation to employ new
visual contrasts – a necessary feature for an appliance that now
boasted 21 control elements and seven dials.

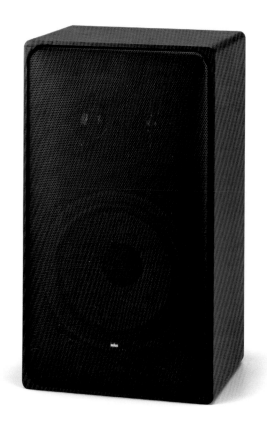

SM 1005
1978 | Design: Dieter Rams
studio monitor, bookshelf or floor-standing speaker
white, black or walnut / aluminium-coloured; black / black

**Hi-fi systems
and components**
1976–1978

In the late 1970s, Braun produced a completely black box speaker. The contrasting radii of the housing edges and cover corners gave it an elegant touch.

studio

1976 | Design: Dieter Rams / Robert Oberheim | *PS 550* record player
1978 | Design: Dieter Rams / Peter Hartwein | *TS 501* receiver | *A 501* amplifier | *C 301* cassette recorder
black, grey

Here we see a black-and-white aesthetic reminiscent of recording studios and slide rules. Now included among the "components" is a cassette recorder, which – due to the height of the cassette drive – does not share the slim format of the other elements.

LA sound
1980 | Design: Dieter Rams /Peter Hartwein
bass reflex speaker
black /black, walnut /brown

SM 2150
1979 | Design: Dieter Rams /Peter Hartwein
studio monitor, floor-standing speaker
aluminium-coloured, black or grey/black

**Hi-fi systems
and components**
1978–1980

Both of these speakers were available with removable front covers. The vertical arrangement of the membranes in the *SM 2150* – in keeping with the stacking principle used in hi-fi systems – resulted in a speaker tower fit for a studio.

PC 1 / RA 1

1978 | Design: Dieter Rams / Peter Hartwein
studio system PC 1 integral / RA 1 analog; record player and cassette recorder
black, grey

A space-saving miracle: no less than 25 control knobs are aligned
side by side across the only 55-mm-high receiver. The equally slim
record player also includes an integrated cassette recorder.

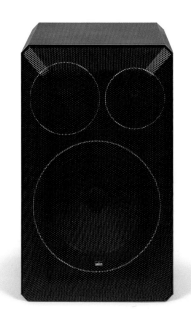

LS 70
1982 | Design: Peter Hartwein
bookshelf speaker
black / black, white / white, walnut / black

**Hi-fi systems
and components**
1980–1982

Both the colour combinations as well as the tapered upper and lower corners of these box speakers corresponded to the housing of the atelier system.

atelier 1

1980 | Design: Peter Hartwein
P 1 record player | *T 1* receiver | *A 1* amplifier | *C 1* cassette recorder
black, crystal grey

Conceived as a moderately priced product for younger consumers,
the *atelier 1* emerged as a formally and functionally sophisticated
system whose design was unequalled in its cohesiveness.

CM 6
1987 | Design: Peter Hartwein
compact monitor
black /black, white /white, grey /grey

LS 150 PA
1983 | Design: Peter Hartwein
powered floor-standing speaker
black/black, white/white

**Hi-fi systems
and components**
1982–1987

The wide variety of special speakers Braun produced allowed users to create personalized sound designs: this in itself was an innovation.

atelier

1982 | Design: Peter Hartwein | *A 2* amplifier | *C 2* cassette recorder | *T 2* receiver
1984 | Design: Peter Hartwein | *P 4* record player
black, crystal grey

Braun's last hi-fi system, in which only the most important control
elements remained visible on the surface, ultimately included a CD
player as well and was available in a luxurious "crystal grey"
colour.

L 308
1973 | Design: Dieter Rams
speaker (8° Series)
white / black

L 260
1972 | Design: Dieter Rams
bookshelf or wall speaker for the *cockpit 250/260*
white / black

**Control units
and components**
1972–1973

The perforations in the convex plastic covers once again pay homage to the *SK 1*. Their relatively large diameter was chosen for acoustic reasons; however, they also bring to mind the halftone dot patterns in Pop Art paintings.

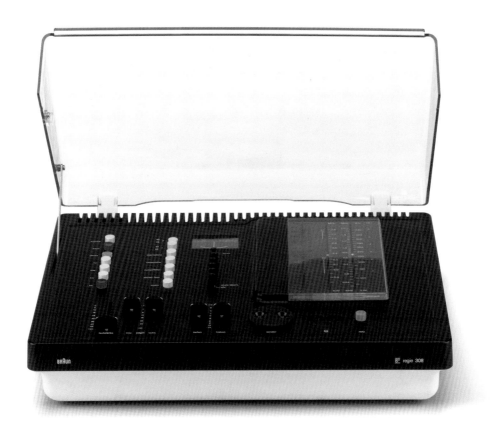

regie 308
1973 | Design: Dieter Rams
control unit (8° Series)
black/white

The look of this receiver, with its eight-degree slope, suggests that
of a mixing desk. Made completely out of plastic, it was inexpensive and designed to complement modern pop-style furniture.

PC 3

1956 | Design: Wilhelm Wagenfeld / Dieter Rams / Gerd Alfred Müller
grey / white

Record players
1956–1957

A portable, sparsely designed "suitcase" record player with practical details: There is a special compartment for stowing the cord, and singles can be secured inside the lid. A second, rounded version of the pick-up arm was also produced.

152

G 12 V
1957 | Design: Hans Gugelot / Wilhelm Wagenfeld
4-speed record player, *PC 3* body
maple

Braun's first separate record player was part of the "building block" system designed by Gugelot. When placed on top of the *G 11* radio, the combined appliances formed a kind of early audio tower. The *FS-G* television set was also identical in height.

PC 3-SV

1959 | Design: Wilhelm Wagenfeld /
Dieter Rams / Gerd Alfred Müller
white / graphite (illus. top)

PS 2

1963 | Design: Dieter Rams
white / graphite | (illus. bottom)

Record players

1959–1968

The first compact stereo record player – which was still configured
for 17 cm singles – fit onto a bookshelf and could be combined with
the *SK 1*. The *PS 2* record player, whose structure was based on
that of the *PC 3 SV*, already featured a tubular steel pick-up arm.

154

PS 500
1968 | Design: Dieter Rams
black/black, anthracite/aluminium-coloured
(illus. top)

PCS 5
1962 | Design: Dieter Rams
light grey/graphite | (illus. bottom)

The first record players of the early hi-fi era, which were soon converted into "building blocks" and which displayed their complex electromechanics beneath the now-obligatory plexiglas cover, once again set a new standard throughout the industry.

PS 358
1973 | Design: Dieter Rams / Robert Oberheim
black / white

Record players
1973–1977

This "semi-automatic" record player was part of the 8° Series. It was equipped with a straight pick-up arm, and the needle had to be lowered onto the record manually by means of a lifter pin.

PDS 550
1977 | Design: Dieter Rams / Robert Oberheim
black, grey

This slender model, part of the *studio* system, had an electronically controlled direct drive. It was operated by means of six sensors and a control disc. The attached cover featured recessed grips.

TG 504

1967 | Design: Dieter Rams
white / aluminium-coloured, anthracite / aluminium-coloured

Reel-to-reel tape recorders
1967–1970

This was one of the few reel-to-reel tape recorders to have a plexiglas cover and be compatible with a hi-fi system. It could even be mounted on the wall. All of the switching operations were triggered electrically.

TG 1000
1970 | Design: Dieter Rams
anthracite / aluminium-coloured, anthracite / anthracite

Conceived as a studio appliance, this tape recorder was a technical
masterpiece. The shape of the buttons and the colour scheme of the
control panel are reminiscent of the *D 300* projector. The colours also
anticipated the look of the 8° Series.

C 301
1978 | Design: Dieter Rams / Peter Hartwein
cassette recorder
black, grey

TCG 450
1975 | Design: Dieter Rams
cassette recorder
anthracite

Cassette recorders
1975–1980

The *C 301* cassette deck, part of the *studio* series, still had a vertically positioned drive. In the more compact *TCG 450*, the cassette was inserted in the top surface.

C 1
1980 | Design: Peter Hartwein
cassette recorder, *atelier 1*
black, crystal grey

The cassette deck for the *atelier 1* system was only 7 cm high; the
cassette could be inserted into a loading tray horizontally. New
features included the LED display and the cinch connector jacks
on the front panel.

CD 3

1985 | Design: Peter Hartwein
CD player, *atelier*
black, crystal grey | (illus. bottom)

CD 4

1986 | Design: Peter Hartwein
CD player, *atelier*
black, crystal grey | (illus. top)

CD-players
1985–1986

The clear linear layout of the joints was an element of the "calmed-down" surface. The slide-out loading tray – first introduced in the *C1* cassette deck – became a standard feature for CD players.

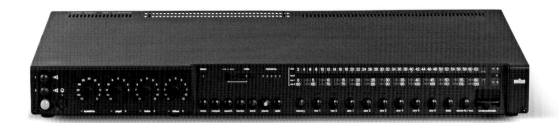

RS 1
1978 | Design: Dieter Rams / Peter Hartwein
Control unit, synthesizer
light grey, black

With its slide-rule dial, this was the slimmest receiver to be produced up to that time. The convex buttons were an innovation that
would later be used in the *atelier 1* as well as in clocks and pocket
calculators

Control units
1978

163

FS-G

1955 | Design: Hans Gugelot
tabletop set
maple, red elm

FS 3

1958
tabletop set (tubular steel stand available as an accessory)
walnut, red elm

Television sets

1955–1959

Gugelot's television set could be combined with the *G 11* radio and the *G 12* record player to form a system. In the *FS 3*, the right angles, simple knobs and tubular steel stand were all inspired by examples from classical Modernism.

164

HFS 2

1959 | Design: Herbert Hirche
television cabinet
walnut, red elm, teak

This television cabinet, which matched Hirche's furniture designs,
had a smooth front surface when the doors were closed. The same
appliance was also available in combination with a radio and a
record player.

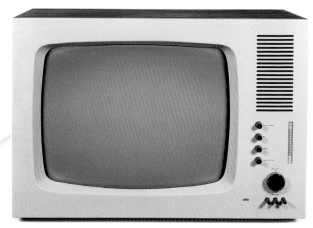

HF 1

1958 | Design: Herbert Hirche
tabletop set (accessory: tubular steel stand)
dark grey / light grey

FS 60

1964 | Design: Herbert Hirche / Dieter Rams
tabletop set (accessory: tubular steel stand)
white / walnut, white / red elm, white / teak

Television sets
1958–1967

Herbert Hirche's *HF 1* was one of the most cohesive designs in the industry; technically, however, it was surpassed within just a few years. With its larger assortment of control knobs on the front panel, the *FS 60* carried the appliance over to the next generation.

FS 80
1964 | Design: Dieter Rams
floor-mounted set with pedestal stand
light grey

FS 1000
1967 | Design: Dieter Rams
tabletop colour television
light grey

Even though Braun bought its technology from other manufacturers,
it succeeded in creating individual types even in the television sector.
The company's own hi-fi appliances – with their columns of control
knobs and parallel grooves – clearly served as design models.

TV 3/Subwoofer/LS 40

1986 | Design: Peter Hartwein
tabletop set + subwoofer + LS 40 satellite speakers
black, crystal grey

Television sets
1986

In this last television set, the display screen was finally freed from the conventional box. The soft curves of the frame are an example of the second, more flowing line in Braun Design. The integration of the appliance with the hi-fi system was the wave of the future.

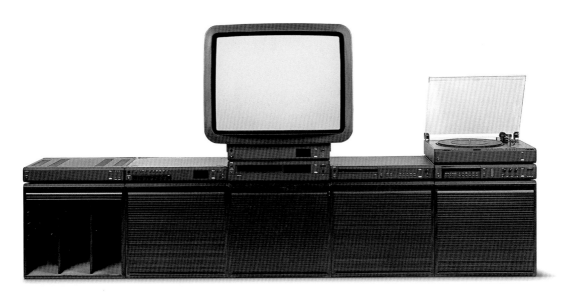

GS 3/4/5/6 with TV 3 television set and atelier hi-fi system

1984 | Design: Peter Hartwein
atelier | black, white, crystal grey

Combinations that go on to infinity: here, the audio-visual world was taking a final step toward totality. There has probably never been a system as harmonious as this one, which also integrated the concept of a private media archive.

Appliance cabinets
1984

GS 1/2 with studio hi-fi system
1978 | Design: Peter Hartwein / Dieter Rams
appliance stand
black, white

AF 1 with atelier hi-fi system
1982 | Design: Peter Hartwein (*atelier* system) /
Dieter Rams (*AF 1* pedestal stand)
black, crystal grey

**Appliance cabinets,
pedestal stands**
1978–1984

A solid pedestal stand allowed the user to place the system in the centre of the room. This had become a realistic option with the release of *atelier* as the first hi-fi system whose design also encompassed a presentable back panel.

170

GS 3/4/5/6 with LS 150 speaker unit and atelier hi-fi system

1984 | Design: Peter Hartwein
atelier appliance cabinet
black, white, crystal grey

A work of audio architecture: the dimensions of the system and
the cabinets were customized to create a harmonious whole. The
components could be arranged either horizontally or vertically.

KH 100
1968 | Design: Reinhold Weiss
mono headphones for the *T 1000 CD*
black | (illus. top left)

KH 500
1975 | Design: Dieter Rams
stereo headphones
black | (illus. bottom left)

KH 1000
1967 | Design Reinhold Weiss
stereo headphones
black

Headphones
1967–1975

Yet another premiere: Braun's first set of headphones, the
KH 1000, had a lightweight, adjustable metal frame and soft
ear cups whose rubber rings were filled with liquid.

Photography and Film

Introduction: **Photography**

1   This explains their marked kinship in form and colour with the pocket radios being produced at the time.

2   With the model *PA 1* (1956), Braun introduced the first projector with remote control and autofocus. In the *D 20* (1962) the company introduced a grip arm, finally finding a good solution for secure slide transport, the cardinal problem with this technology.

3   This allowed complex slide shows to be projected on gigantic screens made up of an assemblage of plastic modules.

4   Braun would not be Braun if the claim to totality had not been asserted here as well. Amateur photographers were offered an extensive range of accessories, from editing and viewing devices to film projectors

Illus.: *Nizo integral 7* film camera, detail

It all started with a visionary idea: Erwin Braun believed there was a market for handy electronic flash units. The still-rudimentary Design Department responded by producing designs in the ascetic style of New Objectivity: neutral grey cubes off Dieter Rams' drawing board.[1] He also designed compact slide projectors in the same light grey or silver, to match the growing product family.[2] In the early 1970s two projectors heralded a conceptual breakthrough: the double-decker *D 300* by Robert Oberheim and Peter Hartwein's two-eyed Tandem projector, an apotheosis of systematic design that verged on the limits of feasibility.[3] Anticipating the new colour trend in the phonograph market, the distinguished dark guise of both devices turned them into magical black boxes.

In his flash units, now also in black, Oberheim developed during the same period a complex and ergonomic formal language that lent expression to the mobility of the flash attachment, redefining the requisite qualities. Just a few years earlier, with similarly spectacular results, he had made his debut in a related field: cine film cameras – whose form Oberheim dictated for two decades – and the matching film projectors.[4] The *Visacustic 1000* and *2000* projectors are among the best ever made for amateur film. The *Nizo S 8* camera, which was presented for the first time in New York in 1965 – one year after the Braun show at the Museum of Modern Art – was the archetype for the modern Super 8 film camera. Braun proceeded to produce some top-of-the-line highlights in the amateur film market: the *S 8*, the *2056*, and finally the *integral* by Peter Schneider – a revolution in operating geometry that failed to evolve only due to the decline of cine film technology itself. Braun sold its film and photography division in 1981.

S 8

Nizo film camera

1965
Design: Robert Oberheim
Variogon 1,8 / 8–40 mm
aluminium-coloured

1 1969 Braun catalogue.

2 The Super 8 cassette film developed by Kodak dominated the amateur film market until the advent of the video camera.

3 The market-leading Munich firm Niezoldi & Krämer was taken over in 1962, after which its products were sold under the Braun *Nizo* brand.

4 In the first half of the 1960s, Braun succeeded several times in creating the paradigm for a whole product group, for example the *sixtant* electric shaver (1961) und the *T 1000* "world receiver" (1963). The concept behind the *Nizo* film cameras remained basically identical all the way through to the final model, the *integral* (1981).

5 The *sixtant* electric shaver was seminal for the colour combination of matte black / matte silver.

6 The same blank, clean surface – in the same materials and colour scheme – can be found in the *studio 2* stereo system.

"The Super 8 cassettes slide into the camera like letters into the mailbox."[1] The fact that time-consuming threading in of film was no longer necessary was good news for all cine film fans – but it wasn't the only innovation in the offing. Nearly simultaneously with the introduction of the new Super 8 format[2] in 1965, Braun presented – in the USA and then in Europe – the first camera developed for use with this film. The *Nizo S 8* would not only set the tone for the *Nizo*-type camera[3] during the next two decades; it was also regarded henceforth as the epitome of the modern cine film camera.[4] Its formula for success, now proven many times over, consisted combining high-level engineering with a rational formal vocabulary purged of the technological, visible-screws aesthetic. Through formal discipline, designer Robert Oberheim managed to achieve both enduring visual appeal and an unmistakable look, which is why *Nizo* film cameras are probably among the most-copied the world over.

By concentrating on the three essential parts of the camera – lens, housing and handle – a clear-cut structure was created, centring on the narrow, cubic camera body, cleansed of all embellishments. On its bright aluminium surface[5] – signifying technical brilliance and high value – the sparingly arranged controls stood out in high contrast, like on a signpost.[6] Their layout is determined by ergonomic considerations as well, as easy and secure handling is key to the use of a film camera. This is why the functions needed during filming – for example, the zoom – are located right above the handle. This means that counter pressure can be exerted by the hand holding the camera, preventing shaky and blurred images – the nightmare of every amateur filmmaker.

D 300

Slide projector

1970
Design: Robert Oberheim
black

1   The price of 329 or 398 DM (with au-tofocus) was justified by such unusual extras as an additional focus control via an optical display and the possibility of using "special effect slides" (e.g. for over-laying texts or filters for colour correction).

2   Black was also used for smaller de-vices such as the *T 2* lighter (1968) and the *manulux NC* flashlight from the same year; later, blackness came into vogue for electric shavers, pocket calculators and clocks as well, along with phonographs, where it was for a long time the industry standard and is still prevalent today.

3   Without lifting the device it could be raised or lowered or tilted to the side using an adjustment wheel.

4   Oberheim would revisit this principle, e.g. on the front and back of the *F 022* flash.

5   The *Synton FP* scoring device was developed for this purpose.

6   Nor was the attempt to accomplish this goal with the *Tandem Professional* double device an economic success.

Braun's last slide projector for standard slide trays was the first with a completely reworked design concept. The highly acclaimed model *D 300*, created by Robert Oberheim, was designed to appeal both to discriminating amateur photographers and profes-sional customers.[1] It replaced the technique used in the conven-tional type of projector, in which the tray rail was at the same level as the housing, with the piggyback principle. Lens and lamp were shifted to a second level, with the tray guided through the device's main body beneath them. The *D 300* is therefore narrower and takes up less space. The double-decker among the projectors was in addition the first major Braun device that was completely black. This first projector in Sunday dress can thus be regarded as trig-gering the "black wave" that soon washed over many other prod-uct areas as well.[2] Although the explanation for choosing this colour sounds thoroughly rational – the device was to be used in a darkened room and should hence not be reflective – it was of course also a question of creating an elegant look.

The *D 300* is a design of unusual density, evincing sculptural quali-ties. Contributing to this self-contained look are both the integrat-ed base[3] and a precisely articulated surface, featuring for example two graphically pleasing opening flaps that meet at the upper edge. The switches, instead of being located at the back (as com-mon up to that time), are arranged clearly along one side. This control panel is then "framed" within a rectangular recess.[4] The slideshow could be controlled and a soundtrack added via a reel-to-reel or cassette tape recorder,[5] laying the groundwork for the multimedia system of the future. The claim that the *D 300* repre-sented "the first step toward audiovision" could ultimately not be met, however.[6]

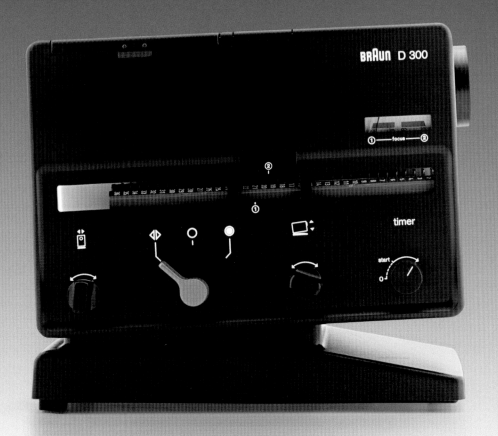

F 022

Flash unit
1972
Design: Robert Oberheim
2000 vario computer
black

1   The contrast is also reminiscent of the silver-and-black combination found in the *sixtant* electric shaver (1962).

2   Scratch-resistant ABS. The first black and anthracite-coloured flash units came out in the early 1960s, inspired by the sixtant electric shaver, e.g. the *F 80 professional* (1961) and *F 65 hobby* (1962).

3   At the time, this material was regarded as inferior and by no means a matter of course.

4   The lower curves also make it easier to operate the photo camera on which the flash is mounted. In the film projector *FP 25* (1971) and the film camera *Nizo S 1* (1972) these same formal features can be seen, likewise combined with black.

5   Between 1972 and 1985 Oberheim designed over 40 models; before him, Dieter Rams had been in charge of this product line.

6   The first completely black device was the *D 300* slide projector of 1970, likewise by Oberheim.

The sparkling light – in the form of a bulging monitor – stands in stark colour contrast to the dark housing. This clearly highlights the main function – the flash[1] – a look that still sets the tone for electronic flashes today. The housing of the *2000 vario* (*F 022*) is made of rigid plastic[2] with a slightly textured surface, connoting reliability[3] and allowing for a good grip – important in a device handled so frequently. Consisting of two shells, the housing possesses a many-layered texture that conveys its qualities tactilely during use. The basic form is dictated by strong curves in the outer edges and the lower corners, forming a "chin".[4] Flat at the top, the case makes an exceptionally integrated impression for its era, while looking extremely robust. The handy *2000 vario*, first in a long series of electronic flashes designed by Robert Oberheim,[5] marked a conceptual breakthrough. It offered a further alternative to what in comparison was the quite trivial box form, while also ushering in the breaking "black wave".[6] The controls are colour-coded in green, red and blue, facilitating comprehension and operation while standing out clearly against the matte black ground.

This compact model introduced a sophisticated formal language and a convenience hitherto unknown in the amateur arena of this product field. Key advantages over previous models were automatic release via a sensor eye, and a light that could be swivelled upward for an indirect flash. The swivel mechanism is executed in the simplest way imaginable: the lamp is attached at the sides by wheels that do double duty as swivel knobs, turning at just a touch of thumb and forefinger.

Nizo integral

Nizo film camera

1979
Design: Peter Schneider
Macro-Variogon 1,2 / 7,5–50 mm
black

1   Between 1979 and 1981, the models *integral 5, 6, 6 S, 7* and *10* came onto the market.

2   With five buttons, from Single-Frame Release (Timer) to Daylight Filter.

3   Instead of the imaginary grid customary up to that time.

This deluxe model was equipped with pretty much everything the amateur filmmaker of the day could dream of, and offered some clever design refinements on top of it. The forward-jutting handle was a landmark innovation. The angle enabled a natural arm position and was henceforth adopted for professional cameras as well. The numerous special features included a microphone that telescoped out of the handle and a built-in, individually adjustable shoulder support. Since more technology meant more weight, the housing was for the first time made of lightweight plastic.

Although formal continuity was preserved, *Nizo integral*, Braun's last camera series,[1] represented a quantum leap for this product group – including in terms of handling. As its most conspicuous feature, designer Peter Schneider developed a function bar[2] to replace the assortment of individual buttons that had prevailed before. This was not only a new organizational layout, bringing all functions in line both conceptually and literally[3] – the visual reduction is at the same time a practical aid that made operation much easier by improving comprehension: when one of the sliding controls is out of line, it signifies that a special setting has been chosen. And when all controls are at the zero position, the user knows that the camera is set to automatic operation. The multifunctional control bar – which stands out in high relief and is placed directly at eye-level with the filmmaker – ends in an indicator showing how much film is left, probably the most important information for the filmmaker.

EF 1
1958 | Design: Dieter Rams
hobby standard
light grey

Flash units
1958–1962

The flash product group was not incorporated into the new design concept until a few years after the phonographs. As with the pocket radios, their style was guided by the idiom of classical Modernism.

F 60/30
1959 | Design: Dieter Rams
hobby
light grey

F 21
1962 | Design: Dieter Rams
hobby
light grey

The first flash unit in pocket format. Advances in condenser technology made the flat shape of the *F 60* possible. The cubic *F 21*, which brings to mind the *HF 1* television, among other things, was the first one-piece electronic flash.

185

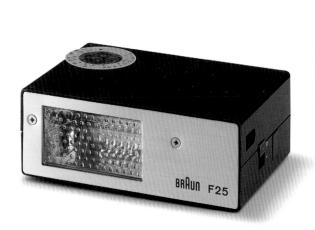

F 25
1963 | Design: Dieter Rams
hobby
grey

F 100
1966 | Design: Dieter Rams
hobby
light grey

Flash units
1963–1969

The horizontal slab shape with glass pane integrated into the flat front was a type all its own. The thumb wheel integrated in one side looks like the dial of a pocket radio.

EF 300
1964 | Design: Dieter Rams
hobby
grey

F 655
1969 | Design: Dieter Rams
hobby
grey

The flash bulb separated from the body of the unit and perched on
a wand became the model for professional applications. A new
kind of modular system was developed for this purpose.

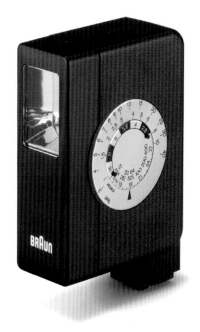

F 111
1970 | Design: Dieter Rams
hobby
black

F 022
1972 | Design: Robert Oberheim
2000 vario computer
black

23 B
1974 | Design: Robert Oberheim
hobby
black

Flash units
1970–1976

The *F 022* is a device type that displays a new approach to the flash unit, bringing together the analytical and organic lines in Braun Design. This strategy would become standard in the industry, not least due to its ergonomic advantages.

F 900
1974 | Design: Robert Oberheim
professional
black

380 BVC
1976 | Design: Robert Oberheim
vario computer
black

In the 1970s professional and semi-professional devices also came
onto the market. In the sensor-controlled 380 *BVC* the batteries are
housed in the thick, wand-shaped handle.

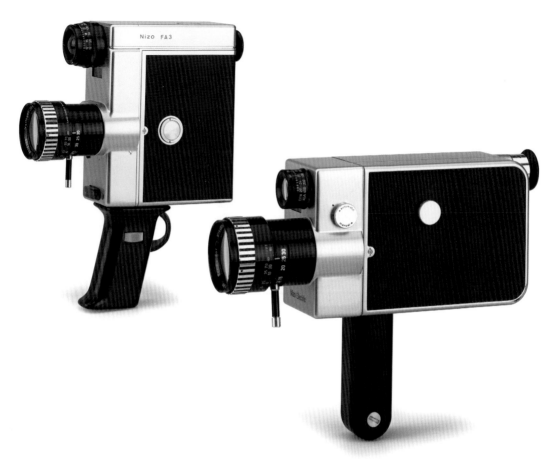

FA 3

1963 | Design: Dieter Rams / Richard Fischer / Robert Oberheim
spring mechanism / *Variogon* 1,8 / 9–30 mm
black / aluminium-coloured

EA 1

1964 | Design: Dieter Rams / Richard Fischer
electric / *Variogon* 1,8 / 9–30 mm
black / aluminium-coloured

Nizo film cameras
1963–1968

There was no new aesthetic or ergonomic concept behind the first
Nizo cine film cameras. The lenses were not yet designed by Braun.

S 8 T
1965 | Design: Robert Oberheim
Variogon 1,8 / 7–56 mm
aluminium-coloured

S 56
1968 | Design: Robert Oberheim
Variogon 1,8 / 7–56 mm
aluminium-coloured

The *S 8* – a later model is shown here – formed the turning point.
Now the main elements of the camera were distinguished from
one another clearly using colour, and the arrangement of the controls was thought through down to the last detail.

191

S 800 set / Schulterstativ ST 3
1970 | Design: Robert Oberheim (Kamera) / Peter Hartwein (Stativ)
Variogon Macro 1,8 / 7–80 mm
black

Nizo **film cameras**
1970–1973

The first black film camera (which came out the same year as the black *D 300* slide projector) was the top-of-the-line product of its day in terms of features. The shoulder tripod, extendable to 26 cm, could be folded up and stowed in a camera bag.

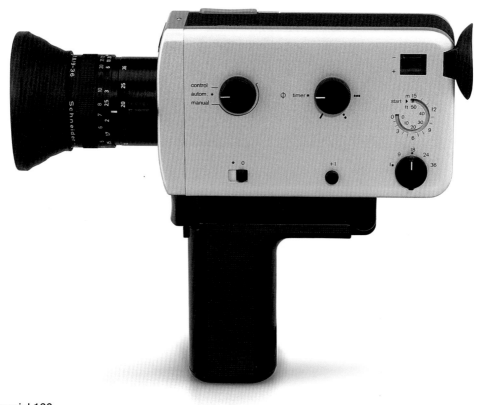

spezial 136
1973 | Robert Oberheim
Variogon 1,8 / 9–36 mm
aluminium-coloured

The cubic form of the body echoes the simple shape of the cassette. The film indicator and dials are arranged clearly, creating a
calm sense of order.

2056 sound

1976 | Design: Peter Schneider
Macro-Variogon 1,4 / 7–56 mm
aluminium-coloured

Nizo film cameras
1974–1979

This model was one of the first sound cameras to make subsequent synchronization of a soundtrack superfluous (the soundtrack was on the film). It already had an ergonomically designed, slanted handle and controls lined up in a neat row.

194

professional
1974 | Design: Robert Oberheim
Variogon Macro 1,8 / 7–80 mm
aluminium-coloured

integral 7
1979 | Design: Peter Schneider
Macro-Variogon 1,2 / 7–50 mm
black

The *integral* – a high-class sound camera in matte black – had an integrated telescopic microphone. With its plastic housing it was cheaper to produce and, because of its light weight and sliding controls, easier to use as well.

FP 1 S
1965 | Design: Dieter Rams / Robert Oberheim
Nizo film projector
light grey

Film projectors
1965–1971

The first film projector, brought out in parallel with the silver camera *S 8*, had a central control button, clearly set off in a different colour.

FP 30
1971 | Design: Robert Oberheim
film projector
aluminium-coloured

For this projector a configuration similar to that of a reel-to-reel
tape player was chosen, allowing important controls to be moved
closer to the operator.

1000
1976 | Design: Peter Hartwein
Visacustic stereo sound projector with speaker
black

Film projectors
1976

For this sound projector developed by Peter Hartwein, a separate speaker unit was available (which could be snapped on for transport). Another speaker could be used to generate stereo sound. Height and lateral adjusters were integrated into the device.

198

FK 1
1968 | Design: Robert Oberheim
film splicer
grey, aluminium-coloured

FK 4
1977 | Design: Peter Schneider
film splicer
black

For *Nizo* cine film fans, just as devoted a group as the phonograph community, there were accessories to be had in similar high design quality: here two much-coveted splicers.

Film accessories
1968–1977

PA 1
1956 | Design: Dieter Rams
automatic projector
light grey

Slide projectors
1956–1963

The vertical layout of the tray shaft and lens, the slanted front and the rounded corners give this device its special look. The buttons are arranged on a "ledge" for easy accessibility.

D 6
1963 | Design: Dieter Rams
Combiscope
light grey

Multifunctionality: a slide projector that, tilted on end, can also be
used as a viewer. A practical, but never again realized combination.

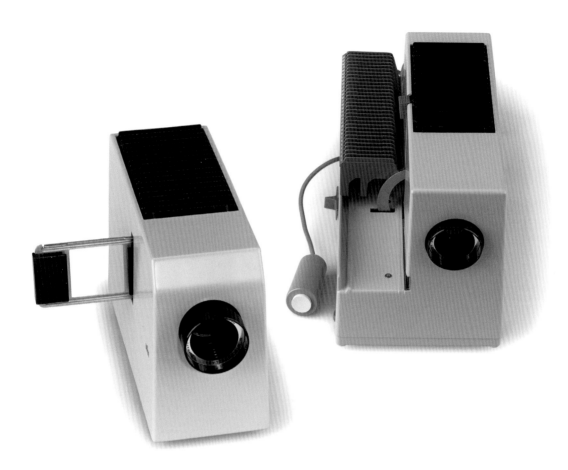

D 10
1962 | Design: Dieter Rams
small projector
light grey

D 20
1962 | Design: Dieter Rams
automatic low-voltage projector
light grey, graphite

Slide projectors
1962–1966

With the slide tray guided along the side on an open rail, parallel to the lens, a layout had been found that would dominate the market for decades.

D 25

1966 | Design: Robert Oberheim
automatic slide projector
light grey / dark grey

The low-height version with extended functionality in the remote
control was a type that was much emulated in the industry. This
slide projector also came out as *D 45 / D 47* in the silver that was
typical for Braun at the time.

D 300
1970 | Design: Robert Oberheim
automatic slide projector
black

Slide projectors
1970–1974

With a form that borrows from Braun's very first slide projector, this device was unique in many ways. It offered more practical advantages than other standard-tray projectors and was made out of various plastics.

Tandem

1974 | Design: Peter Hartwein
Professional (with timer)
black

This double projector, which exploited the benefits of the round
slide tray, formed the core of Braun's sophisticated multivision
system with its various control devices. Projection boxes could be
combined to create picture walls of different sizes.

Nizo 1000

1968 | Design: Robert Oberheim
pocket camera
black / aluminium-coloured

1000

1978 | Design: Robert Oberheim
Nizolux film light
black

Photo camera,
film accessories

1968–1978

Braun's sole photo camera was a compact system with built-in distance gauge. The flattish cube with curved edges came with a carrying case.

Clocks and Pocket Calculators

1971	*phase 1* desktop and alarm clock
1975	*AB 20* desktop and alarm clock
	functional desktop and alarm clock
	ET 11 pocket calculator
1977	*DW 20* wristwatch
	ET 33 pocket calculator
1978	*ABR 21* clock radio
1979	*DN 50* desktop and alarm clock
	ABW 21 wall clock
1981	*ABW 41* wall clock
1985	*AB 312 vsl* desktop and alarm clock
1989	*AW 10* wristwatch
1990	*ABR 313 sl* clock radio
1991	*DB 10 sl* desktop and alarm clock
2001	*AW 75* wristwatch
2002	*ET 100* pocket calculator

1   The line of digital clocks is currently being continued in the radio-controlled alarm clock *DB 10 sl* (1991).

2   With alarm clocks, wall clocks and wristwatches, virtually the entire range of products in this sector was covered. Constant variations within a narrowly defined formal framework led to an amazing variety of types. In the case of alarm clocks, an ergonomic aspect was added, i.e. especially in the design and arrangement of the on-and-off buttons.

illus.: *AW 75* wristwatch

For one of the last of the new product groups to be introduced at Braun, 1975 was a key year. This was the year the *functional* digital alarm clock was launched on the market, the first clock developed totally at Braun, and quite the eye-catcher at that.[1] That same year saw the analogue alarm clock *AB 20* and the first pocket calculator, both successful models with an extremely long aesthetic half-life and corresponding popularity among consumers. The *AB 20*, with its straightforward look of a tachometer plucked from an aeroplane cockpit, left a lasting mark on the appearance of alarm clocks from both Braun and other manufacturers. Later models equipped with special features, such as the radio alarm clock *ABR 21* or the noise-sensitive *voice control AB 312*, were cast in the same mould.

Responsible for all the designs mentioned above was Dietrich Lubs, who put the principle of long service life into practice in a field where it was singularly appropriate: measuring time. Two decades after Max Bill had made rationally designed domestic clocks socially acceptable, Lubs carried forth this approach on a much broader basis, making use of the new quartz technology.[2] Reading the time is a matter of perception, and Lubs optimized the graphic elements needed to do so. These efforts went hand-in-hand with the field of product graphics, in which Lubs was likewise involved – a field that also found application in every other product group, for example in radio or phonograph scales. This attention to visual detail was another of Braun's strong suits. In the bedside and travel alarm clocks, the largest clock segment, the negative lettering and the quartet of hands with their easy-to-read symbolic colours create a simple and clear iconography. At the same time, the clocks, along with the pocket calculators, followed the trend toward black that set in during the 1970s: the colour of the night, of outer space and of spirituality, but also of the finest fountain pens, of festive occasions and exclusive limousines.

functional

Alarm clock

1975
Design: Dietrich Lubs
Digital DN 42
Nr. 4815
black
(*Digital DN 18* velour nickel-plated)

1   This form of time display was introduced in the 1950s (Gino Valle, for example, designed the *Cifra 5* digital clock for Solari in 1955), here in a mechanical variation.

2   A look that belies the actual weight of the metal housing.

3   The basic form for the digits is an "8" formed by stacked squares. This is a gas discharge display, at the time a fairly common but expensive technology. The brightness of the display can be regulated using a dimmer.

4   This physical distinction between important, directly accessible functions and minor, "hidden" ones was first used in the *HF 1* television set (1958) and later in the *atelier* hi-fi system (1980).

5   The principles of perceptual physiology and psychology applied here can also be found in the pocket calculators developed during the same period.

phase 1, the first clock Braun offered, had a digital display.[1] Four years later, the company could boast a genuine self-developed Braun product, this time electronic: *functional*. An early design by Dietrich Lubs, this plug-in alarm clock is unusual in several ways. The major components are not hidden away in a box, but rather expressed separately in the outward form. Display and transformer – in two distinctly separate housing parts – also serve as the front and rear base. Between them "floats" the narrow circuit board, which also functions as the control area.

The slim-waisted, two-centimetre-thick body of the clock looks as lightweight[2] and sleek as an Italian sports car. This effect is underscored by the racy, backward-leaning and therefore easily legible display, whose tinted plexiglas recalls a pair of sunglasses. The six segmented digits[3] are angular but can still be read without effort. The control buttons are on top for easy accessibility, while all setting elements are concealed on the underside.[4] Convex keys facilitate night-time operation, as the millimetre-high bumps can be felt with the fingertips.[5] But that's not the reason *functional* became such a coveted collector's item. The compact metal alarm clock rose to the status of a cult object because it exudes the cachet of a modern sculpture. This is especially the case in the black version, where the display surface melds with the slim housing to form a congenial whole. *functional* is anything but a sombre measuring device – it looks more like a UFO that has just come to rest on the bedside table.

DW 30

Wristwatch

1978
Design: Dieter Rams / Dietrich Lubs
quartz LCD digital
No. 4814
chrome (black not sold)

1   This is a fact not always taken to heart by management. For example, at some point not even one quarter of the customers buying the grass trainer Samba from Adidas were actually wearing the shoes for sport. It took the company a long time to pick up on this.

2   The black watches, produced in smaller numbers, are even more sought-after.

3   With a smooth or ribbed leather strap.

4   The buttons were also used to change from time display to month and day or seconds and minutes; the left button also activated the light.

5   Their clear legibility also picks up on the tradition of Max Bill, who brought out a series of rationally designed clocks in the 1950s that set the standard for "good form" in this product area.

6   One example of the paradox of precision and long life was an advertising campaign in the 1990s for atomic clocks, which supposedly "vary only by one second every million years", but for which the manufacturer was only prepared to give a six-month guarantee.

What do wristwatches and trainers have in common? Although both are purpose-built tools that everyone owns, in the 1980s they became part of the category of "lifestyle products"[1] in which concepts like prestige, luxury and individuality play a major role. Braun's entry into the watch segment was originally a technical experiment, one of the aims being to open up a new field of endeavour for the company's electronics-savvy engineers. Braun wristwatches were latecomers to the lifestyle market and were initially offered only in modest editions. The fact that they are in high demand by collectors today may therefore be attributable to other qualities than merely being fabricated of metal. In particular the digital watches *DW 20* and *DW 30* with LCD display, both of which still cut an elegant figure today, are among the most popular historical Braun objects.[2]

The model *DW 30*, whose metal case[3] came in either black or silver, was the company's first proprietary development. Dietrich Lubs and Dieter Rams succeeded here once again in creating a harmonious, pleasing geometry. In terms of colour, they remained in lock step with the black-and-silver cosmos of Braun products, which had expanded without end since the 1960s. The two push buttons below the display, which are used to set the time,[4] guarantee absolute ease of operation. The design of the analogue wristwatches was modelled on the faces of the Braun wall and alarm clocks.[5] Despite all objectivity, however, an item one wears daily on the body is by nature a very personal affair. And what could express values like discretion and dependability[6] better than a clock?

ABR 21

Clock radio
1978
Design: Dieter Rams / Dietrich Lubs
signal radio
No. 4826
black, white

1   Radio alarm clocks can be considered the new standard radios, both as
regards their widespread use (90% of
the German population has one, according to the Consumer Electronics Society)
as well as their dominance on the
shelves of electronics stores.

2   A round, perforated field for the
speaker was also used in the *T 4* pocket
radio (1959).

3   In the models *ABR 313*, *ABR 314 rsl*
and *ABR 314 df* (1996) with LCD display,
touch-button programming and fold-
down front cover, a more compact format was introduced.

4   They are identical with the rocker
switches in the alarm clocks *AB 20* and
functional (both 1975).

Where there's a bed, a radio alarm clock can't be far off – a device
type[1] that is presumably the audio industry's most variable. For
the ever-popular radio with wake-up function, Dietrich Lubs and
Dieter Rams came up with a convincing formula: they decided to
give both device components equal weight. The dial and speaker
are rendered as circles with the same radius, symmetrically placed
on a rectangular background. This disciplined graphic structure of
almost military severity prompted déjà vu experiences. After all,
the round perforated speaker surrounded by a circular scale – particularly in connection with the two knobs underneath – showed
marked affinities with the small *SK 1* radio.[2]

In later radio alarm clocks[3] the past was no longer quoted. The
convex rocker switches on top of the *ABR 21* were selected from
a building kit of forms that designers drew on for the entire clock
range,[4] as was the matte black colour, the purist dial and the four
hands with their distinguishing colours. The two wide, white hands
show minutes and hours, the slim yellow one seconds and the slim
black one indicates the alarm time (with a coloured point) – long a
combination typical for the brand, with high recognition value. The
yellow second hand in particular became a signet for analogue
clocks, whose rational design recalls an automobile speedometer.
Also participating in this strict neutrality is the Braun corporate
typography – found in every product line. "Akzidenz Grotesk" is
a typeface with only faint serifs in which the verticals and curves
have the same width visually, but not the ends. It thus becomes,
similarly to Helvetica, an unobtrusive "typeface without qualities".

ABW 41

Wall clock

1981
Design: Dietrich Lubs
domodisque
No. 4839
black

1   Max Bill, who in the late 1950s designed clearly articulated, "functional" clock dials, also started with wall clocks.

2   The clock is available in various colours, materials (metal, plastic) and with different dials (in some versions there are no minute markings); in the most reduced version, the plexiglas cover is left off.

The clock per se. If there were such a thing, this is probably what it would look like. The same year that Milan's Memphis Studio was turning all cherished design truisms on their head, ringing in the post-modern age of 'anything goes', Braun delivered yet another example of how restrained design and classical functionalism could be married in a new product. There is a hidden reason why this object lesson took the shape of a wall clock: the fact that it is hung up means there is no need for a base. The clock is therefore all dial.[1] The setting knob as well – which has been brought in front to make it possible to set the time without taking the clock off the wall – disappears in its position as central pivot. The time disk is thus a purely geometrical object that "floats" before the wall, its hands confirming in their steady turning the wisdom of the principle that "form follows function".

While Dietrich Lubs maintained his familiar visual and typographical purity here, he also added a third dimension of depth. The gradation of the dial into three levels was something new. It gives the clock a tangible texture – a small tweak that had significant consequences: the *ABW 41* was the flattest clock in the world. The spatial tiering of the body in addition created shadow rings and gave the hands an extra visual guide. Both increase legibility, especially when seen from far off, as wall clocks tend to be. Although this clock series can be deemed a prime example of applied minimalism, it still comes in an astounding array of variations.[2]

AB 312 vsl

Alarm clock

1985
Design: Dietrich Lubs
voice control
No. 4760
black

1 Affixed above the dial as a metal "ear".

2 It weighs only about 60 grams.

3 The previous model, *AB 312 ts* (1984), had no voice control. The successor, *voice control AB 314 vsl*, had some improved details, e.g. a clear separation of the setting functions (a locked time-set on the back, wake-up time on the side) and the possibility of locking these using a special button.

4 This normative aesthetic was set by the *AB 20* (1975) and prevailed over the following years.

5 The "complete renunciation of special formal features" (*Weniger, aber besser* [Less, But Better], Dieter Rams, Hamburg 1995, p. 95), which Dieter Rams claimed as characteristic for the clocks developed under his purview, is impossible to realize.

"Stop!" "Silence!" "Be quiet!" In the *voice control* clocks just a shout can make the alarm stop ringing. With this innovation Braun revolutionized our morning wake-up ritual in the mid-1980s. Of course, the acoustic sensor[1] also reacts to almost any other kind of noise, such as knocking or coughing. This quality predestined the device as an ideal toy for children, who of course love to test these noisy ways of exercising their control.

The *voice control AB 312 vsl* by Dietrich Lubs, a slim two-and-a-half centimetres and as light as a sheet of paper,[2] fits in any bag, making it the ideal travel alarm clock. This is a universal genius in miniature format, which even works as a flashlight. Its polyglot fold-down front cover, which displays the world time zones, gives it a stable base. And the dial of the voice control echoes the familiar formal repertoire that Braun standardized for analogue alarm clocks.[3] It was modelled on the neutrality of technical instrument panels, but can by no means be considered a case of non-design.[4] This is already demonstrated by the high degree of recognition the clocks enjoy, making them one of the most widespread carriers today of the Braun philosophy of rational design. At the same time, they are an example of how even the most rational product is rife with meaning.[5] We might even see in the product's black housing a metaphor for night, singularly fitting for its function as an alarm clock.

DB 10 sl

Radio-controlled clock

1991
Design: Dietrich Lubs
digital
No. 3876
grey / green, grey

1 In its last version as *DB 12*.

2 Their colours are based on the pocket calculators.

3 This for one thing offers the advantage that the user can see the display while programming the alarm.

4 Especially in the silver version, where the material somewhat resembles corrugated metal sheeting, an idiom familiar from the realm of high-tech architecture. The plastic housing comes in the classic Braun colours of black and silver.

5 An example of the use of plastics of varying degrees of hardness, but without the components being fused as they are in hard-and-soft technology.

Braun's first radio-controlled alarm clock also measures the room temperature.[1] With this versatile informant, the developers took another step into the digital age. Now that technology took up so little space, one might assume that the form of the housing would no longer be dictated by it. But that is at most a half-truth. The face of the nine-cm-high *DB 10* and its successors is dominated by an LCD display in turquoise and the keypad underneath.[2]

As a rule, a display is vertical and the keypad below it flat – for ergonomic reasons. But in order to unite both on one plane, Dietrich Lubs tilted the two elements toward one another.[3] Thus was born the first clock in ski-jump form. The anti-slip ridges on the sides likewise have something architectural about them.[4] For enhanced stability, the monument-like measuring station is equipped with rubber stoppers and an anti-tilt wedge at the back, which also houses the antenna. Features like the 24-hour alarm clock and remote-controlled, and hence absolutely precise, time keeping are things today's consumer simply takes for granted. But what about the incredible ease of operation and attention to detail that can be felt down to the fingertips: small niceties like the friendly click of the rod-shaped night-time alarm and light switch, the way the keypad cover, which can be opened and closed with the little finger, slides so exactly into place, or the tiny programming buttons whose velvety surface caresses the fingers each time they're pressed?[5]

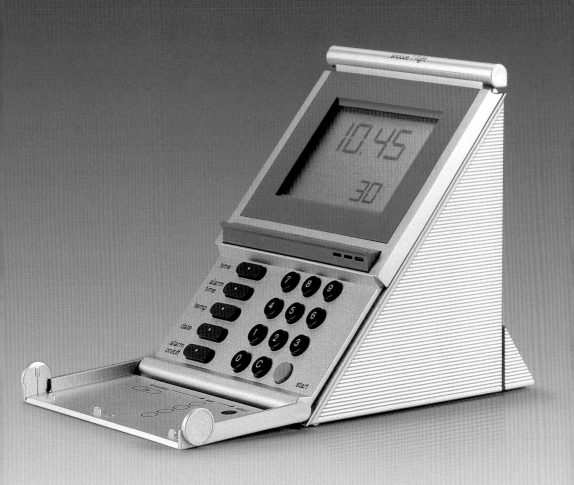

ET 33

Pocket calculator

1977
Design: Dieter Rams / Dietrich Lubs /
Ludwig Littmann
control LCD (slim LCD)
No. 4993
black

1 For example, the device could be made smaller, but this would have a negative impact on ease of handling and the layout of the functions.

2 The number of keys does not necessarily have to be 25. Competitors' products are frequently overloaded with many seldom-used functions.

3 A borrowing from the clock developers, first seen in the alarm clocks *AB 20* and *functional* (both 1975).

4 Meaning keys into which the fingertip "sinks".

5 They emit a silent little "click" when pressed, providing additional orientation.

6 Their design remained virtually unchanged for a good quarter century, which helped them to stand up to the onslaught of cheap imitators.

Order, frugality, harmony, utility. It is no accident that the small arena occupied by pocket calculators tends to gather together all the virtues typical of rational Braun Design. Innate to the small computer that Dietrich Lubs, Dieter Rams and Ludwig Littmann shrunk down to a slim tablet is precisely that brand of mathematical logic that forms the essential basis for the principles of ordered design.

This is manifest in the square formed by the 25 evenly spaced keys – whose different functions are colour-coded – and in the row of numerals above that shares the same dimensions. And yet this size, by no means dictated by technical demands,[1] as well as the reduction in functions,[2] reveal design decisions based not purely on logical considerations, but rather on human factors, where the main concerns are sensation and interpretation. The field of convex keys was a world first[3] whose innovative power is hard to imagine today after it has been emulated countless times. Up until then, the concave solution had seemed more logical.[4] But the sense of touch and the brain work differently than one might think. Fingers can more easily locate and press the smooth domes without slipping onto the neighbouring key.[5] And what's more, the field of solitary raised buttons conveys to our perception a much calmer overall picture. Also contributing to this impression is the warm, decidedly low-key colour scheme. When we take all of these factors into consideration, it's easy to see why the aesthetic of the *ET 33* and its offspring has endured for such a very long time.[6] These are anything but cold calculating machines. They can be more readily compared to the elegant fountain pens that cosy up to them in the jacket pocket.

phase 2
1972 I Design: Dietrich Lubs
No. 4924 / 4925
black, red, yellow I (illus. top left)

digital compact
1975 I Design: Dietrich Lubs
Digital DN 19 I No. 4937
white I (illus. top right)

phase 1
1971 I Design: Dieter Rams / Dietrich Lubs
No. 4915 / 4916 / 4917 / 4928 I pearl white, red,
olive green, transparent I (illus. above)

Desktop and alarm clocks
1971–1976

Braun's early clocks had digital displays and a mixture between
mechanical and electronic technology. While in *phase 1* the digits
were based on prisms, in *phase 2* they consisted of stacked
sheets. In the *digital compact* they ran on tapes.

224

DN 40
1976 | Design: Dieter Rams / Dietrich Lubs
electronic | No. 4967
black, red, white

functional
1975 | Design: Dietrich Lubs
Digital DN 18 | No. 4958
velour nickel-plated (Digital *DN 42* black)

The model functional featured a new kind of convex switch on top,
while in the *DN 40* the switches were at the back. The *functional*
was equipped with an elaborate gas discharge display and the
DN 40 with fluorescent numerals.

AB 20 / 20 tb

1975 I Design: Dieter Rams / Dietrich Lubs
exact quartz / travel I No. 4963
black

AB 21/s

1978 I Design: Dieter Rams / Dietrich Lubs
signal quartz I No. 4821 / 4836
black, red, white

Desktop and alarm clocks
1975–1979

The small, lightweight and very successful analogue alarm clocks, which were produced for a long period of time, were originally designed for the bedside table. The fold-down front cover made them into travel alarm clocks.

226

DN 50

1979 | Design: Ludwig Littmann
visotronic | No . 4850
black

The first alarm clock that forms a triangle when viewed from the
side. It featured a double display and long keys that were easier to
locate in the dark.

AB 11

1980 | Design: Dietrich Lubs
megamatic quartz | No. 4834
black, white

AB 30

1982 | Design: Dietrich Lubs
alarm quartz | No. 4847
black, white, black / white

Desktop and alarm clocks
1980–1988

The model *AB 30* and the 24-hour alarm clock *AB 11* have a switch-off button that extends across almost their entire width, while previous models had been switched on and off using a toggle switch.

228

AB 2
1984 | Design: Jürgen Greubel / Dieter Rams
quartz | No. 4761
black, white, yellow, green, grey and others

KTC/KC
1988 | Design: Dietrich Lubs
combination quartz clock + timer | No. 4863 / 4859
white

The *AB 2* alarm clock has a round housing that echoes the shape
of the dial. This form idea is also the starting point for the double
clock / timer *KTC/KC* (where each part can be used separately).

AB 312 vsl
1985 | Design: Dietrich Lubs
voice control | No. 4760
black

AB 1
1987 | Design: Dietrich Lubs
quartz | No. 4746
black, white

AB 40 vsl
1992 | Design: Dietrich Lubs
voice control | No. 4745
black

Desktop and alarm clocks
1985–1996

The *AB 312 vsl*, a later version of the first flat alarm clock, model *AB 310*, proved to be the ideal travel alarm clock. The integrated acoustic sensor makes for a more relaxed awakening.

DB 10 sl
1991 | Design: Dietrich Lubs
digital | No. 3876
grey / green, grey

DB 12 fsl
1996 | Design: Dietrich Lubs
time control temperature radio-controlled clock | No. 3875
black

The first radio-controlled alarm clock owes its striking appearance
to a slanted front. In ease of use and reduction to key functions,
this high-tech clock resembles the family of pocket calculators.

DAB 80 fsl
1993 | Design: Dietrich Lubs
time control radio-controlled clock | No. 3863
black

AB 60 fsl
1994 | Design: Dietrich Lubs
time control radio-controlled clock | No. 3850
black

Desktop and alarm clocks
1993–1995

This model was a fusion of the *DB 10 sl* with the analogue alarm clock, in classic Braun form. The programming keys are located on an easy-access slanted base that can be closed with a flap.

AB 6
1993 | Design: Dietrich Lubs
quartz | No. 4747
black

AB 314 sl
1995 | Design: Dietrich Lubs
quartz | No. 3864
black, white

Out of the vocabulary of rational, easy-to-use and technically advanced clocks developed at Braun, it was possible to derive a number of variations, for example the *AB 6*, where the outside curve mimics the round dial.

233

ABR 21

1978 | Design: Dieter Rams / Dietrich Lubs
signal radio | No. 4826
black, white | (illus. top left)

ABR 11

1981 | Design: Dieter Rams / Dietrich Lubs
megamatic radio | No. 4846
black | (illus. top right)

ABR 313 sl

1990 | Design: Dietrich Lubs
radio alarm quartz | No. 4779
black | (illus. above)

Clock radios

1978–1996

Clock radios are today one of the most widespread forms of radio, one to which Braun – here in analogue form – lent its familiar functional touch. The round perforated speaker is an element with a long tradition.

234

ABR 314 df
1996 | Design: Dietrich Lubs
radio alarm quartz | No. 3869
black, Millennium Edition in silver

The combination of analogue alarm clock and digital radio unites
the advantages of station programming with simple clock operation and the good legibility of the classic round dial.

ABW 21

1979 | Design: Dietrich Lubs
domo quartz fix + flex | No. 4833
black, white | (illus. left)

ABW 21 set

1980 | Design: Dietrich Lubs
domoset quartz clock with barometer
No. 4855 | black | (illus. top right)

ABW 21 d

1980 | Design: Dietrich Lubs
domodesk quartz desktop version
No. 4833 | black, white | (illus. below right)

Wall clocks
1979–1982

This clock model came in several variations: with base, as double display with barometer or with a bellows at the back so the dial can be rotated in the desired direction.

ABW 41
1981 | Design: Dietrich Lubs
domodisque | No. 4839
black

ABK 30
1982 | Design: Dietrich Lubs
quartz | Nr. 4861
white / white, -/ yellow, -/ blue, -/ red, -/ brown, black / black

This slimmest of clocks (which borrowed its works from the alarm
clock *AB 310*) is an example of practical minimalism, but allowed for
variations in colour and in the relationship of the ring to the face.

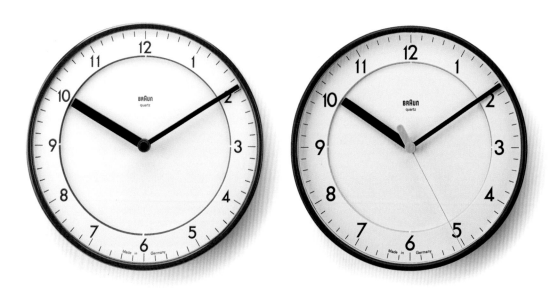

ABK 20

1985 | Design: Dietrich Lubs
No. 4780
red, white, blue, black, brown

ABK 31

1985 | Design: Dietrich Lubs
No. 4781
white / white, red / grey, brown / brown

Wall clocks

1985–1988

These wall clocks with their coloured rings and numerals in slightly modified Univers typeface can facilitate legibility in certain conditions.

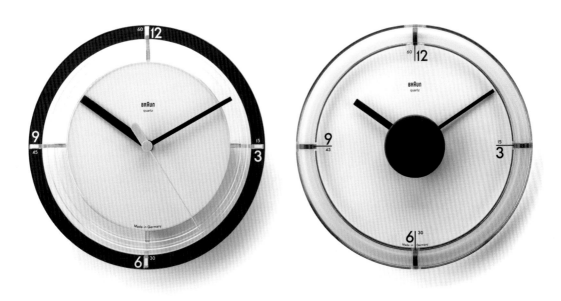

ABW 21

1987 | Design: Dietrich Lubs
No. 4782
grey / blue / transparent

ABW 35

1988 | Design: Dietrich Lubs
No. 4778
grey / transparent

The reduction to four markings and the use of a transparent material that lets the wall behind show through introduced an experimental element to the clock programme.

DW 20
1977 | Design: Dieter Rams / Dietrich Lubs
quartz LCD digital | No. 4812
chrome, black

AW 10
1989 | Design: Dietrich Lubs
quartz analog | No. 4789
chrome, black

AW 50
1991 | Design: Dietrich Lubs
quartz analog | No. 3805
platinum, titanium ceramic

Wristwatches
1977–2003

Like the first clocks, the first wristwatches also had digital displays. It was not until the following decade that analogue versions followed them, bringing the clarity of the analogue alarm clock and wall clock faces onto the wrist.

240

AW 60 T
1995 | Design: Dietrich Lubs
Chronodate | No. 3806
titanium ceramic

AW 22
2003 | Design: Peter Hartwein
quartz | No. 3812
silver / black

AW 24
2003 | Design: Peter Hartwein
quartz | No. 3814
blacky / blue

A further visual reduction consists in leaving out the numerals. By contrast, the model *AW 60 T* shows how even the extra functions of a chronograph can be incorporated without forfeiting a clear overview.

ET 11
1975 | Design: Dieter Rams / Dietrich Lubs
control | No. 4954
black

ET 22
1976 | Design: Dieter Rams / Dietrich Lubs
control | No. 4955
black

ET 33
1977 | Design: Dieter Rams / Dietrich Lubs /
Ludwig Littmann | *control LCD* | No. 4993
black

Pocket calculators
1975–1987

The quest for the ideal form: in the mid-1970s it took several development steps to come up with the first pocket calculator perfectly suited for daily use.

ET 44
1978 | Design: Dieter Rams / Dietrich Lubs
control LCD | No. 4994
black

ETS 77
1987 | Design: Dietrich Lubs / Dieter Rams
control solar | No. 4777
black

Even a minimalistic design can be varied in a number of ways, for example by slightly modifying the shape of the keys or by integrating a modern power source such as solar energy.

ST 1
1987 | Design: Dietrich Lubs
solar card | No. 4856
black

ET 88
1991 | Design: Dietrich Lubs
world traveller | No. 4877
black

Pocket calculators
1987–1991

While the mini-calculator in credit-card format fits in any wallet, the *world traveller* offers useful extra functions for people who are often on the go.

Lighters and Flashlights

Introduction: **Lighters and Flashlights**

1   Later, piezoelectric igniters were
used, and the engineers also worked
with solar cells.

Illus.: *T2 / TFG 2* table lighter, from above

In the mid-1960s Braun set up a department called "New Products" to develop innovative products based on new technological processes. The first brainchild of this idea incubator was an electro-magnetically igniting table lighter. The *TFG 1 permanent*, which Reinhold Weiss conceived as a slab shape resting on one of its narrower sides, was also available in a Director's Version plated in 18-carat gold. Even more interesting than the technology involved[1] is the psychology of giving someone a light, which apparently exercised a vital influence on the design, although a detailed analysis of this association is beyond the scope of this book. The fact is that this action, performed in passing, is quite an ambiguous gesture, in which doing someone a favour is coupled with the flaunting of a status symbol.

Designing an object meant to connote prestige was something new for Braun Design, but, with the mythical status the department had already attained, this was certainly a logical development. The symbolic purpose of the lighter is reflected in fine materials and finishing, along with a variety of different versions and the recourse to simple, basic forms perceived as "eternal". What emerged from the team's efforts is a stately series of lovely table and pocket lighters, even including the Pop object *T3 domino*. In this product group, shaped for the most part by Dieter Rams, the cuboid form with textured facade dominates. Flashlights also give light. But that's about the only thing the two product groups have in common. The portable lighters are by contrast purely objects of practical use, which only summon feelings of pride in little boys.

T2/TFG2

Table lighter

1968
Design: Dieter Rams
cylindric
No. 6822
silver-plated metal, with longitudinal
grooves
silver-plated, smooth
chrome-plated, with ring texture
chrome-plated, polished surface
chrome-plated, with longitudinal
grooves
black, with ring texture
silver-plated, with diamond pattern
red, blue or orange plastic
black, black top
black, chrome-plated top
acrylic

1 Lighters had been part of the product
range since 1966.

2 8.5 cm high, 5 cm in diameter, in
metal about 250 grams.

3 The original magnet ignition was later
replaced by a piezo igniter.

Silver-plated metal, smooth, or with a diamond pattern or longitudinal grooves. Chrome-plated metal, polished smooth or with a ring texture. Black metal, polished smooth or with a ring texture. Thermosetting plastic in black, blue, orange or red. The model *T 2* came in 13 different variations over the years. This kind of variety – not exactly typical for Braun – is a clear indication of one vital purpose of this product, one that goes beyond the mundane lighting of cigars or cigarettes: to demonstrate good taste. The metal cylinder in ceremonious black or silver with its fine pin-stripe grooves is guaranteed to make a good impression. Like good pens, lighters frequently serve as status symbols – and now they became design objects as well, thanks to Braun.[1]

The *T 2 cylindric* table lighter, the first one Dieter Rams designed, is straight out of the geometry textbook, even carrying an elementary geometrical figure in its name: the cylinder. The little tabletop tower[2] can be fully enclosed within the average male hand. As a bit of pressure is required to operate the igniter,[3] the switch embedded in the side had to be relatively large, and it was given curved ends to make it even easier to press. For the ostensibly trivial act of giving someone a light – which lasts just seconds but is sometimes rife with meaning – the *T 2* delivers an audible click that adds a nice acoustic touch.

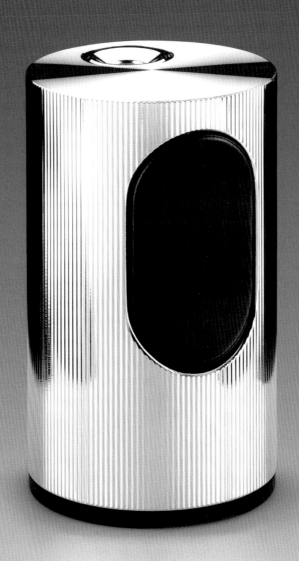

T 3

Table lighter

1970
Design: Dieter Rams
domino, battery ignition
No. 6740
red, yellow, blue, white plastic

1 The lighter is about five-and-a-half centimetres high and wide and not quite six centimetres deep.

2 The relationship between purpose, engineering and the form of the housing seems quite random in lighters (as it is today in electronic devices). The decision in favour of geometric purism is therefore by no means a "functional" necessity, but rather an aesthetic decision.

3 It's worth mentioning here the colour series created by the above-mentioned artist, Victor Vasarély. An endless range of colours also turned up on book-shelves everywhere in the legendary paperback series *Edition Suhrkamp* designed by Willy Fleckhaus.

4 Well-known examples are the stack-able *Panton Chair* by Verner Panton (1960 for Vitra) and the, likewise stack-able, ashtrays by Walter Zeischegg (1967 for Helit).

5 At Braun, bright Pop colours first made their appearance in the wand-shaped *B 2* electric shaver (1965), and later in the *KSM 1/11* coffee grinder (1967), the *HLD 4* hair dryer, the cassett shaver and the diskus flashlight; all three debuted in 1970, i.e. the same year the *T 3* came out. Another product area where colour suddenly showed up was in plastic door handles manufactured by Hewi.

6 This dot was later omitted.

7 The *cassett* shaver (1970) already sported a dot. Accentuated or lined-up dots, a feature of Op Art, were also used in advertising and for political ends ("Red Dot Campaign").

Slab, cube, cylinder. Simple geometry prevails in Braun lighters. The father of this minimalism is Dieter Rams, who is also the author of the model *T 3 domino*. Against a changing historic backdrop, even eternal forms ended up taking on new frames of reference, through the geometric patterns created by Victor Vasarély for example, the artist who popularized Op Art. *domino* is a small cube[1] – a striking, quite unconventional form for this product type.[2] Edges and corners are rounded to different degrees. On the top the black hollow where the flame emerges is set off markedly from the rest – all the more, as the plastic block came in a series of primary colours, a spectrum one does not necessarily expect from Braun. But at the boiling point of the rebellious 1960s, the world simply took on a new set of hues.[3] Objects of daily use were now likewise immersed in "shocking neon colours".[4] Braun was not immune from this infectious relish for colourful new surroundings.[5]

In an era when Pop Art was consecrating consumer products as art and when so many everyday things suddenly looked like art objects, the functionalist Rams delivered a Pop sculpture that is still treasured primarily in its fire-engine red or egg-yolk yellow versions. On the side is a circular button labelled with a black dot,[6] another graphic accent typical of the times, which turns the product's surface into a picture screen.[7] *domino*, designed as an inexpensive alternative for young people, was complemented by a set of stackable ashtrays that we can see as a reflection of the systematic Ulm tradition – or as lifestyle utensils in a day when the Beatles and Jimi Hendrix were calling the tunes.

manulux NC

Flashlight

1970
Design: Reinhold Weiss / Dieter Rams
rechargeable
No. 5903
black

[1] In the poorly lit era during and after the Second World War, in which batteries were scarce, Max Braun purchased the manulux dynamo-powered flashlight. Later, Hans Gugelot designed a new version, the manulux DT 1 (1964), which strongly echoed the sixtant shaver (1962).

[2] It was two centimetres high and about twelve centimetres long.

[3] This includes shavers and flash units, whereby the Braun sixtant (1962) and the F 022 flash (1972) also share their black colour with the manulux NC.

[4] The manulux NC and the D 300 slide projector from the same year were the first completely black products.

This product type, last reworked by Reinhold Weiss and Dieter Rams, was a reminiscence of the company's history.[1] A flashlight is an object people carry around with them. Therefore, the rechargeable model *manulux NC* was quite small[2]: an elongated slab as flat as a pack of cigarettes, which could be encircled by even the daintiest of hands and stowed in the smallest shirt pocket. The tiny plastic light weighed only 70 grams, as much as a medium-sized letter.

Since flashlights are mainly used in the dark, the long sliding switch integrated into the body is fitted with ridges that can easily be felt and pushed forward with the thumb. The housing is slightly wider at the front to indicate the direction of the light emitted. The plexiglas lamp cover has a reflective bulge that changes the dispersion of the light. This "lens" can easily be slid off with a finger, so the bulb can be changed in seconds. The rear section of the housing – a removable cap under which the battery and socket are found – forms a semi-circle when viewed from the front. *manulux NC* has a "chin", like all of Braun's mobile appliances[3] designed to nestle in the palm of the hand. The black colour may allude to darkness, but in those days it was also a fixed element of the corporate image,[4] part of its livery, so to speak. *manulux NC* is one of those loyal, discreet servants prescribed by the classic Braunian design ethos.

TFG 1
1966 | Design: Reinhold Weiss
permanent table lighter | No. 6826
See Appendix for colours and versions

Table lighters
1966–1968

In the mid-1960s, when Braun was implementing its "Grand Design" scheme, the first lighter was introduced, a small slab that also came in black-and-silver. It was operated with a new kind of sliding switch.

254

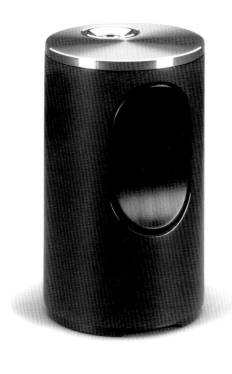

T 2 / TFG 2

1968 | Design: Dieter Rams
cylindric table lighter | No. 6822
See Appendix for colours and versions

Table sculptures: the standing lighters, named for their cylindrical
form, were modern members of this product group and relatively
inexpensive to make.

T 3
1970 | Design: Dieter Rams
domino table lighter, battery ignition | No. 6740
red, yellow, blue and white plastic

Table lighters
1970

This type of lighter was created in the late 1960s out of the combination of simple geometric shapes and a rainbow of colours typical of the period – perfect for the Pop age.

F 1
1971 | Design: Dieter Rams
mactron pocket lighter | No. 6902
See Appendix for colours and versions

mach 2
1971 | Design: Dieter Rams / Florian Seiffert
pocket lighter | No. 6991
See Appendix for colours and versions

electric
1972 | Design: Gugelot-Institut
pocket lighter (*mach 2 slim*) | No. 6060
See Appendix for colours and versions

In the early 1970s the pocket lighters took on a narrow, elongated rectangular shape. Braunian black-and-silver and the textured surface signal high quality.

pocket lighters
1971–1972

T 4
1973 | Design: Gugelot-Institut
studio pocket lighter | No. 6809 / 110
See Appendix for colours and versions

weekend
1974 | Design: Dieter Rams
pocket lighter | No. 6813 / 062
See Appendix for colours and versions

centric
1974 | Design: Jürgen Greubel
pocket lighter | No. 6817 / 338
See Appendix for colours and versions

pocket lighters
1973–1980

In model *T 4* the ignition button was not on top as usual but instead took up almost an entire narrow edge. Black was the dominant colour in these years.

dino

1975 | Design: Busse Design Ulm
(Redesign) | pocket lighter
No. 6110 / 302 | black plastic

duo

1977 | Design: Busse Design Ulm
pocket lighter | No. 6070 /302
See Appendix for colours and versions

dymatic

1980 | Design: Dieter Rams
pocket lighter | No. 6120 /301
See Appendix for colours and versions

Design in miniature: based on a clear formal vocabulary, different variations were played on the basic theme, sometimes by external designers such as the Rido Busse design agency.

variabel
1981 | Design: Dieter Rams
wand lighter | No. 6130 / 700
brushed chrome, brushed stainless steel

Wand lighter
1981

The unusual concept of a long lighter enables the user to access hard-to-reach objects while keeping his hand at a safe distance.

manulux DT 1
1964 I Design: Hans Gugelot / Hans Sukopp
dynamo flashlight I No. 826
dark olive, black

manulux NC
1970 I Design: Reinhold Weiss / Dieter Rams
rechargeable flashlight I No. 5903
black

Two flashlights without batteries: while the *manulux DT 1*, like its
successful forerunner from the 1940s, could be operated by
dynamo, the *manulux NC* was fed with electricity from the mains.

Flashlights
1964–1970

diskus

1970 | Design: Hans Gugelot (1964)
battery-powered flashlight | No. 904
black, yellow, orange, white

Flashlights
1970

These circular flashlights have an innovative, futuristic design.
The glowing UFOs came in the bright colours typical of the times.

Electric Shavers

Introduction: **Electric Shavers**

1 The *S 50* came out in 1950. The first prototype for a "dry shaver" had already been developed in 1943, in the midst of the Second World War – a rough draft with nowhere near enough power.

2 In 1953 only 1.5% of German men used an electric shaver; by 1960, 40% did.

3 This basic form was adopted at that time by other manufacturers, with slight variances, for example in the models *Dual* (1955), *Remington For-Most* (1956) and *Siemens SEH 63* (1958), but Braun was the only one to make the shape part of its corporate identity. The *300 Deluxe* also already had a rocker switch on the left side.

4 For example, the *300 Spezial* was given a plug designed after Wilhelm Wagenfeld's ideas.

5 The *SM 3* also came in anthracite.

6 Ronson marketed its electric shavers licensed from Braun in a black-and-silver version as early as the 1950s; both the chrome-plated head and the black body were American developments. Ronson also patented the beard trimmer – which Braun first brought out with the *combi* (1957) (cf. Artur Braun, *Max Brauns Rasierer. Erinnerungen von Artur Braun*, Hamburg 1986, p. 77 f.).

7 While the box idiom otherwise dominated classical Modernism, Braun also brought into play natural forms and ergonomic aspects – such as in the *KM 3* food processor (1957). This formal repertoire was being developed during the same period in Scandinavian design.

Illus.: *micron plus universal* electric shaver detail

The man and his machine. The tool with which millions of men crop their beard daily is surrounded by an aura of associations ranging from high-tech to archaic, from the wallet to the subconscious. It's no coincidence that some new electric shavers are taking on shapes reminiscent of a hand axe and also of the new generation of cell phones. The post-war model *S 50*[1] with shear blade and an American-style housing kicked off a product line that was at the time still in its infancy.[2] Three years later the model *300 Deluxe* was launched on the market, a hybrid being that still bore the old logo, while its case already sported the new, rationalized lettering. Seminal here was the separation of the chrome-plated shear head from the plastic cube below, already round-cornered and rid of its sharp edges. The fact that the easy-grip lower part of the housing forms a "chin" is not exactly out of place on a razor[3] and is a feature that still distinguishes Braun shavers today.

By the late 1950s, the sea change in design had already begun.[4] The simplification of contours effected by Gerd Alfred Müller led to the combi and Standard types and finally to the *SM 3*, which tapers symmetrically from middle to top, providing the model for the later *sixtant SM 31*.[5] The shaver's sculptural incisiveness and its sales success earned razors an independent standing within the product range.[6] The sixtant, which nestles in the hand like a smooth stone, became an icon because Müller and Hans Gugelot succeeded in enhancing the symbolic power of the advances made in the shear blade and flexible shaver head by changing the product's colour scheme. From now on, the colour black, heretofore alien to this product milieu, would dominate, and the electric shaver would henceforth be regarded as an object of value.[7] The years around 1970, a turbulent and yet creative period, witnessed approaches such as the longer-format shaver by Richard Fischer

8   Due to its extraordinary significance, *sixtant* was updated regularly, especially by Richard Fischer. Besides technical improvements, subsequent models were given easy-grip textures, smaller radii, straighter lines and a ribbed sliding switch, like the one in the *mayadent* toothbrush (1963).

9   Examples are the sure-footed *cassett* (1970) and the *Intercontinental* (1972), which introduced silver as a housing colour.

Illus.: *FreeGlider 6680* electric shaver, detail

and various models by Florian Seiffert[8] that foreshadowed conceptual alternatives. This phase also saw the first designs by Roland Ullmann, based on which vital subsequent steps would lead to the modern Braun shaver. The grip bumps typical for the brand as well as the user-friendly beard trimmers were established in the early 1980s with the *micron plus*. These innovations would endure, along with the centrally placed plug and the sleeker design – attributes first realized in the *micron vario*. Thanks to an automatically regulated discharging rhythm and the display featured in the *Flex Integral*, dry shaving became even more convenient in the 1990s.

The top-of-the-line models with their silver shells articulated by minute seams finally metamorphosed into luxury sedans for the bathroom shelf.[9] Toward the end of the millennium, in an epoch marked by progressive globalization and increasing individualism, a series of special razor types was developed, including the models Pocket *Twist plus* and *FreeGlider*, featuring a new translucent look. The dawning of the 21st century also brought a departure from the simple block form, which gave way to a more complex formal vocabulary. Hard-and-soft technology was expanded to become multi-component technology, and the spatial coexistence of housing and shear blade was redefined. But the real sensation was the introduction of the self-cleaning shaver. By solving the problem of how to dispose of beard waste through the development of the *Syncro* and *Activator*, complete with their own *Cleaning Center*, Braun once again achieved an innovative breakthrough.

BRAUN

FreeGlider

sixtant SM 31

Electric shaver

1962
Design: Gerd Alfred Müller /
Hans Gugelot /Fritz Eichler
No. 5310
black /brushed matte finish

1 They could for the first time be
snapped onto the shear head rather than
screwed on.

2 Three years instead of the usual six
months.

3 Some see here echoes of American
streamlining. But these formal features
are above all a reference to the organic
qualities of Scandinavian design, in
which natural forms were reconciled with
functionality – an approach that was also
applied to industrial design. One example is the Ford *Taunus 17 M* (1960). The
shaver segment thus evolved its own formal vocabulary within a product range
that was otherwise informed by the
model of box-happy classical Modernism.

4 Both the first Braun razor, the *S 50*
(1950), and the Ronson *300 Special*
(1955), which was licensed from Braun
for manufacture in the USA, had been
available in a black version, but this was
at a time when the still-tiny shaver market hardly attracted much public attention. A vital contribution was apparently
made by Fritz Eichler, notoriously a stick-
ler about colour; he had seen Danish sil-
verware with brushed plastic handles
that gave it a much more upscale air.
Cf. Note 7.

If a child were to draw a razor, this is what it would look like. Even today, *sixtant* is still something like the electric shaver per se. Already regarded as the best-designed and most aesthetically pleasing device of its kind when it first came out, it has now achieved iconic status – a rare honour for a banal everyday small electrical appliance. With its hexagonal holes, the newly developed shear foil gave the razor its memorable name: *sixtant*. These foils[1] were no longer punched, but rather fabricated using a chemical galvanoplastic process and then coated in platinum. This was what allowed dry shaving to compete with wet for the first time in terms of protecting the skin. The small, sleek *sixtant* packed a wealth of technical know-how, for example in its confidence-inspiring hum and practically indestructible pivot motor, or in its very durable die-cast frame – features that made an unusually long guarantee[2] possible and that made the *sixtant* the very incarnation of solid German "quality workmanship".

This razor possesses indisputable ergonomic qualities with its dimensions and curves shaped to perfectly fit the human, that is to say male, hand. The domed shear head is likewise ingeniously simple and effective. The *sixtant's* pioneering design was based on the *SM 3* by Gerd Alfred Müller, a standing slab with very rounded corners and edges that tapered both upward and downward.[3] Hans Gugelot gave the housing of the sixtant even larger radii. More decisive still, however, was the change in colour – a step as radical as those marking the early Braun designs, but one that by no means came without precedent.[4] While the white of Müller's predecessor model still bowed to the usual colour codex of the bathroom, the new black guise succeeded in lifting the razor completely out of this context and into a new realm of associations peculiar to the world of the electric shaver. The unusual colour choice had further repercussions as well. There was now a divid-

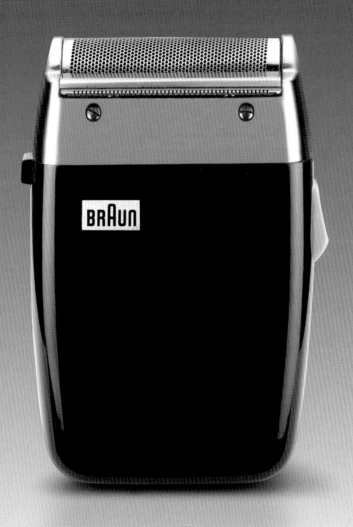

5 The BMW *1500* that came out the same year also had a ruler-straight waist-line, a feature that began to spread throughout automobile design.

6 Ever since the *Leica*, silver-and-black had been standard in the camera field, later also seen, for example, in the mid-format *Hasselblad* camera.

7 This brushed matte surface was at first created by hand. Cf. Note 4.

8 This colour scheme expresses such diverse qualities as engineering and luxury, but also understatement and timeless design.

9 Starting in 1968 with *sixtant S*; up until then the shear head had to be removed and replaced.

ing line between light and dark that clearly articulated the device.[5] We can only guess whether the changeover to black-and-silver for high-end cameras[6] played a role here. At any rate, men were now given something weighty, even existential, to hold in their hand every morning, an aura that was henceforth transferred onto the trivial activity of shaving. The electric razor, which was long seen as a mere stopgap when no water was available – and whose image was therefore about on the same level as the lawn mower – was now elevated to the status of a prestige object.

Contributing to this upgrade in no small way was another minor tweak: the dulling of the surface[7] of what were the basically ordinary materials of plastic and chrome-plated steel created a fine, irregular matte sheen that enhanced the emotional impact even further. Not only in the field of razors, but also in a number of other product genres – from coffee grinder to hi-fi tower – the black-and-silver duality spread in subsequent years, becoming – though initially borrowed from other brands – part of the Braun corporate identity.[8] The *sixtant* was also a commercial success. This Volkswagen among shavers, which was gradually equipped with extras such as a snap-on beard trimmer, was sold to over eight million customers,[9] making the electric shaver an indispensable part of the Western lifestyle.

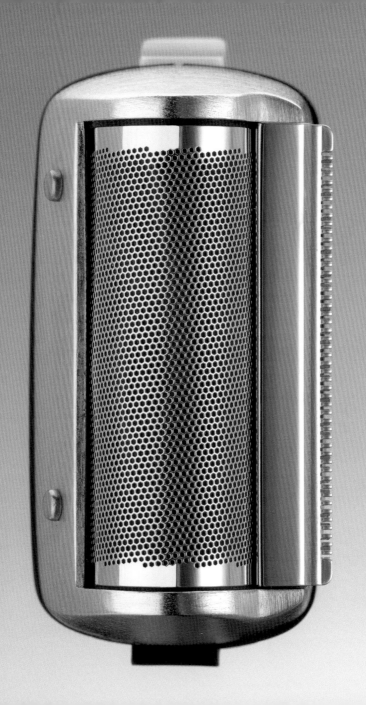

micron plus universal

Electric shaver
1982
Design: Roland Ullmann
mains, rechargeable battery
No. 5561
stainless steel

1 This technology involves binding soft plastics to metal or harder plastic, a process that has become standard in a wide range of product areas.

2 Up until that time, a screwdriver was needed to replace the shear blade.

This was the first shaver with a beard. Its outer skin is covered with a regular pattern of dark grey dots reminiscent of industrial structures or a work of the Art Informel period, but which also look like beard stubble clinging to the chin of the housing. Furthermore, there are parallels to classic Braun products, such as the *SK 1* radio, whose demonstrative perforated metal surface inevitably comes to mind. What seemed from the very beginning to be a matter of course is in fact a daring feat of manufacturing technology and an idea that made design history. This was the dawn of hard-and-soft technology,[1] a proprietary development by Braun that was used here for the first time in an appliance. The practical advantages of this bumpy texture are obvious: the device is easier to grip and can't slip and fall off even the smoothest of surfaces. The conspicuous pattern formed by the microdots, which ever since then has distinguished Braun shavers from all others, is based on an ambitious process that was not easy to master at first, especially in the micron plus with its seamless covering of 500 bumps.

Roland Ullmann's design for the *micron plus* evinced even further trailblazing innovations that today are long since considered routine. Of course, no user could have noticed that the inner workings of the shaver had been completely rearranged. But people did appreciate the shear foil tray[2] that could now be removed with just two fingers, as well as the first trimmer that could be separately switched on according to the "switch in switch" principle. This patented sliding mechanism, still in use today, is a classic example of an ingenious innovation that users soon took completely for granted. Nor should we neglect to mention that all these new developments worked out by engineers and specialists stemmed from impulses coming from the Design Department. Which just goes to show what industrial design is capable of.

272

micron vario 3 universal

Electric shaver

1985
Design: Roland Ullmann
mains, rechargeable battery
No. 5564
black

1 With the help of a few enthusiastic engineers of course.

2 The socket also worked as a switch, i.e. it could be turned from 220 to 110 volts.

3 Production now entailed only a vertical integration process. Pre-assembled components could be slipped into the sleeve (instead of having to mount shells on top of each other).

Shavers used to be short and wide. It was only with the *micron vario 3* that things changed dramatically. Roland Ullmann replaced the squat and stout type, long since out of step with the times in the days of the "economic miracle", with a new, pared down ideal of beauty. The longer and slimmer model not only looks more sophisticated; it also lies better in the hand and has clear design advantages. Realizing this attenuated form was much more complicated than a layman might imagine, however. The previous models had an outlet for the power cable on their underside. It was not located in the middle, but rather off to one side – opposite the button used to switch on electric power. This dual configuration seemed unalterable until Ullmann took it upon himself[1] to develop the first central socket,[2] which became the essential prerequisite for slimming down the appliance.

The *micron vario 3*, a gentleman in grey pinstripes, was also a milestone in terms of manufacturing technology. It marked the transition to sleeve construction,[3] which inaugurated a revolution on the factory floor. At the same time, it was the key requirement for giving the shaver a stable cap on its underside. The *micron vario*, an unusually cohesive-looking appliance, achieved over several years the highest daily production rates of all shavers. With over 20 million sold, it is the most-produced Braun shaver ever. And this VW *Rabbit* among the shavers is still part of the product range today.

Flex Integral 5550

Electric shaver

1994
Design: Roland Ullmann
mains, rechargeable battery
No. 5504
grey /matte chrome-plated finish

1   This automatic system (*Syncro-Logic*) discharges the battery completely before recharging.

2   The result is a visualization of the function of shaving as a kind of vehicle that drives over the skin.

3   This makes the appliance childproof.

In the late 1980s electric shavers went mobile as rechargeable batteries finally offered an acceptable lifespan. Starting with the model *Flex Integral 5550*, the devices were equipped with a display showing the charging status. Another innovation that really made a difference – along with the first flexible shear head – but which was invisible, was an electronic system that automatically regulated the battery's discharging rhythm, no matter what the user did.[1] Ever since then, battery lifespan has been virtually endless. The looks of the Flex Integral series didn't betray this innovation, but they did constitute a milestone in their own right.

Roland Ullmann, who shaped the image of Braun shavers for decades, dared to depart from the obligatory black in favour of grey-silver, a combination with weak contrasts and a distinguished air. The much-reduced bumps are also light grey. The discrete, relatively large dots are now arranged in four parallel lines that follow the direction of shaving.[2] The line dividing the facade in half at the border between grip area and sliding control is an example of harmonious proportions. The locking switch on the right, which prevents the razor from being switched on by accident,[3] is likewise as inconspicuous as possible. The *Flex Integral* is a master of understatement. But once switched on, it does not emit a reserved whisper as might be expected. Instead, the frequency experts, who are well able to eliminate any disruptive noises, gave the *Flex Integral* a surprisingly powerful-sounding motor hum.

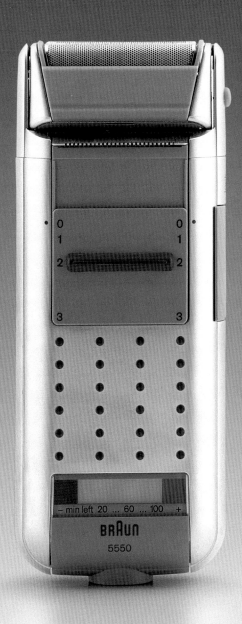

Activator System Clean & Charge

Electric shaver and Cleaning Center

2003 | Design: Roland Ullmann
Activator System 8595
mains, rechargeable battery
+ *Clean&Charge* System
No. 5643
silver

1   This system was developed by Braun.

2   This variation is additionally much less expensive to manufacture.

Toward the end of the 20th century the technology of dry shaving was so highly developed that no one could imagine serious progress still being made. That is, until Braun eliminated a source of annoyance that people had evidently regarded as God-given up to then: the disposal of the remainders of the beard after shaving. The *Syncro Clean&Charge* system offers total cleaning that – so the promise goes – revolutionizes the shaving experience. The first self-cleaning dry shaving system was an unprecedented product type. Designed by Roland Ullmann, the system consists of a 13-cm-high cleaning device in which the electric shaver is inserted. In the base is a replaceable cartridge[1] holding the circulating liquid that forms the key to this compact cleaning station. The plastic container holding the liquid remains visible as a blue line at the base of the device, thus telegraphing the principle inherent to the system. The casual reclining pose the shaver assumes in the cleaning device has a functional purpose: in this position it's easier to insert the shaver, and the cleaning liquid can flow out better. The *Syncro* shaver and the first *Cleaning Center* were developed independently – as there was no way of ensuring the success of this new idea. This is why the *Syncro* was still powered from the mains and needed a hook-shaped, upward-protruding extension for power supply.

Only after consumer acceptance had been confirmed at the cash register was it possible to take the next logical step: the *Activator* had electric contacts integrated on the reverse, a sensible and elegant solution.[2] This made it possible to get rid of the extension arm. While in the previous model the cleaning and charging process had to be activated by pressing a button, now everything worked automatically. The *Activator* "notices" when it's inserted in the station and starts to work. During the process a blue control diode lights up. Technical blue is now used in Braun shavers as an

278

3   This variation, less expensive to make, is also used in many mobile phones.

4   In the *Syncro* the slightly raised head was completely blue.

5   First used in 1999 in the *Syncro*.

6   The silver-and-grey colour scheme goes back to the *sixtant*.

7   This arrangement should delight any Braun traditionalist.

orientation and signal colour, including in LED displays.[3] The central push-and-slide switch, flush with the surface, is also framed in blue.[4] The *Activator*, whose sleek lines are emphasized by the black soft plastic grips along the side, has a shear head that is distinctly separated from the body of the device.[5] Its optimized foil structure, which for the first time has different-shaped openings, recalls patterns found in nature. Another new, microsized, innovation is that the bumps sparingly arranged in a curve have two different diameters.

The *Activator* is a work of innovative fine-tuning. But it also displays Braun's efforts to maintain continuity, whether in its signature silver-and-black combination[6] or its straight-lined central function bar.[7] Parallel seams shape the look of the shaver like the hood of a luxury sedan. This deft play with precise separations and the flow of line – which plays a key role in modern product aesthetics, most obviously in contemporary automobile design – accounts to some extent for what we like to call a "high-tech" look. And that impression does not deceive. After all, a single *Activator* contains over 100,000 transistors.

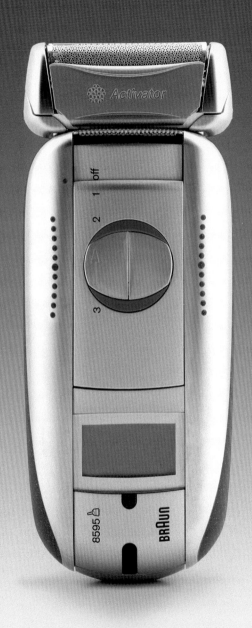

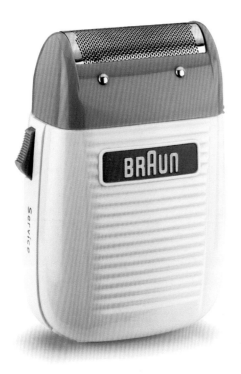 

300 special DL 3
1955
white / brown / red

combi DL5
1957 | Design: Dieter Rams / Gerd Alfred Müller
No. 5249 | white

Electric shavers
1955–1962

Among the first assignments given to Gerd A. Müller, Braun's first in-house designer, was to revise the shaver. The appliance was given finer ribs, a metal shear head and a more understated logo.

282

S 60
1960 | Design: Gerd Alfred Müller
Standard 2
white / chrome

SM 3
1960 | Design: Gerd Alfred Müller
No. 5300
white, anthracite

sixtant SM 31
1962 | Design: Gerd Alfred Müller / Hans Gugelot
No. 5310
black / brushed matte finish

The *SM 3* marked the inception of a new form: an example of the organic line in Braun Design. The transition from soap colours to manly black-and-silver also signalled a technical quantum leap.

commander SM 5
1963 I Design: Richard Fischer
mains, rechargeable battery
No. 5500 I dark grey

S 62
1962 I Design: Gerd Alfred Müller
Standard 3 I No. 5620
white / olive

parat BT SM 53
1968 I Design: Dieter Rams / Richard Fischer
battery 6 / 12 V, battery 12 / 24 V I No. 5230
olive / chrome

Electric shavers
1962–1969

The metamorphosis of the shaver into a high-class object continued. In the *commander*, the first model with rechargeable batteries, a great deal of engineering had to be packed into the rectangular device

stab B2
1966 | Design: Richard Fischer
battery | No. 5964
yellow, light grey, blue, red

stab B3
1968 | Design: Richard Fischer
battery | No. 5970
aluminium-coloured

stab B11
1969 | Design: Richard Fischer
No. 5969
aluminium-coloured

The cylindrical shaver, designated as an extra device, had its own round shear head system. It was operated via a ribbed sliding control. The model *B11* ran on a standard 1.5-volt battery.

sixtant BN
1967 | Design: Richard Fischer
No. 5511
black

sixtant 6006
1970 | Design: Richard Fischer
No. 5340
black

Electric shavers
1967–1972

Introducing the stars of the show: the *BN*, a long-time top-seller with snap-on hair cutter, had an elegant centrally placed control button. The *6006* on the other hand pleased customers with its circular recessed grips on the main body and shear head.

286

cassett
1970 I Design: Florian Seiffert
battery I No. 5536
red, yellow, black

rallye/sixtant color
1971 I Design: Florian Seiffert
No. 5321
red/black, yellow/black, black/black

intercontinetal
1972 I Design: Florian Seiffert/Robert Oberheim
No. 5550
black/chrome

The funky extra shaver *cassett* had a shape verging on the triangular.
In the classy *intercontinental* a band of chrome shifted the proportions, moving the button for operating the hair cutter to the centre.

vario-set
1973 | Design: Hartwig Kahlcke
No. 5350
creamy white (not sold)

sixtant 8008
1973 | Design: Dieter Rams /
Florian Seiffert / Robert Oberheim
No. 5383 | brown, black

micron
1976 | Design: Roland Ullmann
No. 5410
black

Electric shavers
1973–1979

Premieres: *vario* had an adjustable shear blade. In the *8008*, a best-seller in a leather case, the screws were invisible. The *micron*, manufactured using a simple system of shells, was the first shaver with an extendable hair cutter.

288

intercity
1977 | Design: Roland Ullmann
rechargeable battery | No. 5545
black

sixtant 4004/compact S
1979 | Design: Dieter Rams/Robert Oberheim /
Roland Ullmann | No. 5372
smootht /chrome, ribbedt /black

sixtant 2002/synchron standard
1978 | Design: Roland Ullmann
No. 5209
dark blue, grey

The *intercity* travel razor had a new kind of sure-grip structure and
was nearly symmetrical. The *sixtant 4004* – like the *2002* – was
also available with a black shear head.

micron plus universal
1982 | Design: Roland Ullmann
mains, rechargeable battery | No. 5561
stainless steel

sixtant 2004
1984 | Design: Roland Ullmann
No. 5213
black/chrome, black/black

pocket
1984 | Design: Roland Ullmann
battery | No. 5526
black

Electric shavers
1982–1986

The bumpy surface of the *micron* not only introduced hard-and-soft technology; it also had the first one-button controls and could be tested during manufacture before the housing was mounted thanks to the arrangement of its inner workings.

micron vario 3 universal
1985 I Design: Roland Ullmann
mains, rechargeable battery I No. 5564
black

linear rechargeable/linear 275
1986 I Design: Roland Ullmann
rechargeable battery I No. 5365
grey/black, grey/red

linear 245
1986 I Design: Roland Ullmann
mains I No. 5235
black/red, -/grey, -/yellow, -/green

The new sleeve construction made the slim figure of the *vario 3*
possible. The soft bumps were arranged in rows here, while in the
linear series they form parallel lines set off in a different colour.

micron S universal

1986 | Design: Roland Ullmann
mains, rechargeable battery | No. 5556
black

Flex control 4515 universal

1990 | Roland Ullmann
mains, rechargeable battery | No. 5585
black

Flex control 4550 universal cc

1991 | Design: Roland Ullmann
mains, rechargeable battery | No. 5580
grey / chrome-plated finish

Electric shavers
1986–1994

The *Flex control 4550*, the first Braun razor with an LC display showing charging status, is clothed in a tasteful silver-grey. Its twin-foil flexible head was a world first.

action line
1992 | Design: Roland Ullmann
mains | No. 5479
black

Flex control 4010
1993 | Design: Roland Ullmann
mains | No. 5437
black

2540 universal
1994 | Design: Roland Ullmann
mains, rechargeable battery | No. 5596
black

Flex control models accentuated their slim figures through a rigorous
structure that placed the emphasis on longitudinal lines. In the *2540
universal* – both a perfect hair cutter and foil shaver – the long parallel
sliding controls fill the bill

Flex Integral 5550 universal
1994 I Design: Roland Ullmann
mains, rechargeable battery I No. 5504
grey / matte chrome-plated finish

2560 universal
1995 I Design: Roland Ullmann
mains, rechargeable battery I No. 5596
black / metallic anthracite

Flex Integral 5414
1995/2001 I Design: Roland Ullmann
No. 5476
silver

Electric shavers
1994–1999

A slightly enlarged display in the *5550* drew attention to the substantially improved automatic charging function. The *5414* has minimized and obliquely arranged soft plastic stripes, along with lateral LEDs.

Flex Integral ultra speed 6525
1997 | Design: Roland Ullmann
No. 5703
matte chrome-plated finish

370 PTP TB
1999 | Design: Roland Ullmann / Corne-
lia Seifert | *Pocket Twist Plus 370*
No. 5615 | transparent blue

375 PTP
1999 | Design: Roland Ullmann
Pocket Twist Plus 375 | No. 5615
black / matte chrome-plated finish

Thanks to a more powerful motor, the *ultra speed* made shaving
even more effective. The *Pocket Twist* stood out due to its translucent housing and the central rotating switch that give it its name.

Flex Integral ultra speed 6512
2000 | Design: Roland Ullmann
mains, rechargeable battery | No. 5706
black

2540 S TB Shave & Shape
1999 | Design: Roland Ullmann / Cornelia Seifert
mains, rechargeable battery | No. 5596
transparent blue

4615 TwinControl
2000 | Design: Björn Kling /
Duy Phong Vu | mains,
rechargeable battery | silver

Electric shavers
1999–2004

The model *Shave & Shape* fulfils the double function of shaver and
beard trimmer (with an attachment for styling partial and designer
beards). The graceful, wasp-waisted *4615* was designed especially
for the Far East.

FreeGlider 6680

2002 | Design: Roland Ullmann
mains, rechargeable battery | No. 5710
silver/blue

Flex XP 5612

2002 | Design: Roland Ullmann
mains, rechargeable battery | No. 5720
silver/black

2675 cruZer³

2004 | Design: Roland Ullmann | Concept:
Oliver Grabes/David Wykes | mains, rechar-
geable battery | No. 5732 | silver/black

The *FreeGlider* is Braun's first electric wet razor. Its transparent
skin reveals the fill level. Sleek, organically formed cases are easier
to grip. This also goes for the wedge-shaped tapering grip zones

Syncro 7516
2001 | Design: Roland Ullmann
mains, rechargeable battery | No. 5494
matte chrome-plated finish/black

Syncro Logic 7680
2000 | Design: Roland Ullmann
mains, rechargeable battery | No. 5491
champagne

Activator 8595
2003 | Design: Roland Ullmann
mains, rechargeable battery | No. 5645
silver / grey

Electric shavers
2001–2003

The *Syncro*, the first shaver with *Cleaning Center*, picks up again
the softer lines that were already typical in the early phase of
Braun shavers. The *Activator* likewise combines curves and
straight lines. The colour blue signalizes technical perfection.

Syncro System 7680
2001 | Design: Roland Ullmann
mains, rechargeable battery + *Clean&Charge*
No. 5491 / No. 5301 | champagne, black

Activator System 8595
2003 | Design: Roland Ullmann
mains, rechargeable battery + Clean&Charge
No. 5645 | silver, grey

The self-cleaning electric shaver is an innovation that gave Braun a
unique selling point, one that was further simplified in the *Activator*
model. The jaunty tilt accelerates the outflow of cleaning fluid.

exact universal

1986/1990 | Design: R. Ullmann
mains, rechargeable battery
No. 5280 | black

EP 15

2005 | Design: B. Kling / B. Wilson
R. Ullmann | *exact power EP 15*
No. 5602 | black / light grey

EP 100

1999/2005 | Design: B. Kling /
R. Ullmann | *exact power EP 100*
No. 5601 | 1999: blue
2005: silver / grey / blue

HC 20

2001/2005 | Design: B. Kling
hair perfect | No. 5606
2001: blue / light green
2005: blue / grey-brown / orange

**Beard
and hair trimmers**
1986– 2005

The trend toward more complex and emotional designs can also be
seen in the beard trimmers. The means used are softer shapes, sub-
tler blends of materials and more distinctive colour combinations.

Body Care

Introduction: **Body Care**

1 The German word for blow dryer, *Fön*, is copyrighted by AEG, which brought the first such appliance onto the market in 1900. Some of the models from this era quoted the perforated field that first surfaced in the *T 4* pocket radio (1959).

Illus.: *BC 1400* hair dryer; detail

While appliances such as epilation devices, underarm shavers and curling irons are geared toward a female clientele, the hair dryer is a largely genderless product. Like the iron and the toaster, it is one of the very early electrical appliances and can hence look back on a long history of formal evolution. At the same time, it is closely associated with the Braun brand, which has played a major role in moulding this product type ever since the 1960s. In principle, the hair dryer is nothing more than a handy, more focused variation on the heater, in which a fan is mounted between the intake and exhaust openings. The fact that quite a large number of Braun designers had a hand in shaping this product area only seems remarkable at first glance, because this not particularly complicated device leaves scope for a huge degree of design freedom.

The first hair dryers from Braun did not have a handle – in keeping with the cubic form that was dominant in that era. As time went on, the designers oriented themselves more on the traditional form of the blow dryer.[1] With the unusually compact *PGC 1000*, in which the technical parts were logically organized, Heinz Ullrich Haase managed to create a lasting type in the late 1970s. This efficient and travel-ready hair dryer with a slanted handle was a touchstone that would be continually differentiated in subsequent years. In the late 1990s the designers articulated themselves on the basis of the same configuration, but in a much wider variety of materials and with a new formal vocabulary. The *PRSC 1800 Professional Style* is exemplary for this trend; its "global design" was instantly comprehensible the world over. In the same period this product sector was joined by two home-diagnosis devices that made measuring temperature and blood pressure much easier.

PGC 1000

Hair dryer
1978
Design: Heinz Ullrich Haase
super compact
No. 4456
white / grey

1   The hair dryer was invented by AEG, who copyrighted the word it coined to describe it: Fön.

2   The plastic housing is only 15 cm long (the diameter of the upper housing is 6 cm) and weighs only 220 grams.

3   The air intake opening.

4   For example, in the model *HLD 1000* (1975).

5   A quote from the Braun canon that picks up formally – like the *ABR 21* radio alarm clock from the same year – on the perforated fields of the *SK 1* transistor radio (1958) and the *T 4* pocket radio (1959).

The electric wind-maker has been with us since 1900.[1] More than three quarters of a century later, it was reinvented from the ground up. The model *PGC 1000 super compact*, designed by Heinz Ullrich Haase, seems so normal to us because it has defined what a hair dryer looks like over an amazingly long period of time. The whitish-grey drying turbine is much reduced in size compared to its forerunners, visibly slimmer and weighs not more than half a pound.[2] These qualities are joined by an altered overall configuration. Up until that time, the ventilator and grill[3] were usually placed at the vertex of handle and housing and were frequently shifted off to the side like in a paddle-steamer.[4] Now, the air intake was at the back instead and formed the termination of the housing, an intelligent formal solution that also offered greater safety, reducing the likelihood of hair being sucked in. The fact that the screen is designed as a field of round holes reflects the form of the ventilator wheel and has a long tradition at Braun.[5]

The handle of the *PGC 1000* caused a small sensation. Hair dryer handles had always been either perpendicular to the flow of air or, like a pistol, slanted backward. Tests showed, however, that exactly the opposite inclination brings ergonomic benefits. A forward-tilted handle is easier to hold and therefore less tiring. The "blow dryer" became an arrow: a case of reverse aerodynamics with a forward-thrusting silhouette that was thereafter copied so often and so closely that this pioneering innovation was soon regarded as a matter of course.

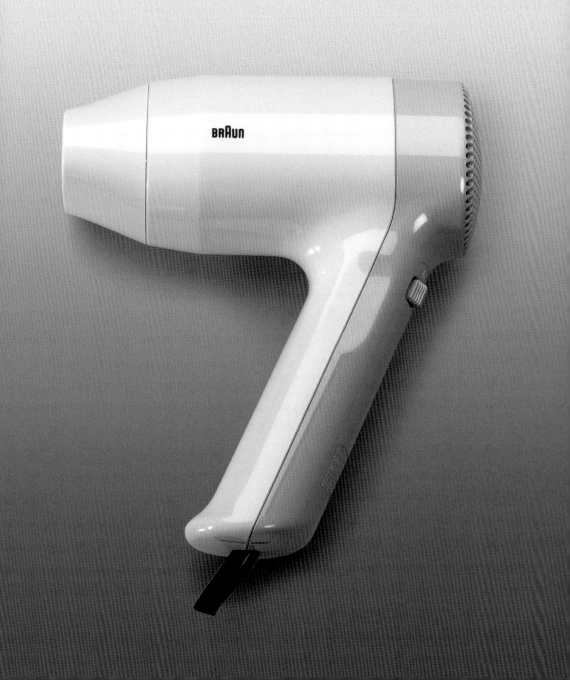

PRSC 1800

Hair dryer

1998
Design: Björn Kling / Jürgen Greubel
professional 1800
No. 3522
black / grey / chrome

1   In order to keep the diameter of the handle small, a new switch was even developed.

2   Dirt can't penetrate and can simply be wiped off instead.

3   To make sure the outer shell of polypropylene doesn't get too hot, the heating element has an inner shell constructed so that the fan can be inserted into the housing as a self-contained unit.

4   A special variation on hard-and-soft technology: it looks like three separate parts put together, but is actually only two. This combines the advantages of three parts in terms of colour options with cost savings – which was a mandatory specification for the project.

When a product is conceived today, those responsible have to keep an eye on all the different markets across the globe, which seldom converge. The Professional Style hair dryer is a design that emerged as a synthesis of these diverse sets of expectations. It is comparatively large because it packs plenty of power – a central aspect for American consumers. But its flowing lines ensure that the portable wind machine still looks graceful. The handle is relatively small,[1] a nod to customers in the Far East. There are also some functional reasons explaining the choice of this particular configuration: for example, the vaguely funnel-shaped form optimizes the flow of air. The various premises were brought together to create one common denominator – a prime example of "global design" able to prevail around the world.

A few surprises were in store, however: for one, a range of materials never before seen in a hair dryer, including the removable, tightly woven mesh over the air intake grill[2] and the fine, silvery finish on the upper side. Finally, there are some special features of the housing that are hard to discern even upon closer scrutiny. This applies to the construction itself[3] as well as the look. Externally, the Professional Style is made up of three segments. In reality, though, the front surface of the handle – which looks like an independent part of the housing – is actually only a moulded-on piece of softer material.[4] This is a visual, tactile and also an ergonomic advantage in terms of an easier grip. Continued up and back over the lower edge of the appliance, this soft section forms an arch, a discrete graphic element that gives the new hair dryer line a distinctive look.

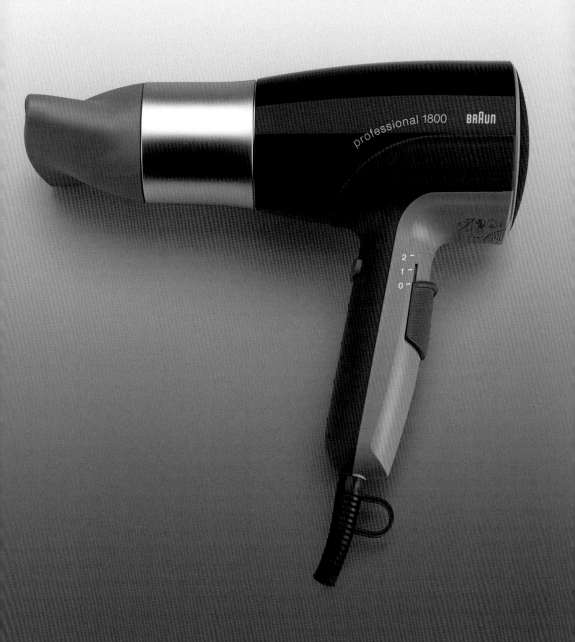

Silk-épil eversoft

Epilation device

2002
Design: Peter Schneider / Jürgen
Greubel
eversoft 2470 | mains
No. 5316
lilac / metallic, violet / metallic,
yellow / silver

1   References to style trends such as
Jugendstil from the turn of the last century
and to the Scandinavian idiom of the mid-
20th century are obvious. Flowing forms
had hardly been used yet for technical
products.

2   This entailed an easy-grip curve at the
back and the sleekness of the upward
taper. Viewed from the front it measures
seven centimetres at the bottom (at the
large bulge), six at the top, and from the
side three at the bottom and two at the
top.

3   This goes for non-European countries
as well, because *Silk-épil eversoft* is to a
great extent an export article.

4   About 120 grams.

5   Here in the variation hard-and-hard
technology. Cf. the introduction of multi-
component technology in the *micron plus*
electric shaver.

6   These are joined by smaller translucent
elements.

This appliance seems to have cast off everything machine-like about it. Peter Schneider and Jürgen Greubel gave the palm-sized epilation device an expressive droplet shape and furnished it with an abundant array of forms, a new paradigm for design in the dawning 21st century.[1] Right angles are the exception here. The product body has an undulating figure.[2] The small volume is geared toward what are as a rule the smaller hands of the female clientele for this product.[3] But the one-finger operation is standard in Braun products for all genders. *Silk-épil eversoft* weighs not much more than a CD in a jewel case.[4] A lightweight object that from the side resembles the sweeping curve of a feather.

The multicoloured surface is articulated by flowing planes and radii – a graceful look that is further enhanced by delicate pastel tones and which forms a contrast to the not-entirely-pain-free procedure for which the *Silk-épil* is used. The multicoloured look goes hand-in-hand with the multi-component technology.[5] Smooth plastic zones are flanked by the somewhat rougher surface of the grip areas.[6] *Silk-épil* is a classic example of how current product design is rediscovering sculptural and emotional qualities. Even symbolism, long banished from the temple of functionalism, is being rehabilitated: the appliance has a face with cheeks and nose and the V-shape is a typically feminine emblem. Belying its soft looks, the *Silk-épil* operates with a high degree of mechanical precision. Snapping the various attachments in place with thumb and forefinger, you can feel the tension in the spring and hear a short, satisfying click.

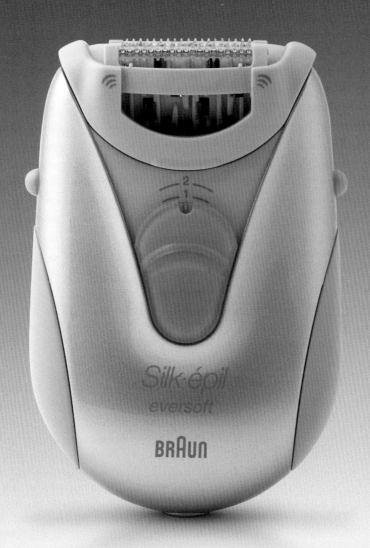

IRT Pro 3000

Ear Thermometer

1999
Design: Björn Kling / Dietrich Lubs /
Till Winkler
Braun ThermoScan
No. 6014
metallic silver / grey

1 A safety advantage that is hard to overestimate. The reduced level of fear alone increases measuring accuracy.

2 The original technology came from the American company *ThermoScan*, which was acquired by Braun's parent company, Gillette. At first, Braun was merely able to revise their product somewhat, resulting in the model *IRT 1000* (1997).

Braun has not only succeeded several times in creating enduring classics; the company's new product concepts have actually changed people's habits and everyday lives. That is, after all, the deeper meaning of innovation. The *ThermoScan* has the best of chances to become a classic – if indeed it isn't one already – and it has applied technical innovation to eliminating what used to be an unpleasant and seemingly unavoidable routine procedure. Using this digital ear thermometer is lightning-quick and so uncomplicated that babies simply go on sleeping while having their temperature measured.[1] This effective method makes grandpa's fever thermometer obsolete. The first device of its kind on the market was a foreign product[2] in a still somewhat clumsy guise. A comparison with the model *Pro 3000*, Braun's first proprietary development in this sector, shows a completely different approach. Behind it are two diametrically opposed attitudes toward product design. In the original model a technical invention was given physical form and the actual usage situation not completely thought through, complicating handling during measuring. In shaping the Braun product, on the other hand, ease of operation was a primary consideration. The result is an abundance of details that come together to make a harmonious whole. This outcome can only be achieved when development, design and manufacture are not isolated endeavours but are instead understood as a single process – a fundamental idea that informed Braun Design from the very start.

The difference can be seen in the smaller circumference of the device and the resulting loss of weight, which facilitates secure placement in the ear – anything but trivial when treating the sick. A hollow into which the main control button is set also helps to raise accuracy of operation to nearly 100 percent. From the side, the *Pro 3000* forms a slightly upward-bending, forward-leaning paral-

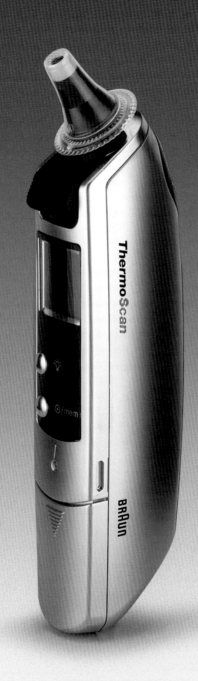

IRT Pro 3000

3   There is also a professional version for doctors and hospitals, with features such as built-in theft protection.

4   *ThermoScan* has a memory function showing temperature sequences. This allows the user to determine if the temperature has risen or fallen.

5   Cf. the entry on the *micron vario 3 universal* electric shaver (1985).

Illus.: *IRT 3520*

lelogram, whose two main elements – the "trunk" and the housing with its "back" – summon anthropomorphic associations. At the same time, the angle between the two parts allows the thermometer to be held correctly, making accurate measurement possible in the first place. The handy analysis device for home use,[3] which can be operated with just thumb and forefinger, is a veritable incarnation of Braunian design virtues such as simplicity, comprehensibility and user-friendliness.[4]

White, and later silver, as neutral background colours are also firmly entrenched in the company history. The lower functional parts are set off in light grey – a reserved colour scheme that likewise had precedents[5] and which radiates the kind of staid respectability that is singularly appropriate to the thermometer's task and context. The two round control buttons are light pastel green – hard to overlook. A small, unprepossessing masterstroke is the transparent plastic hood on the measuring tip, which offers protection against earwax, but is also of vital importance as a "lens" ensuring precision measurement. *ThermoScan* detects by means of a small red button if this "little hat" is present, which can then be flicked off after use at the touch of a button.

Silk-épil EE 1
1989 I Design: Serge Brun
mains I No. 5285
white

Silk-épil duo / plus EE 30
1992 I Design: Serge Brun
rechargeable I mains, rechargeable battery
No. 5295, 5272 I white

Epilation devices
1989–1997

The first epilation devices had a "chin", parallel bevels at the sides and a feminine switch made up of three balls. With cap on, the appliances are symmetrical.

cosmetic EF 20
1993 | Design: Peter Schneider / P. Eckart
battery | No. 5293
white

Silk-épil EE 300
1995 | Design: Peter Schneider
select rechargeable | mains, rechargeable
battery | No. 5298 | white

Silk-épil EE 90
1997 | Design: Peter Schneider
Silk-épil comfort
No. 5306 | white / yellow

A new variation especially for facial hair was offered with the slim,
wand-shaped hair remover. The second *EE* series has a calmer
look and uses a central, easy-to-operate switch reminiscent of that
in some shavers, such as early *Syncro* models.

Silk-épil EE 1020
2000 I Design: Peter Schneider / Jürgen Greubel
SuperSoft I mains I No. 5303
sunshine

Silk-épil 2170
2001 I Design: Peter Schneider / Jürgen Greubel
eversoft Solo I mains I No. 5316
yellow / silver

Epilation devices
2000–2004

The apron – coupled with a tongue-shaped switch with soft surface – became the basic shape for epilation devices. Here again
new colours and easy-grip surfaces go hand-in-hand.

316

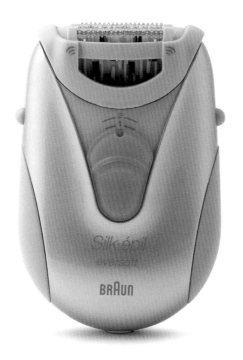

Silk-épil 2470

2002 | Design: Peter Schneider / Jürgen Greubel /
Cornelia Seifert | *eversoft Easy Start* | mains | No. 5316
lilac / metallic

Silk-épil 3270

2004 | Design: Peter Schneider / Jürgen Greubel / Cornelia
Seifert / Björn Kling | *SoftPerfection Easy Start* | No. 5318
amethyst, silver

A change of pace came in the late 1990s, when a soft, flowing line
took the stage. The "cheeks" were sometimes chubbier and other
times more narrow. Noticeable is a new boldness in colour choice.

BM 12/BL 12
1972 | Design: Florian Seiffert
underarmshaver | battery | No. 5967
orange, yellow, red

ladyshaver
1971 | Design: Florian Seiffert
No. 5650
white, orange

Lady Braun elegance exclusive
1982 | Design: Roland Ullmann
mains, rechargeable battery | No. 5565
red-transparent

Epilation devices
1971–2005

Ladyshavers usually borrowed their design from their male counterparts. The underarm shaver *B 12* likewise echoed the wand shaver of the late 1960s.

Lady Braun elegance 2
1985 | Design: Roland Ullmann
No. 5667
white

Lady Braun style
1988 | Design: Roland Ullmann
mains / G | No. 5577
white

Silk&Soft LS 5500
2005 | Design: Björn Kling | *BodyShave*
rechargeable battery, mains | No. 5328
translucent-blue / silver, translucent-white / silver

The wand shape was taken up once again, both in a classic interpretation and in an elongated version with a widening shear head at
the top for hard-to-reach parts of the body.

HLD 2/20/21, HLD 23/231

1964 | Design: Reinhold Weiss
No. 4410, 4414
white, black

Hair dryers
1964–1970

Braun's first hair dryer visualizes its technical structure in a rear curve, which also made a good handle. Intake and outflow grill form a single optical unit.

HLD 4

1970 | Design: Dieter Rams
No. 4416
red, blue, yellow

The successor device was a rectangle with the shorter sides
slightly rounded. Parallel slits recall the early phonographs. The
compact appliance came in the bright colours that were popular in
those years.

HLD 6/61
1971 | Design: Jürgen Greubel
No. 4418
white, orange

Hair dryers
1971–1974

In some cases the hair dryers harked back to the classic form of the Fön (blow dryer), with two "legs" and a laterally placed intake opening between them, in this case covered. New here was the concentrator nozzle for accelerating the airflow.

 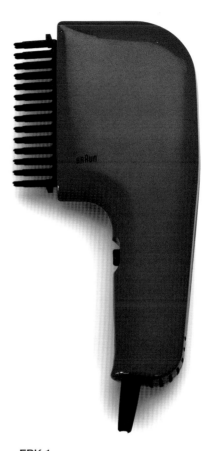

HLD 5
1972 | Design: Reinhold Weiss / Jürgen Greubel / Heinz Ullrich Haase
Hairstyling-Set / *Man styler* | No. 4402 / 4406
orange, brown, black, white

EPK 1
1974 | Design: Jürgen Greubel
Swing-hair, detangler comb | No. 4431
orange

The hair care segment began to branch off into an assortment of
specialized appliances. Both the hairstyling set and the hair dryer
with detangler comb have a vertical layout here.

HLD 1000 / PG 1000
1975 | Design: Jürgen Greubel
Braun 1000 | No. 4407
white

HLD 550
1976 | Design: Heinz Ullrich Haase
No. 4422
orange

Hair dryers
1975–1991

Hair dryers grew thinner and were given a pattern of holes that called up associations with the early days of Braun (cf. for example the *SK 1* and *T 4* radios). A new idea was the empty handle for storing the cord – a step in the direction of the travel hair dryer.

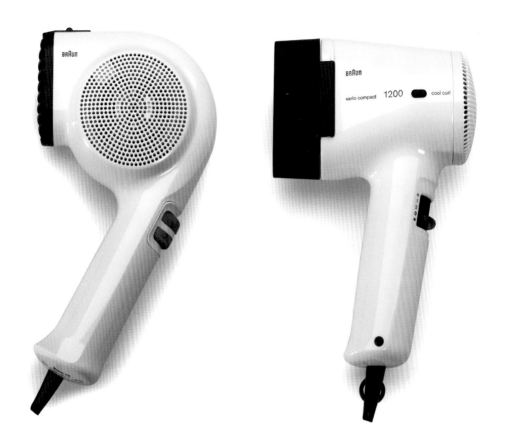

PGE 1200
1978 | Design: Heinz Ullrich Haase
Protector electronic sensor hairdryer | No. 4455
white

PSK / PK 1200 / B
1982/1991 | Design: Robert Oberheim
silencio 1200 / vario plus / plus cool | No. 4479/4548
white, black, blue

The noise of the air blower was also a design challenge. The ambitious goal was to make the dryer quieter at higher performance levels. A cold level was integrated into the *PSK 1200*.

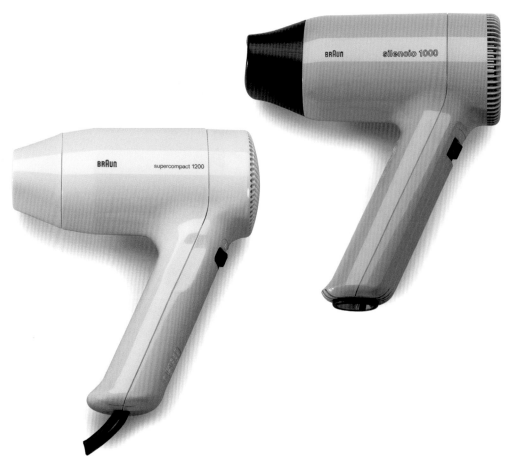

PGS / PGC 1200
1982 | Design: Heinz Ullrich Haase
softstyler / super compact | No. 4457
white, green

P 1000
1988 | Design: Robert Oberheim
silencio 1000 | No. 4588
grey, blue, violet

Hair dryers
1982–1988

The slanted handle has ergonomic advantages. The compact form of the *PGS / PGC 1200* constituted a new hair dryer type – achieved through a rearrangement of the components that was made possible by new technology and accentuated by the lettering.

BP 1000

1983 | Design: Robert Oberheim
mobil mini / international mini /compact 1000 | No. 4578
brown, aubergine, blue, white

PC 1250

1988 | Design: Robert Oberheim
silencio 1200 / 1250 | No. 4549
blue

The hinged handle, which also held the cord, made the compact
appliance even smaller, allowing it to fit in any travel bag.

C 1500 E/P

1992 I Design: Robert Oberheim
Professional power Salon Master I No. 3503
white

HL 1800

1991 I Design: Robert Oberheim / Jürgen Greubel
Control 1800 high-line I No. 4493
white / black

Hair dryers
1991–2002

Formal variations, such as the tapering of the air-conducting part of the housing, were joined by innovative details. A ring on the handle for hanging and a flexible cord connection are convenient touches that everyone can appreciate.

328

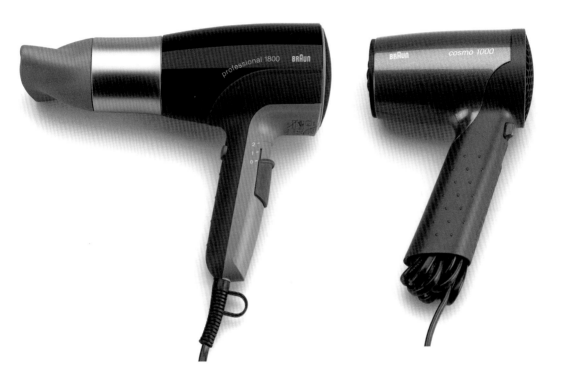

PRSC 1800
1998 | Design: Björn Kling / Jürgen Greubel
professional 1800 | No. 3522
black / grey / chrome

A 1000
1999 / 2002 | Design: Jürgen Greubel / Cornelia Seifert / Till Winkler
cosmo 1000 | No. 3533
1999: aqua | 2002: metallic silver

Higher power is connoted by a slightly larger format and new type
of composite material. Ridges or bumps on the handles for a better grip were also a new feature.

BC 1400
2000 I Design: Till Winkler
swing cool I No. 3519
metallic

Hair dryers
2000–2001

The perpendicular angle between the two housing sections was realized here as a gentle S-curve. An arch soaring upward separates the ergonomic handle from the functional blower tube, emphasized by the contrast between smooth and rough surfaces.

330

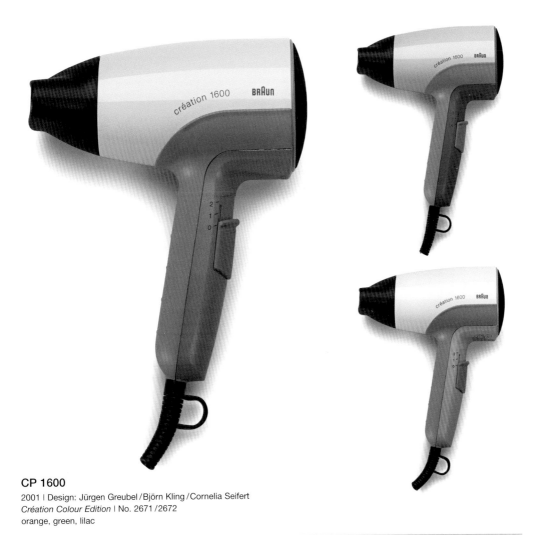

CP 1600

2001 | Design: Jürgen Greubel / Björn Kling / Cornelia Seifert
Création Colour Edition | No. 2671 / 2672
orange, green, lilac

This hair dryer series features a rear handle surface in a contrasting colour that continues onto the rear part of the blower tube. The division into three varicoloured parts and the ergonomic soft lines are further optical signals. A new fluff screen allows dust to be simply brushed off.

Pro 2000
2002 | Design: Dietrich Lubs
FuturPro 2000 solo | No. 3537
pearl-metallic

Pro 2000 Ion DF
2004 | Design: Duy Phong Vu /Dietrich Lubs
FuturPro Ion-Care diffusor | No. 3539
ocean-blow

Hair dryers
2002–2005

Appliances that express their performance in their form and proportions. The *Pro 2000* has a globe-shaped power centre and a
look characterized by the contrast between a powerful-looking
"tube" and a more graceful handle.

C 1800 Ion DF

2005 | Design: Duy Phong Vu
creation2 IonCare C 1800 DF | No. 3542
silver-blue

Bold colour and the balance of opposing lines lend the IonCare a dynamic air with subtle emotional undertones. The switch as well, which curves outward like a leaf on a stem, is a complex structure made up of freehand forms.

RS 60/65

1977 | Design: Heinz Ullrich Haase
roundstyler set | No. 4429
orange | (illus. top)

RS 68

1978 | Design: Heinz Ullrich Haase
roundstyler hood set | No. 4449
red | (illus. bottom)

Roundstylers
1977–1991

Wands for styling and freshening up hairstyles when dry were added to the product programme in the mid-1970s. The combination with attachable brush offers the functionality of two appliances in one.

RSK 1005/1003

1982/1991 | Design: Robert Oberheim
cool curl roundstyler set | No. 4522
white, black

The roundstyler with sensor technology to protect the skin, a cool-down phase and five-part accessory set – all stored in a practical carrying case – is a further example of a systematic idea put into practice.

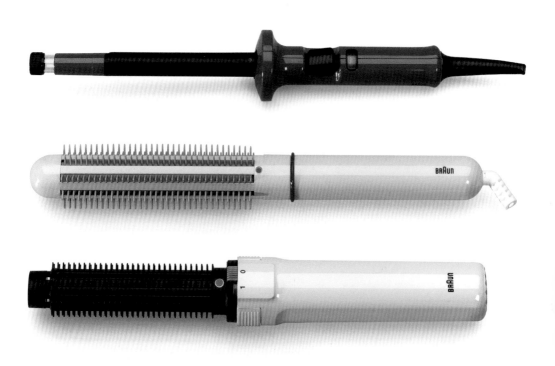

DLS 10
1975 | Design: Heinz Ullrich Haase
Quick curl | No. 4441
orange | (illus. top)

LS 35
1979 | Design: M. S. Cousins
quick style | No. 4504
white | (illus. middle)

GC 2
1982 | Design: Robert Oberheim
independant styler | No. 4506
white | (illus. bottom)

Air stylers
Curling irons
1975–1995

The *independent styler* is a battery-powered air styler for high-volume, wavy hairstyles. It has an automatic temperature regulator.

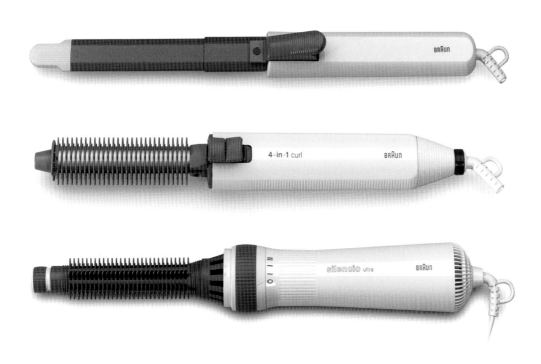

FZ 10
1990 I Design: Robert Oberheim
ZZ-look I No. 4495
white / grey I (illus. top)

TCC 40 / A
1992 I Design: Robert Oberheim
4-in-1-curl I No. 3563
white / grey I (illus. middle)

AS 400 / R
1992/1995 I Design: Robert Oberheim
silencio ultra I No. 4485
white / grey I (illus. bottom)

The *silencio* styles damp or dry hair with warm air, and does it
quietly. Thanks to an automatic curl release operated with a ridged
ring, it can be removed from the hair without pulling.

AS 1000

2000 I Design: Robert Oberheim / Cornelia Seifert
power styler professional I No. 4522
black / chrome I (illus. top)

C Pro S

2004 I Design: Till Winkler
Cordless Steam Styler I No. 3589
silver I (illus. middle)

ASS 1000 Pro

2003 I Design: Ludwig Littmann
Steam & Style pro I No. 3536
silver / lavender I (illus. bottom)

**Air stylers
Curling irons**
1998–2005

Through the combined use of new and different materials, further accentuated through new colours and the application of hard-and-soft technology, these appliances take on a whole new, more deluxe appearance.

338

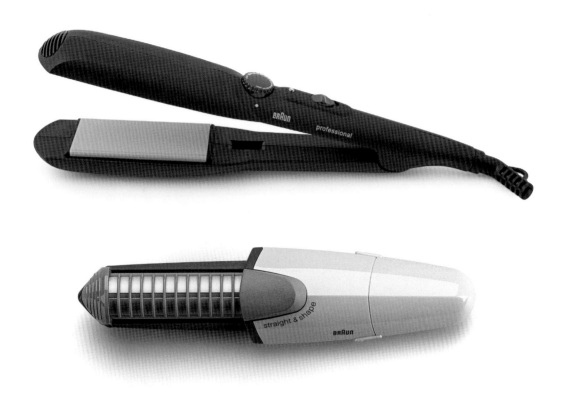

ES 1
2005 | Design: Duy Phong Vu
professional ceramic hair straightener
No. 3543 | black | (illus. top)

BS 1
1998 | Design: Cornelia Seifert
Straight & Shape | No. 3588
lilac | (illus. bottom)

Travel-ready, battery-powered air stylers for women have been
available since the 1980s. In the meantime, they have also been
given a feminine colour palette. The model *ES 1* with its attenuated, almost "mouth-like" form functions based on ceramics.

HUV 1

1964 | Design: Dieter Rams / Reinhold Weiss / Dietrich Lubs
Cosmolux irradiation device | No. 4395
white / aluminium-coloured

HW 1

1968 | Design: Dieter Rams
Personenwaage | No. 4960
aluminium-coloured / black

Body care
1964–1968

The irradiation device and personal scale were new items introduced in the experiment-happy 1960s. The clearly articulated
scale is a classic example of successful de-cluttering and careful
design down to the last detail.

340

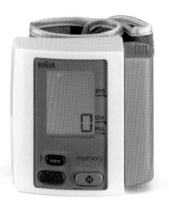

BP 1500

1998 | Design: Björn Kling /
Dietrich Lubs | *VitalScan Plus*
No. 6052 | white / grey | (illus. l. t.)

BP 2510

2000 | Design: Dietrich Lubs
PrecisionSensor
No. 6954 | white | (illus. r. t.)

BP 1650

2002 | Design: Peter Hartwein
VitalScan Plus
No. 6057 | anthracite | (illus. l. b.)

BP 3560 Pharmacy

2005 | Peter Hartwein
SensorControl EasyClick
No. 6085 | silver (illus. r. b.)

Braun's blood pressure monitoring devices are equipped with easy-
to-use buttons, a large display, easy-to-read digits and icons as
well as a host of functional extras, such as an abbreviated measuring process and the ability to store up to 60 readings.

Blood pressure monitors
1998–2005

IRT Pro 3000

1999 | Design: Björn Kling / Dietrich Lubs /
Till Winkler | *Braun ThermoScan Pro 3000*
No. 6014 | metallic silver / grey

IRT 3520

1998 | Design: Björn Kling / Dietrich Lubs /
Till Winkler | *Braun ThermoScan plus
IRT 3520* | No. 6013 | white

IRT Pro 4000

2004 | Design: Jürgen Greubel /
Ludwig Littmann | *Braun ThermoScan*
No. 6021 | silver

Infrared ear thermometers
1998–2004

The ear thermometer Braun introduced in the 1990s is a good
example of the step-by-step metamorphosis of a product toward
enhanced ease of use and an organic, hand-friendly, more emotional form.

342

Oral Care

Introduction: Oral Care

1   The ratio of regular to electric tooth-brushes today is about 50/50.

2   This is also the case with e.g. shavers, coffee grinders, flashlights, lighters and hand blenders.

3   This sleek line was made possible primarily by a newly engineered drive.

4   For example, in the toothbrushes designed by Björn Kling and Duy Phong Vu.

5   These are designed for *Oral-B*, a Gillette subsidiary, and are no longer sold under the Braun brand name.

Illus.: *D 10.511* electric toothbrush for children; detail

Electric toothbrushes first entered the product range in the experiment-enamoured 1960s – a development that was not systematically pursued until the 1980s, however, when Braun played a major role in popularizing this product type.[1] With a brush and a handle that holds the motor, these appliances fuse two main elements. The variables are the form, composition and the flexibility of the bristles. In order to ensure easy and effective brushing in the narrow oral cavity, the appliance should weigh as little as possible and be small and easy to handle. Toothbrushes are among those products in which the housing itself serves as a handle.[2] While Braun's original electric toothbrush, *mayadent*, looks somewhat like a soda bottle, the silhouette was soon slimmed down significantly, until Peter Hartwein's electric toothbrushes equipped with *Plak Control* technology achieved a new ideal of sleekness in the 1990s.[3] The new hard-and-soft technology also put in an appearance here. In newer models, the soft zones, behind which the control buttons are safely "welded", or which serve as ergonomic grip areas, have expanded to become graphically dominant aprons.[4]

In the dental field, which is all about hygiene, classic white prevails. A high point of this concentrated aesthetic was the *OC 3* combination toothbrush and oral irrigator, which demonstrated competence by turning the bathroom into a dental hygienist's office. The fact that the new, more complex set of tools that designers had at their disposal could also inspire the desire for haptic effects and bright colours is demonstrated by the electric toothbrushes for children. Regular toothbrushes,[5] which not too long ago were about as exciting as a dishwashing brush, were transformed into small colourful sculptures, not least by the use of hard-and-soft technology, which made them especially easy to grip. Models such as the *Cross Action* by Peter Schneider and Jürgen Greubel are skilled finger exercises in volume penetration.

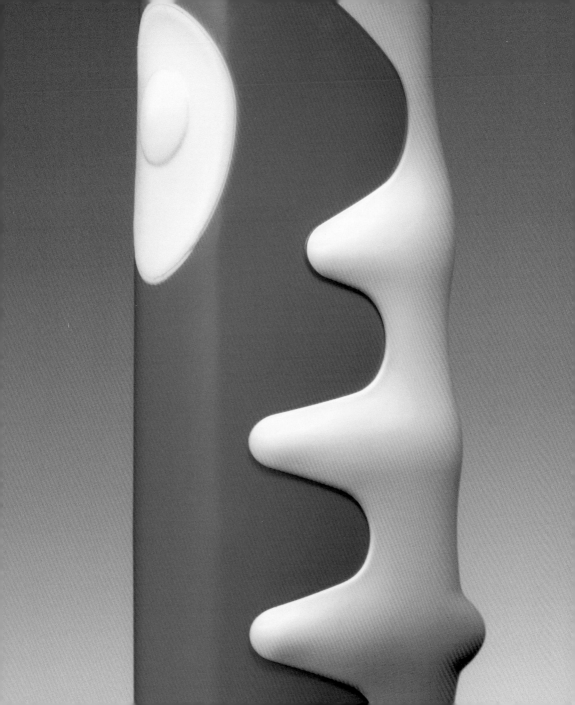

mayadent

Electric toothbrush

1963
Design: Willi Zimmermann
white

1   This era also saw achievements such as the introduction of the *T 1000* short-wave radio, the hi-fi system and the *sixtant* electric shaver.

2   The maximum diameter is four centimetres.

3   Cf. the entry for the *D 7022 Plak Control* electric toothbrush.

It was a pioneering achievement. But in the exciting, productive phase Braun experienced in the early 1960s,[1] it seemed more like a sideshow. Later, this assessment would prove completely wrong. While other business areas had to be discontinued, the concept of fitting a toothbrush with an electric motor turned out to be the spark igniting a market that is still burning brightly today. In hindsight, Willi Zimmermann's design seems disarmingly simple and even provocatively naked. *mayadent* looks like the rough idea of the electric toothbrush in material form.

The 16-cm-high archetype is made up of three visibly separated functional elements: the base as a cylindrical battery holder and in the middle the tapering motor housing, segueing smoothly into the vibrating head with its two separate bundles of bristles. Overall, the result is a figure with sloping shoulders that could be a cubist design for a chess piece. An easy-to-hold housing[2] with a ridged sliding control that could be operated with one finger was already an ergonomic standard at Braun by then. The case of *mayadent* is a classic illustration of a more comprehensive approach to product design, which, if it is to deserve its name, goes far beyond the mere layout of pleasing surfaces. Zimmermann not only created in *mayadent* a product type; he changed people's habits, ushering in a development that surely still holds some surprises in store.[3] Ever since the electric toothbrush became part of our everyday lives, it has been enshrined in the catalogue of achievements of Western civilization.

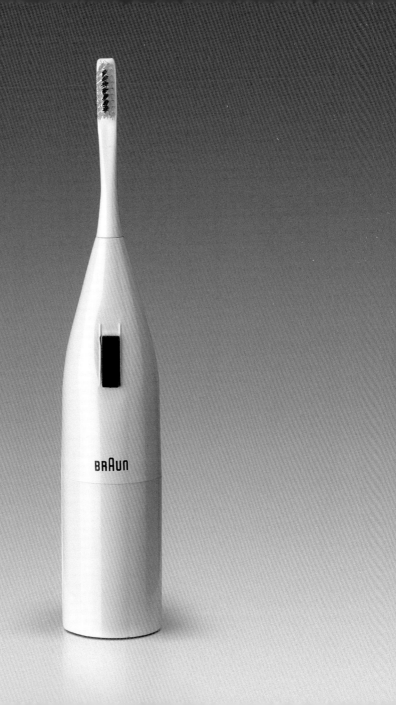

OC 3

Dental Center

1984
Design: Peter Hartwein
Dental Center/Timer,
toothbrush and oral irrigator
No. 4803
white

1 The toothbrush is equipped with two contacts underneath and recharges automatically when put in place. An indicator lamp shows the charging status.

2 It's interesting to note that rest stops along the motorway with their all-round service are a German invention.

Systematic thinking, perfection, inventiveness. If these ostensibly German virtues grab the spotlight anywhere in Braun Design, then it's here. The *OC 3 Dental Center*, designed by Peter Hartwein, offers an abundance of innovation in a compact package. Such details as the cleverly conceived hidden storage space for the electric cord on the back, which also serves as a wall attachment, are in themselves a joy for all those whose fussiness doesn't end in the bathroom. And this is only one of at least four different attachment solutions that can be found in this hygiene tool – a different one for every part that is to be held in the hand: the toothbrush nestles in an encircling ring,[1] the oral irrigator is held upright by a magnet, and for the water container there is a simple yet effective plug attachment using a rubber gasket.

OC 3 was the first complete oral hygiene set. This irrigation and brushing station shares its laboratory aesthetic with the typical dentist's office. The same association is summoned by the row of irrigation nozzles and brush heads standing at the ready. Small masterpieces are the removable ring-shaped magnetic power controls, which are easy to clean and naturally – as goes without saying for the company's design principles – can be easily operated with one thumb. *OC 3* is not integrated into a housing. Its four main components – the toothbrush, the oral irrigator, the cup and the power supply unit – remain discrete objects with distinct geometries. Iconographically, the ensemble with its two miniature columns at the sides forms a kind of filling station[2]: a small supply post with 24-hour service.

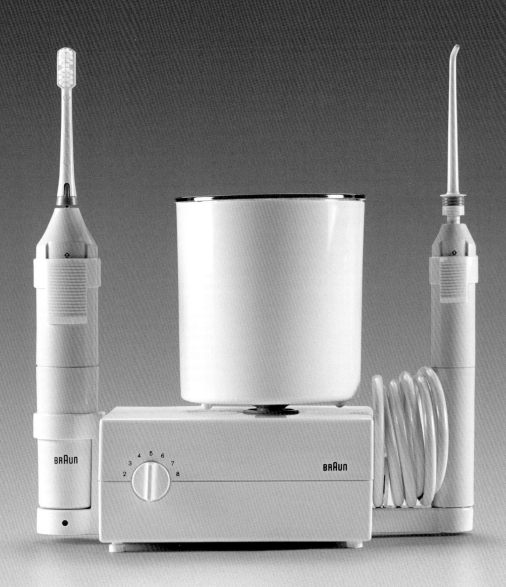

Oral-B Plus

Toothbrush

1987 | Design: Peter Schneider /
Jürgen Greubel

1   This was the strategy elected for compensating for the loss of the film and photography sector.

2   It was in particular a matter of creating symmetrical lines of communication between engineering and design. This was nothing other than a repetition of the same process that had been tackled at Braun itself in the early years. Peter Schneider, who had also been the contact person for the camera-maker Niezoldi & Krämer, had experience in these things.

3   The narrow neck had to stand up to some resistance in manufacturing (thin necks break more easily).

4   A dip into the repertoire of early Braun Designs; cf. for example the cross-slits in the radios by Hans Gugelot.

5   It is still being produced under license today.

Not that long ago, all toothbrushes looked alike – banal and boring. Until well into the 1980s the small, manually guided cleaning tools were not the focus of any targeted design efforts. They only changed when the people at Braun began to scout out new fields of endeavour[1] and discovered the toothbrush-maker *Oral-B* in their very own corporate group. Peter Schneider, in charge of external cooperative ventures, made contact with the Californian sister company, launching the first chapter of a story that is exemplary in at least two ways. First, it demonstrates the successful establishment of product design, which had not yet taken hold at *Oral-B* and for which the laborious development of a communication structure was necessary, not least in the form of a convergence process between two corporate cultures.[2] And second, it involved the virtual reinvention of a product type.

The model *Oral-B Plus* by Jürgen Greubel and Peter Schneider was the first professionally designed toothbrush and at the same time the archetype for a whole product family. It still has the flat, straight handle toothbrushes always had, but this one already displays some distinctive features: the narrow neck,[3] the shoulders that result, and finally the cross-ribs[4] that make for an easy grip and that still shape the face of Oral-B toothbrushes today. The *Plus* model, which came in various colours and also in a smaller, travel version, as well as being available in a translucent material, made the change significant. With well over one billion sold, it is the best-selling toothbrush of all time.[5]

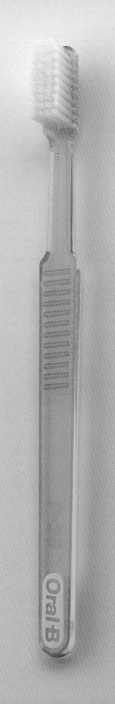

D 7022

Electric toothbrush
1994
Design: Peter Hartwein
Plak Control / duo timer
No. 4727
white / blue

1   The concept is based on the idea that the bristles' cleaning action is most effective at the moment when they change their direction. The bristles are then under greater pressure and necessarily penetrate into the spaces between the teeth. In order to reap the maximum benefit from this principle, the head of the *Plak Control* oscillates back and forth at a small angle of rotation as fast as possible – up to 3,600 changes of direction per minute. *Plak Control* also entailed a change in a non-visible area: the bristles were given rounded ends, making them gentler on the gums.

2   115 grams, 21 centimetres.

3   This new switch concept was an optimal solution for creating a tight seal, as the material components are fused together.

4   A circle stands for "on" and a dot for "off".

5   A form familiar from the Wankel engine.

This toothbrush was slimmer, worked extremely efficiently and had an unmistakable round head. When in the early 1990s Braun engineers developed a new technology for cleaning teeth,[1] which they dubbed *Plak Control*, Peter Hartwein designed a new model to go with it. The most obvious difference from the previous toothbrushes is the marked forward-slanting ledge between the handle holding the motor and the thin, upward tapering "neck", which corresponds roughly to the proportions of a regular toothbrush and is thus easier to move in the mouth.[2]

Hartwein made use of a second technical innovation, hard-and-soft technology, to create a characteristic look for the new implement. Dominating the front side is an on-and-off switch[3] hidden behind a "shield" of soft plastic[3] with a simple, easy-to-understand circle and dot symbolism.[4] This focal point is framed at the edges by two vertical parallel lines. These millimetre-thin longitudinal stripes, likewise in soft material that can be felt even by sleepy morning-time fingers, not only elongate the handle optically but also fulfil a very practical purpose. The toothbrush – which, according to scientific studies, is turned some 30 times each brushing – can be better held and guided. Also contributing to ease of handling is the unusual, haptically optimized form of the housing, which in cross-section forms a regular, rounded triangle, i.e. has slight edges.[5] At the bottom this form transitions into a cylinder, which makes for greater stability. Hartwein emphasized the handle's slim lines using yet another trick: he placed the toothbrush in front of the charging station, which it hides. As a figurehead in the fight against plaque.

Oral-B Cross Action

Toothbrush

1996 | Design: Peter Schneider/
Jürgen Greubel
2-component material

1   Around 200 million are sold in Germany per year. In the USA alone, sales reach the billions.

2   For Oral-B.

The radical metamorphosis that the small bristled tool has undergone during the last two decades has, remarkably enough, gone almost unnoticed – although, or perhaps precisely because, we all hold it in our hand every day. The toothbrush is an underestimated product, regarded as boringly pedestrian. In fact, however, it is a case of pure design, for this cleaning instrument contains hardly any technology and no electronics whatsoever. That's why form is a crucial factor in the classical non-electric toothbrush. Design is painstaking work here. At the same time, the toothbrush is a mass-market product[1] that calls for high investments in production technology.

A major step toward the new image of the high-tech toothbrush was taken by Peter Schneider and Jürgen Greubel with the model *Cross Action*. *Cross Action* represented a paradigm change: away from the straight stick with bristles and toward a complex, three-dimensional object at the edge of what was possible at the time. *Cross Action* was given a carefully thought-out body that nestles snugly in the hand and feels pleasant to the touch. Its composition out of two different plastics plays a major role in achieving this effect. Viewed from the side, the hard, semi-translucent material inscribes a curved line, tapering continuously toward the head. This hard element lies atop a soft back cushion on the handle, which provides both a nice feel and a secure grip.[2] The toothbrush was given volume and became a sculpture manifesting an expanded concept of functionality. Clarity, simplicity and harmony are still important, but they are joined by a host of additional dimensions such as the penetration of space, sensuous appeal and optimized ergonomics. Countless tests had determined, for example, that a modified arrangement of the bristle bundles made brushing more effective. With the *Cross Action* the designers not only ventured onto new ergonomic territory in terms of the form and placement of the grip zones; they also made the resulting advantages in handling

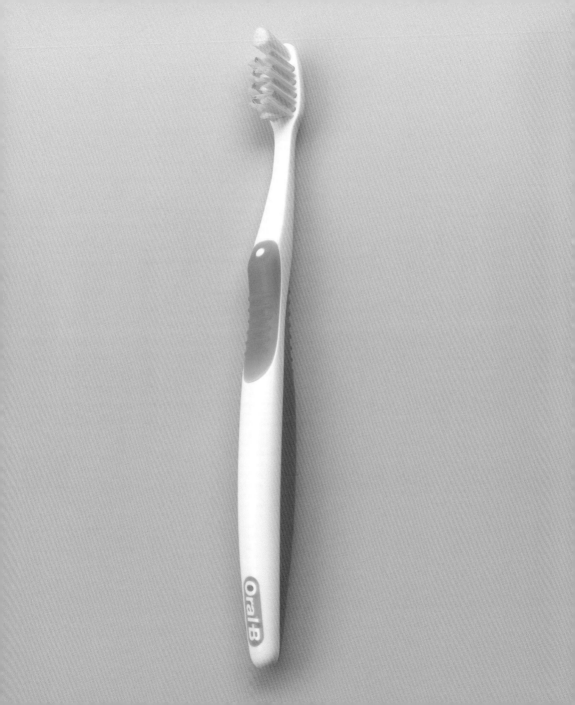

visible as well as palpable. Requisite to this comprehensive approach to product design are today's technologies, such as 3-D software, which allow design boundaries to be extended further and further. As a tangible counterpart to these immaterial behind-the-scenes workshop efforts, we see a construction created using a multi-component process,[3] resulting in a multi-coloured variety of shapes. Here as well, the *Cross Action* was pioneering. Sleights of hand such as the composition of the brand name from both hard and soft materials were once inconceivable.

Braun Design redefined the toothbrush and therefore the rules of this market. Consumers appreciate this progress and – perhaps unconsciously – reach for the more complex product. What the teeth-conscious customer of today expects is an optimal synthesis of state-of-the-art technology and subtle aesthetic, as well as a high level of practicality – and all of it of course at an acceptable price. Toothbrushes are not only an example of a previously nondescript product emerging from its cocoon – they also represent the way in which a consumer demand spiral is set in motion.

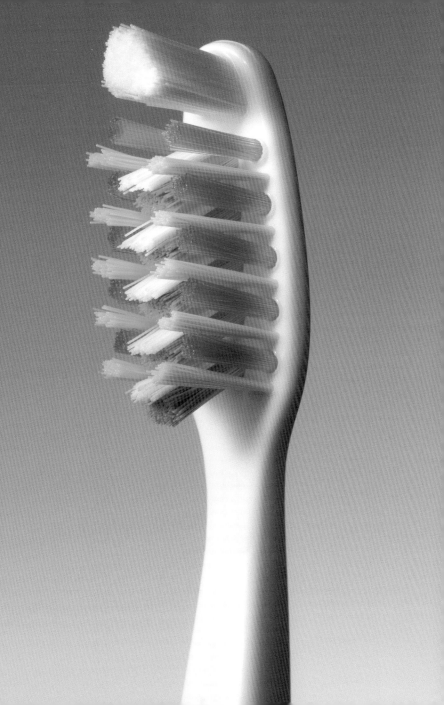

mayadent
1963 | Design: Willi Zimmermann
white

md 1
1979 | Design: Robert Oberheim
dental oral irrigator | No. 4802
white, black

**Electric toothbrushes
and dental centers**
1963–1980

The archetype of the electric toothbrush dates back to the early 1960s, an epoch in which Braun developed a number of "new products". Hardly less innovative is the oral irrigator dating from the following decade.

zb 1t/d 1t
1980 | Design: Robert Oberheim
travel set with rechargeable battery
electric toothbrush | No. 4801 | black

md 2
1980 | Design: Robert Oberheim
aquaplus oral irrigator | No. 4946
white

The *zb1* is slimmer than its precursor, *mayadent*, and has a larger switch. Hand-friendly curves like those of the *md 2* oral irrigator can also be found in Oberheim's flash units.

359

md 30

1984 | Design: Peter Hartwein
Dental oral irrigator | No. 4803
white

OC 3

1984 | Design: Peter Hartwein
Dental Center / Timer, toothbrush and oral irrigator | No. 4803
white

**Electric toothbrushes
and dental centers**
1984–1991

Braun's dental hygiene stations for everyman were a world first
and an example of systematic design. Their laboratory aesthetic is
meant to signal that they are thought through carefully down to the
last detail, as well as demonstrating medical competence.

360

d 31
1984 | Design: Peter Hartwein
Dental / Timer, toothbrush and travel set | No. 4804
white

OC 5545
1991 | Design: Peter Hartwein
Plak Control Center | No. 4723
white

When the *Plak Control* technology made dental hygiene more
effective, the brushing and irrigation station was given a more self-
contained form. Now the fluid level can be seen in the semi-
translucent tank – a completely new concept.

361

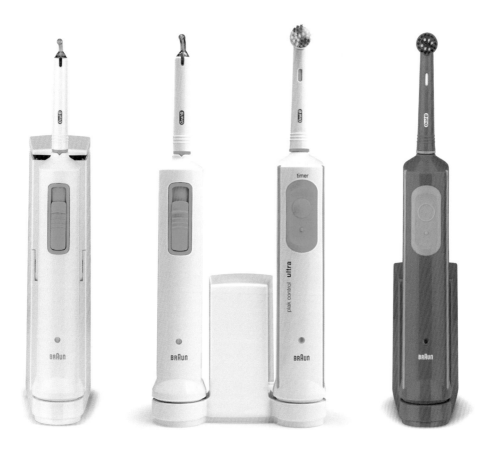

ID 2025
1996 | Design: Peter Hartwein
Interclean Tower | No. 3725
white / mint

IC 2522
1996 | Design: Peter Hartwein
Interclean Ultra System | No. 3725
white / mint

D 7521 K
1995 | Design: Peter Hartwein
Plak Control Kids | No. 4728
blue / turquoise

**Electric toothbrushes
and dental centers**
1995–1996

The *ID* interdental cleaning set removes plaque from the spaces
between the teeth. The application of hard-and-soft technology in
oral care appliances offered new graphic possibilities, a better grip
and increased safety.

362

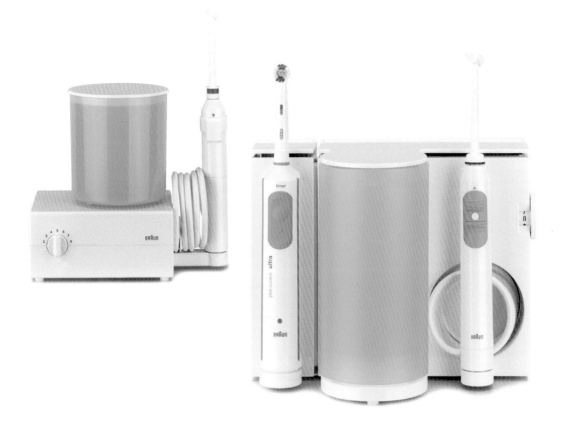

MD 31
1996 | Design: Peter Hartwein
Munddusche | No. 4803
white / blue

OC 9525
1996 | Design: Peter Hartwein
Plak Control Ultra Center Timer | No. 4714
white / mint

In the *OC 9525* the components were rearranged and the motor
block set on end, which makes space above to store nozzles and
brushes. Now equipped with a rotor, the oral irrigation nozzle
works like a high-pressure cleaner.

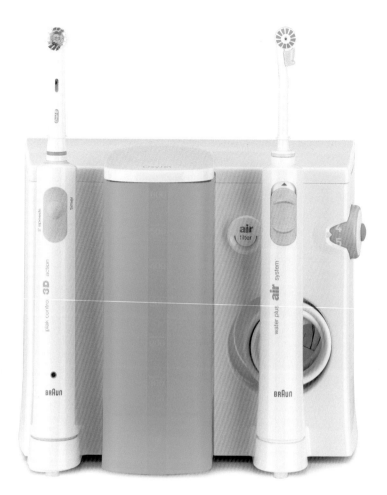

OC 15.525
1999 | Design: Peter Hartwein
OxyJet 3D Center | No. 4715
white / silver-grey / cyan

**Electric toothbrushes
and dental centers**
1999–2001

The oscillating movements of the brush head and the new air-bubble technology (for fighting plaque bacteria) found expression in the redesign of the system, featuring gentle curves and softer transitions.

D 10.511
2000 I Design: Peter Hartwein / Till Winkler
Kinderzahnbürste I No. 4733
dark- / light lilac, blue / yellow

D 2010
2001 I Design: Björn Kling
AdvancePowerTM Kids I No. 4721
light blue / orange / red

For the *D 10.511* a four-component injection moulding process
was used for more colour ("Lego colours"). In designing children's
toothbrushes, the designers drew on a fresh colour scheme and
biomorphic, associative forms.

D 4010

2001 | Design: Björn Kling / Duy Phong Vu
Plak Control battery-powered toothbrush
No. 4739 | white / green

D 17.525

2001 | Design: Björn Kling / Duy Phong Vu
3D Excel standard | No. 4736
white / blue

D 4510

2002 | Design: Duy Phong Vu
Advanced Power 4510 | No. 4740
white / blue

**Electric toothbrushes
and dental centers**

2001–2004

Differentiation between the various devices took on increasing
importance. Soft material was used to achieve optimal ergonomic
qualities and for visual accentuation.

D 17.525 XL

2004 | Design: Björn Kling
Oral-B Professional Care 5500 XL | No. 4729
blue / white

S 18.525.2

2004 | Design: Duy Phong Vu
Oral-B Sonic Complete | No. 4717
blue / white

The even slimmer toothbrushes in the *sonic* series signalled their new brush head technology and other extra functions through a variety of colours and surface treatments. Their rubber backs minimize vibrations.

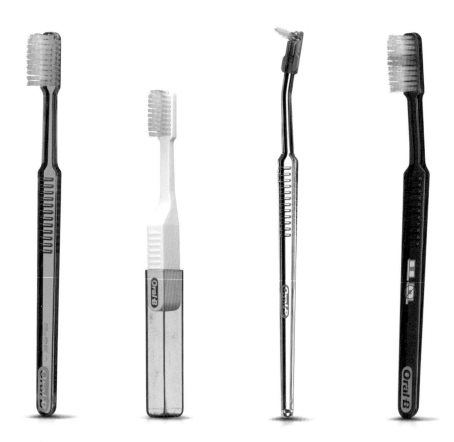

Oral-B Plus
1987 | Design: Peter Schneider/
Jürgen Greubel
toothbrush

Oral-B Travel
1990 | Design: Peter Schneider/
Jürgen Greubel
travel toothbrush

Oral-B Interdental
1987 | Design: Peter Schneider/
Jürgen Greubel
interdental cleaner
transparent

Oral-B Angular Indicator
1989 | Design: Peter Schneider/
Jürgen Greubel
toothbrush with indicator bristles
1-component material

Toothbrushes
1987–2003

Oral-B Plus inaugurated the toothbrush as a professionally designed product. The model came in various versions: in transparent plastic, with inclined neck and as a compact travel toothbrush with cap.

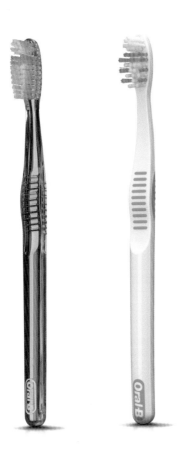

Oral-B Advantage
1991 | Design: Peter Schneider/
Jürgen Greubel
1-component material

Oral-B Advantage
1994 | Design: Peter Schneider/
Jürgen Greubel
2-component material

Oral-B Cross Action
1996 | Design: Peter Schneider/
Jürgen Greubel
2-component material

**Oral-B Cross Action
Vitalizer**
2003 | Design: Peter Schneider/
Jürgen Greubel/Till Winkler
3-component material

While *Oral-B Plus* was still a stick, the *Cross Action* had a complex
body composed of differently shaped volumes – one that can only
be illustrated on a computer screen since soft and hard materials
intertwine here: a new level of formal freedom.

Oral-B New Indicator

2002 | Design: Till Winkler /
Duy Phong Vu
toothbrush
2-component material

Oral-B New Classic

2003 | Design: Björn Kling
toothbrush
2-component material

**Oral-B Advantage
Next Generation**

2003 | Design: Björn Kling
toothbrush
2-component material

**Oral-B Cross Action
Power**

2003 | Design: Till Winkler
electric battery-powered toothbrush
2-component material

Toothbrushes

2002–2003

The battery-powered *Cross Action* is among the smallest of electric toothbrushes. The model *Indicator* is a virtuoso example of three-dimensional penetration of space. Its lightness also comes from the use of transparent material.

370

Household Appliances

Introduction: **Household Appliances**

1   *Multimix* food processor (1950).

2   Large appliances such as refrigerators, washing machines and vacuum cleaners were not tackled.

3   There was already an "electric model kitchen" in Chicago in 1893.

4   Although both involved a kitchen reform as well. The "Frankfurt Kitchen" in particular rose to fame.

5   This also applied to the first *Multimix*.

Illus.: *KSM 1/11* coffee grinder; detail

It all started with a kitchen machine that company founder Max Braun constructed himself.[1] Later this machine spawned a nearly complete set of household tools. Today household appliances are still one of the largest product groups in the Braun catalogue. The emphasis has always been on small appliances.[2] These motorized helpers were among the first electric devices for private use and were invented for the most part in the USA.[3] In Europe's sweeping early-20th-century design reform, they were simply neglected. Neither the workshop movement nor the "New Building" campaign took them on.[4] The appliances of the 1950s therefore often imitated the streamlined US style.[5] This is why the *KM 3* food processor by Gerd Alfred Müller caused such a sensation. It was the first device that also cut a fine figure sitting on the shelf. This curvaceous star plainly betrayed the touch of someone who had put thought not only into its functionality, but also into its proportions. That put this electromechanical kitchen helper into a whole different quality category. Braun was the first manufacturer to lend household appliances an aura. The *KM 3* ultimately evolved into a little factory, with a shredder, citrus press, meat grinder and coffee mill.

This type of multifunctional solution, in which the systematic approach seemed to take on material form, is still offered today, for example in handblenders. The majority of household appliances – for example, mixers, juicers, water kettles, toasters and coffee machines – are used to prepare food. Since in most cases it is a matter of processing one or more substances, the way they are fed into the machine naturally plays a role in its conception. Another central element of the design is the mechanics necessary for cutting, whirling or pressing, as well as their operation and regulation. The variety of foods is reflected in the diversity of these tasks, and these in turn in the number of different types of appliance. Since these devices usually leave the designer a wide scope

BRAUN

Introduction: Household Appliances

6   Both were designed by Reinhold Weiss.

7   The trend toward processed foods is decreasing the demand for kitchen appliances, while competition both from Europe and abroad is rising. Of the German household appliance manufacturers that once led the market, only Braun has been able to stand its ground.

8   Through the almost complete seal.

Illus.: *Impression* water kettle; detail

for variation, they frequently represent challenging design tasks. The crucial contribution of the Braun design team, which consists almost entirely of men, is to rethink the logic of these machines, which are usually used by women, down to the last detail, and to come up with a distinctive and practical design for each one of them. The *KM 3* food processor is a perfect example of this process, as is its contemporary, the *Multipress* juicer. Hygienic white was the logical colour to use when it came to food – a rule that still applies today. The ensuing decades witnessed a series of seminal designs: from the *HT 2* toaster or the *KSM 1/11*[6] coffee grinder, to the *KF 20* and *KF 40* coffee machines, all the way to the *MR 500* handblender and the *FreeStyle* iron, both designed by Ludwig Littmann, the old master of Braun household appliances. A steady series of new fields of application opened up in this product range beginning in the 1960s. And Braun made many an excursion into areas that were later abandoned. Who still remembers grills, dishwashers, clothes dryers, freezers and espresso machines that bore the famous logo with the big "A"?

In an environment that has grown increasingly difficult,[7] the household appliance market has recently been set spinning again by technical innovations. The possibilities offered by digitally assisted design and the hard-and-soft technology that Braun developed – one that inevitably imposes itself when it comes to handling heat and liquids – have led to a paradigm change. Products like the *MR 5000* handblender demonstrate optimized handling and complex volumes, allowing them to offer not only more safety,[8] but also different silhouettes and a new sensory appeal.

KM 3

Food processor

1957
Design: Gerd Alfred Müller
No. 4203/4206
white/blue

1 1957 catalogue.

2 Kitchen Aid had already brought the first mixer with base and bowl onto the market in 1920, a product genre that was popularized in the 1930s primarily by the *Mixmaster* from Sunbeam.

3 The American term for the standing mixer also emphasizes the production aspect: "food processor". The German Küchenmaschine, "kitchen machine", by contrast, still resonates with the enthusiasm that accompanied the inroads made by technology into the household. Something similar had happened a few years previously with the Tanksäulen ("filling station columns"), which in the USA were prosaically called "pumps".

4 The housing is made of thermosetting plastic and the bowl, for the first time, of an impact-resistant plastic.

5 The *SK 4* had been launched a year earlier.

6 Among the best-known representatives of this style were the Finn Alvar Aalto and Arne Jacobsen from Denmark.

7 Including Braun's own *Multimix*, which had been in production since the early 1950s. This appliance could be transformed into a *Multimix* combination device with the addition of a baseplate, mixing attachment, brackets and bowl, already displaying the principle of the "food processor" (cf. October 1955 product catalogue).

8 The right edge of the bowl and the left edge of the housing (which seamlessly continued underneath the bowl) inscribed the same parabola-like curve – again as parallel lines. The relatively large radius supports the harmonious impression while underscoring the mobility of the bowl.

It wasn't really an "earth-shattering novelty",[1] the company modestly claimed. As a matter of fact, the technology for electric mixing and chopping of food comes from the USA.[2] But Gerd Alfred Müller's model *KM 3* caused such a stir for good reason. Not least because this food processor[3] demonstrated for the first time that the new design ethos at Braun, until then applied only to radios, could be transferred to other products. The white appliance,[4] which in its plainness must have looked to contemporaries as naked as the *SK 4* radio-phonograph combination, was another culture shock.[5] But that's where the similarities end. These two first Braun classics speak different, indeed even contradictory, formal languages. The boxy *SK 4* pays tribute to the 90-degree rationalism of the "New Building" movement, while the *KM 3* displays flowing forms and a voluminous approach, a "natural" element with a Scandinavian pedigree.[6]

Braun's Küchenmaschine, which established this word as the operative term in Germany, suddenly made all previous models look ungainly.[7] Never before had there been a design that integrated all the parts in such a self-contained figure while still remaining clearly recognizable for what it was. Müller chose the stacking principle. Parallel seams separate the functions – i.e. motor, drive and attachments – as clearly identifiable "storeys" in the housing. It is the dialectic between strict formal configuration and the lightness of the details that accounts for the appliance's straightforward appeal – just as can be said for major artworks. One secret behind the aesthetic quality of the overall design can be found in the balanced proportions of the mixing bowl and housing, the machine's two main components. Their upper edges form a continuous line. The housing hugs the bowl and both fuse to become one formal unit.[8] The broad-surface base attached to the housing conveys stability. The conically tapering housing seems to con-

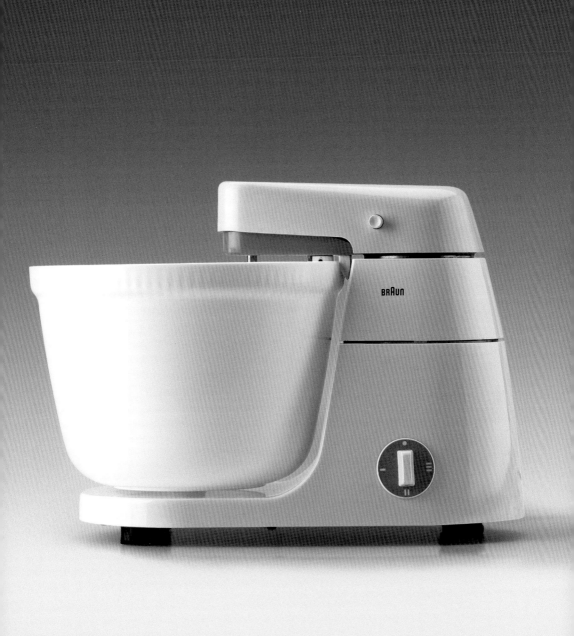

KM 3

9   We mention in passing here that this shape could also evoke other, much more archaic forms, such as a church spire or crane (the mixing arm is slightly tilted).

10 The appliance can be disassembled in just a few steps, and all of the main parts stand on their own without tipping over.

11 American "flying machines", such as the *Douglas DC 3* (1936) and the *Boeing 707* (1954), which had not only similarly smooth surfaces but also shapes that were functional through and through, became fetishes of Modernism.

dense the power of the motor,[9] whose loudness was a notorious feature of the *KM 3*. Only two control buttons are found on the otherwise virginal outer skin, whose immaculate surfaces broadcast the fact that the machine is abwaschbar, a German signal word in those years meaning that the surface can be wiped down with a wet cloth. After all, the mostly female clientele were interested primarily in the practical benefits of the household miracle-worker: the rotating mixing bowl, the easy-to-remove mixing arm (in mixers from other manufacturers, the arm was lifted out of the bowl on a hinge), and the unusually well-thought-out and uncomplicated handling, up to and including cleaning.[10]

The *KM 3* continued to be produced, with slight modifications, for over three decades, and is hence one of the longest-lived industrial products of all time, and one of the most copied. Some people regard it for this reason as the epitome of "timeless" design. But its rounded forms also fit effortlessly into the 1950s style panorama with its big-busted beauties and sweeping cantilevered concrete roofs. The *KM 3* was an apotheosis of the streamlining era and, at least in the kitchen, exuded a similar symbolic value as the cigar-shaped passenger aircraft[11] that in those years began circling the globe. Müller had discovered a middle path between sober functionalism and the mythic machine, creating the Marilyn Monroe of food processors.

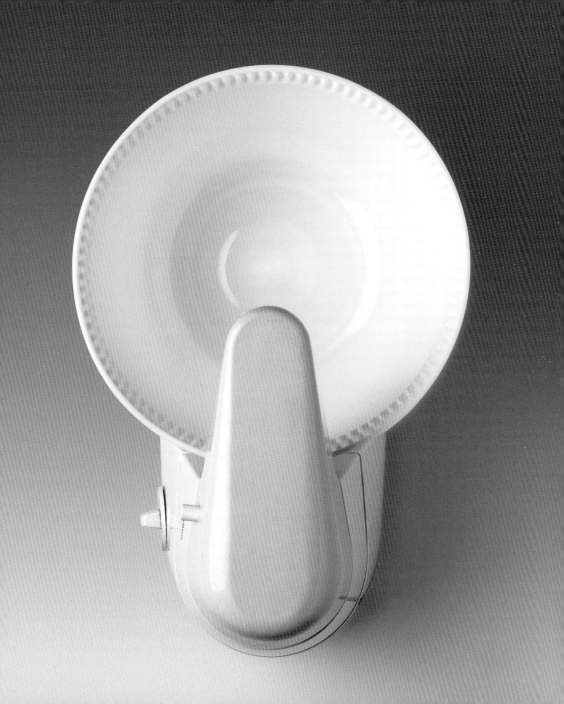

H 1/11

Heater

1959
Design: Dieter Rams
Thermolüfter
No. 4305
white / grey

1   Width, height and depth were 26.5 x
8.5 x 13.5 cm.

2   First seen in the new radios designed
by Hans Gugelot.

3   The *SK 4* (1956) was already conspicuous for its angular shape.

It was known as the "brick". Braun's first heater was one of those devices from the early days of design whose unorthodox form inspired an affectionate nickname. The disrespectful moniker went right to the heart of the matter: the model *H 1*, designed by Dieter Rams, was the smallest heater on the market up to that time, whose slab-shaped form as well as its dimensions[1] indeed called to mind a lowly brick. Other 2000-watt heaters were much larger. That sales got off to a slow start is no doubt attributable to the fact that people simply didn't believe that the small appliance packed sufficient power. It was only when word spread of the heating performance of the *H 1* that things changed. The secret of its effectiveness was a cross-flow blower, a technical innovation that brought such additional benefits as a larger heating range and low-noise operation. The mighty mite was equipped with a thermostat and an adjustable base to modify the direction of heat. The metal housing was grey and white with plastic sections on the sides and slats on the front and top. They underscore the extremely simple geometry based on 90-degree angles. Parallel ventilation slits of this kind were part of the company's corporate image in the late 1950s.[2]

The rectangular box,[3] an idiom that plays an important role in classical Modernism, in particular in architecture, is given a new spin here by Rams in the form of an industrial product with a facade. The *H 1* is an under-table bungalow in the style of Mies van der Rohe.

KSM 1/11

Coffee grinder with
hammer mechanism
1967
Design: Reinhold Weiss
Aromatic
No. 4024/4026
white, orange, red, yellow, green,
chrome/black

1   A mail-order catalogue brought out by
the Tietz company around 1900 contains
ten models, three of them wall-mounted
mills and one "Children's Coffee Grinder"
(Maribel Königer, *Küchengerät im 20.
Jahrhundert*, Munich 1994, p. 57).

2   The first motor-driven coffee grinder
came onto the market in 1903, produced
by the Hobart company in Chicago. The
mid-1950s appliances (*Siemens KSM 2* in
1955, *Moulinex* in 1956, *Onko D4* in 1958)
all had a relatively simple basic shape.

3   The sensuous pleasure people take in
electrically engineered devices is comparable to the visual pleasure of the washing
machine, whose bull's eye exerts a certain
fascination even for adults.

4   Two years previously, a standing version had already been developed, the
model *KMM 1/121* (1965).

5   This solitary button was also featured
in the *H 1* television (1958) and later in the
Aromaster *KF 20* coffee machine (1972).

6   The circumference varies between
25.5 (glass and base at the bottom) and
26.6 centimetres (base at button level).

7   A similar colour palette was realized for
the first time in the stab *B 2* shaver (1966),
and later in the model *cassett* (1970).

8   The *sixtant* electric razor introduced
five years before (1962) had made the
black-and-silver colour scheme popular.

9   This was a new use for plexiglas. A
wall thickness of 5 millimetres had never
been realized before, nor had such a finely
differentiated inner structure.

Coffee grinders, like meat grinders or eggbeaters, were common early mechanical household helpers.[1] The fact that they were capable of sparking such euphoria in Europe when they came out in electric versions[2] is easy to understand for anyone who has ever ground his own coffee. The naïve joy provided by this "little factory" – one of the first electrical appliances that was affordable for broad sections of the populace – may perhaps be attributable to its minimal dimensions. The small size means, namely, that the user holds the device in his hand, and can feel the vibrations of the motor when it takes off like a race car in the Grand Prix.[3]

When Braun brought out the model *KSM 1/11* in the mid-1960s[4] – designed by Reinhold Weiss – this cylinder was the simplest object yet to bear the Braun logo. The most noticeable feature of the minimalist monument is the lonely red dot-shaped control button.[5] Upon closer observation, we can also detect a slight downward tapering in the housing.[6] This nearly intangible touch makes the grinder easier to grip and elevates it above the banal character of a mere tube. The slightly bulging body, which weighs much more than a pound of coffee, lies snugly in four fingers, to be operated with the thumb. *KSM 1/11* came in the obligatory white, but also – we are, after all, talking about the Pop sixties – in red, yellow, orange and green[7] as well as in an exclusive black-and-silver version, a quote of the company's own success.[8] The dual colours make the tiered structure visible: the black base holds the motor, the band encircles the bowl in which the coffee is ground, and the thick-walled plexiglas top, which also works as a safety catch, makes the grinding process transparent.[9]

Multipress MPZ 22

Juicer

1972 | Redesign 1994
Design: Dieter Rams / Jürgen Greubel
citromatic / de luxe
No. 4979
white

1 There were four generations between 1957 and 1994.

2 By Gerd Alfred Müller in 1957; it was considered somewhat complicated to operate.

3 From 1970.

4 This makes them lightweight and easy to clean.

5 Cf. coffee grinders and electric shavers.

When looking at this citrus press expressions like "good design" or "German quality workmanship" inevitably come to mind, phrases that were once common parlance and had thoroughly positive connotations, but that today are used, if at all, only in quotation marks. The values associated with them – such as technological perfection and ease of handling combined with ascetic reserve – are manifested in the model *MPZ 22*. It is also a good example of a product that is regularly updated. Like the VW *Rabbit*, this kitchen appliance saw a steady stream of new versions demonstrating careful rethinking.[1] But the cylindrical form always stayed the same.

Braun's first electric juicer, the model *MP 3*, had a metal bracket and what was already an unusually compact form. *MP 50*, the next juice extractor,[2] was a redesign by Jürgen Greubel, one that was conspicuous for large radii at the edges.[3] It had a recess in the front to accommodate the container catching the juice. The *MPZ 22*, likewise by Greubel, brought further simplification: now there was only a horizontal seam between the two main sections of the appliance, the press and the motor housing. The press, into which the spout is integrated, is made up of three very lightweight nesting plastic parts that are not fixed in place.[4] Since the motor is started by downward pressure, this appliance needs no switch. During the pressing process, the power of the motor can be both felt and heard.[5] The little *MPZ 22* sounds as robust as a German mid-sized car.

KF 20

Coffee machine

1972
Design: Florian Seiffert
Aromaster
No. 4050
white, yellow, orange, red,
dark red, olive

1   The Ford *Model T* from 1908 is
regarded as the epitome of technical
perfection, in which the structure deter-
mines the form and is plain to see.

2   In the basic version for eight cups, or
as *KF 21* for 12 cups.

3   Older staff members like Fischer and
Weiss retired and were replaced by a
whole host of newcomers, such as
Hartwein, Kahlcke, Schneider, Ullmann
and Seiffert.

4   This trend was prompted by rising
wages accompanied by falling coffee
and electricity prices.

5   Compared to the much more basic
electric coffee grinder, for example,
whose basic form is identical from every
manufacturer.

Once upon a time, the comforting gurgling sound of the coffee
machine was as yet unknown in kitchens and offices. Although
automatic coffee-making looked back on a long history, it took
Braun to overcome the "Model-T stage"[1] and to turn the electric
coffee machine with filter into a universal appliance. The model
KF 20[2], designed by Florian Seiffert, was considered from the outset to be one of those classics that define a whole product genre
for a certain period of time. Likewise classic was the arduous
communication process that was apparently needed before the
new product could be implemented. This involved the not entirely easy back-and-forth between the masterminds in the Design
Department and the technicians with their professional and empiri-
cally based scepticism. This fraught but crucial relationship was
aggravated further by the upheaval of the 1960s and the urge felt
by a new generation of designers at Braun to flex their creative
muscles.[3] And then there were technical hurdles, such as the
development of a glass coffee pot in which details like an effective
spout were completely unexplored territory for both the glass
manufacturers and Braun.

These were the days when coffee drinking – which had always
been something of a festive, ritualized act – gradually became part
of the everyday routine.[4] The inevitable result of this change in
lifestyle and purchasing habits was the coffee machine, one of the
numerous everyday products that took shape during this era. An
apparatus for the automated brewing of the dark brown beans
leaves a relatively large degree of freedom in terms of layout.[5]
Many different constellations are conceivable. Seiffert's product
concept is based on the elementary idea that liquids always flow
downward. This is why he selected a structure oriented around the
hierarchical principle of the water tower: on top is the tank, in the
middle the filter that snaps in at three labelled points (it is hung

6   For coffee machines based on the German coffee filter.

7   The wires for the upper heating element are also conducted therein.

from below into the housing), and at the base a glass pot standing on a hotplate to hold the finished beverage. The cylindrical cross-section was the obvious choice for both pot and filter.[6] From these premises there logically emerged a stately column some 40 centimetres in height. With its choice of colours, some of them neon-bright, this coffee maker was no shrinking violet, betraying in its simple shape the principles on which it was predicated. The base-plate and the upper section that "floats" above the pot are connected by two bent metal pipes, an eye-catching detail to which the machine owes its graceful appearance.

This material with such a loaded design history (tubular steel!) underscores the mechanical character of the coffee-making process. The pipes were also needed, however, because two heating elements were required – one to heat the water and another to keep the coffee hot.[7] This dual role harboured a structural weakness that by no means dampened the passion design fans felt for the grand design. In practice, the *KF 20* rationalized the process of coffee-making considerably, not least due to extremely easy operation from the front by means of a solitary rocker switch with a clearly visible on-off lamp for the forgetful.

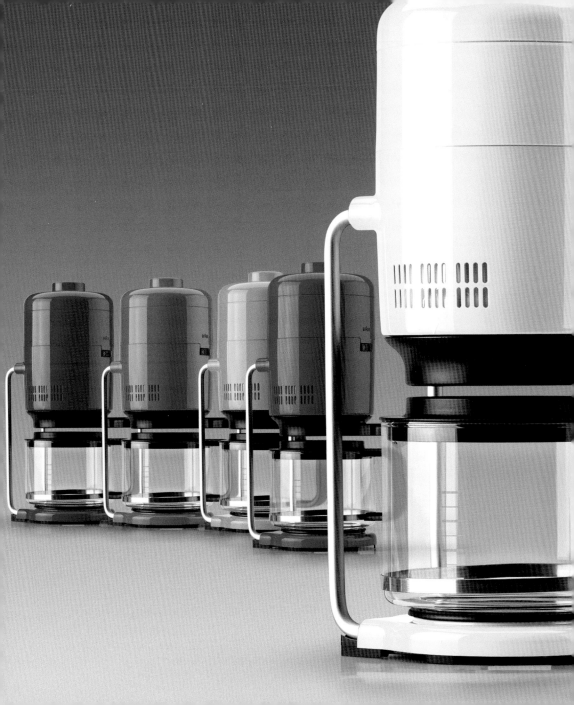

KF 40

Coffee machine

1984
Design: Hartwig Kahlcke
Aromaster 10/plus, 10/12/plus, 12
No. 4057/63
white, red/grey, red/black, black

1   In the literature this is also referred to
as an L-shape, which ignores the water
supply section that forms the "roof" of
the filter.

2   The free space in the lower part of
the enclosure was used to stow the
cord.

The most logical and easiest-to-produce layout for an automatic coffee machine based on the filter system is the C-shape[1]: the pot with filter on top is accompanied by a separate tank at the side. This configuration is not very pleasing formally or aesthetically, however, and usually looks ungainly. When Hartwig Kahlcke faced the task of eliminating this shortcoming in the early 1980s, he came upon one of those ingeniously simple solutions that are probably so hard to conceive of precisely because they are so obvious. The model *KF 40* is a prime example of how to solve a problem by looking at design from a different angle. Take two and make them one: Kahlcke did not depart from the tried-and-true layout, but instead simply integrated the two separate elements by telescoping the cylinders and melding them into a single unit.

Seen from above, the – formerly freestanding – tank hugs the filter-and-pot tower. In elevation, this structure looks like a "C" or a sickle.[2] The sure-footed *KF 40* represented not only a formal adjustment, but also a substantial rationalization, achieved not least through two hinge mechanisms: the feather-light lid atop the tank and the swivelling filter, both of which can be operated with one finger, considerably accelerating and facilitating daily coffee making. The same can be said for the frontal rocker switch. The ridges on the back of the water tank mask any indentations, which are not entirely avoidable in the inexpensive polypropylene used here. The *KF 40* is an affordable product appreciated both by consumers and by curators of design collections.

KGZ 3/31

Meat grinder
1982
Design: Hartwig Kahlke
No. 4242
white

1 With a different attachment, the device, under the name *KGM 3/31* (1986) could also be used as a grain mill.

2 Which unfortunately has a tendency to yellow.

The meat grinder was one of those mechanical appliances that belonged to the arsenal of basic kitchenware as early as the 19th century. It took another century, though, before this most fundamental of household helpers lost its rough, industrial look and found its way to a carefully thought-out and, in the classic sense, "good" form. The model *KGZ 3/31* dates from the early 1980s – a coherent design by Hartwig Kahlke – and has been in production ever since with only minor modifications.

The housing has a "back", a new topos in the Braun canon that also offers a practical advantage: the shelf on which the bowl is placed can be removed, turned over and perched there after use.[1] Thought was thus given to the problem of storage – something designers sometimes neglect. Further details sure to delight cooks are the recessed grips on either side and the recess at the front, which hugs the bowl for greater stability. When working with fat and meat, hygiene is vital. *KGZ 3/31* is easy to take apart and hence easy to clean – an aspect conveyed by the elegant smooth surfaces and virginal white.[2] The overall design likewise makes a clear statement. This machine still looks like a machine, even with its expressive physiognomy. The rump and neck-shaped feed tube give the *KGZ 3/31* an anthropomorphic air.

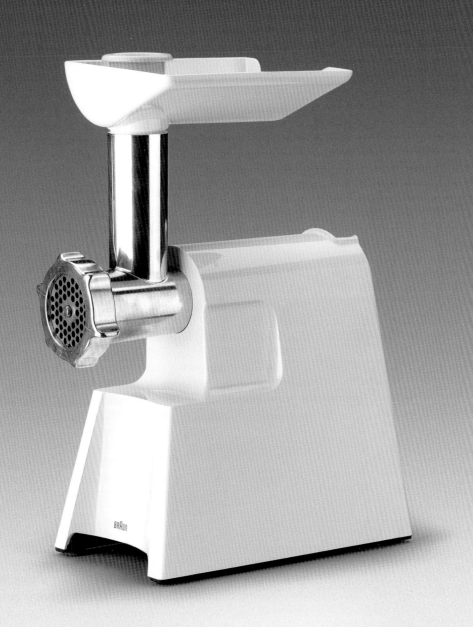

MR 500

Handblender

1995
Design: Ludwig Littmann
Multiquick control plus
No. 4187
white / anthracite

1　The first handblender is considered to be the *Zauberstab* (Magic Wand) from the Swiss company Esge.

2　Braun's current *Multimix*, for example, has a handblender attachment.

3　Model *MR 6* (1981), and then *MR 30* (1982), *MR 7* (1985) and *MR 300* (1987).

4　Cf. here the entry on the model *MR 5000* (2001).

5　This cap protects against both splashes and injury.

6　Starting with the *MR 30*. Some current models still have a metal wand, however.

This is, for a change, not a proprietary Braun development.[1] But Braun has substantially sped up the mutation of this appliance in recent years. Equipped with a foot, but still by no means able to stand on its own, the handblender represented, along with the handmixer and food processor, a further variation on the mixers that were introduced in Europe in the 1950s and whose areas of application to a great extent overlap. This functional similarity is especially the case with the hand-held appliances.[2] In the early 1980s the first handblender bearing the Braun logo came onto the market,[3] which, like all subsequent models, came off Ludwig Littmann's drawing board.

Handblenders are among the devices that must be held in and guided by the hand, but which don't have a separate handle, instead themselves forming a kind of handle. The German name, Stabmixer, has a double meaning: referring to both the technical principle (the effect achieved through a rotating Stab, or wand), and to the slim, elongated form of the housing. Interestingly enough, a process of formal melding is part of the genesis of this product, a duality which tends to be disguised.[4] The adjustments in the design consisted over the years – apart from slight variations in format – of a modified foot, which was soon furnished with a semi-circular protective cap,[5] as well as the introduction of plastic housing cast from a single mould.[6] A soft, funnel-shaped transition between the upper part, which encloses the motor, and the actual mixing wand gave the device a unified look. The *MR 500*, which spelled the first conceptual about-face in the development of this product genre, is a classic example of the interplay of technical and formal innovation in a single design. The main modifications compared to previous models were based on hard-and-soft technology, the application of which Littmann raised to a new level. Not only the surfaces and controls were affected, but even

MR 500

7   In formal terms, this recalls the
micron plus (1980).

8   The optimization of the injection
moulding process is an example of the
close cooperation between design, engineering and production.

the construction itself. The most conspicuous feature on the
facade of the *MR 500* is the dark, ridged strip of soft plastic into
which the switch is integrated. The machine thus carries the technology within as if on a shield before it.[7] The concept of the invisible switch, which is marked by a round recess but is protected
from moisture beneath the soft plastic, was just as new as the
other benefits provided by the soft material: a better sealing of the
housing, the new kind of unlocking button, and the connection
with the motor mounting inside. The motor "floats" in a rubber
mount that prevents it from rattling and makes it purr instead.
Several functions could hence be covered by a single injection
moulding process.[8]

The complex design of this handblender, which provides advantages in handling as well as in manufacture, is a textbook case of
industrial design. The first handblender in which the seams
between the main elements are strongly accentuated with contrasting materials and colours is still by no means optically rent
apart. And, as far as colour is concerned, the *MR 500* exercises
classic Braunian constraint.

396

control plus

SI 6510 FreeStyle

Steam iron

2000
Design: Ludwig Littmann/
Jürgen Greubel
FreeStyle
No. 4696
white / lilac

1   The electronic elements can otherwise be housed in the rear section of the
handle.

2   Whereby the details in the flow of line
are debatable in face of such complexity.

3   The iron won a plastics industry
award for best design with the highest
degree of difficulty.

4   Similar to how the fill level can be
read in *Dyson*-brand vacuum cleaners.

5   Doubted by some nostalgic Braun
purists who don't acknowledge that the
company's signature style also under-
went a development process in the pioneer days.

Imitation is the sincerest form of flattery. When the *FreeStyle* came onto the market, it was the first steam iron with an open handle. It took some time, but the competition finally followed suit. After all, the open-ended handle was not an easy solution in terms of construction,[1] but it did represent a breakthrough in ease of operation. And it gives *FreeStyle* an unmistakably dynamic silhouette, somewhere between mobile phone and luxury yacht. Everyone understands what this connotes: high-tech and tempo.

This streamlined form adequately expresses the fact that the steam iron, with its combination of electricity, heat and water in a compact space, is among the more technically demanding of the small appliances. And it does so in a texture that also pleases the eye with a virtuoso combination of different materials. In terms of its surface landscape, comparing *FreeStyle* with older irons is like pointing out the differences between a Porsche *911* from the 1960s and the current version of sports car, smoothed and polished on the computer screen.[2] By bringing together two different plastics, Littmann and Greubel delivered a case study in advanced multi-component technology[3]: soft, hard and translucent materials are interwoven in a variety of ways. The soft parts improve the grip and stability and provide better sealing around the buttons. And the use of transparent surfaces, something we have been accustomed to since the 1990s, is more than just aesthetically pleasing; the transparent tank allows the user to see the water level.[4] What we commonly call functionality appears here in an up-to-date guise.[5]

MR 5000

Handblender

2001
Design: Ludwig Littmann
Multiquick / Minipimer professional
No. 4191
white / grey

1 Cf. entry on model *MR 500* (1995).

2 Based, however, on the most sensible arrangement of the individual elements.

3 They also fulfil specific purposes: for example, the bends in the "hip skirt" make possible the obvious and hence easier snapping together of upper and lower parts.

4 The oblique recesses in the foot symbolize the rotating movement. And the open arches at the bottom make it easier to turn the implement during operation.

5 Some Braun traditionalists lament the loss of the former simplicity.

6 With all its accessories, this handblender becomes a complete food processor.

For decades, the history of the handblender didn't offer anything new and exciting. But after a small quantum leap had already been achieved in the 1990s, prompted by advances in technology,[1] Ludwig Littmann lent further emphasis to the unexpected revival of the wand-shaped mixer with the *MR 5000* – in particular as regards handling and appearance. An obvious change was the melding of the motor housing and mixing wand to form a single unit. But the details also betray a design with an unusually high degree of integration. For example, a graphic structure is generated with the help of hard-and-soft technology.[2] The product body consists of flowing surfaces and lines, in which bends and transitions are the exception.[3] This leads to a surface landscape that is as interesting as it is balanced: an organic formal language that sees itself as an aesthetic and ergonomic counterpart to the human body, which as we know doesn't include many regular geometric shapes. The *MR 5000* is as sexy as a voluptuous mermaid, an association that is summoned not only by the curves of its hips and back, but also by the tail fin at its feet.[4]

The fact that this artificial character makes the scene in the classic Braun colours of grey and white lends it an air of respectability, emphasizing its high level of performance. As there is no accounting for taste where erotic matters are concerned, however, it is hardly surprising that not everyone is susceptible to the charms of the sensuous *MR 5000*. Some see too much styling in the new sculptural approach.[5] Perhaps it's a case of an industrial larva emerging from its cocoon as a butterfly that is not only more beautiful, but also more capable.[6]

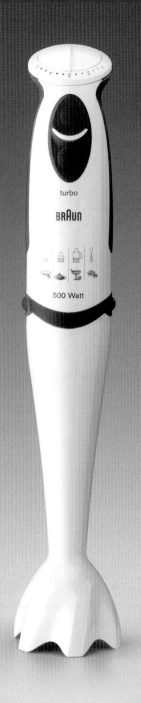

KM 3/31

1957 | Design: Gerd Alfred Müller
food processor | No. 4203
white / blue

MX 32

1962 | Design: Gerd Alfred Müller / Robert Oberheim
Multimix | No. 4142
white / green

Kitchen machines
1957–1965

The mother of all food processors is still regarded as a beauty.
With a removable mixing arm and various attachments, it is also
a perfect example of a product system.

KM 32
1964 | Design: Gerd Alfred Müller / Robert Oberheim
food processor | No. 4122 / 4123
white / green

KM 2
1965 | Design: Dieter Rams / Richard Fischer
Multiwerk | No. 4130
white

The *Multimix* jug also fit onto the *KM 3* and its carefully modified
successor. The *KM 2* was a multifunctional food preparation
machine based on a handmixer.

ZK 1
1979 | Design: Hartwig Kahlcke
Multiquick series | Nr. 4249–4250
white

MC 1/2
1983 | Design: Hartwig Kahlcke
Multiquick compact / electronic | No. 4171
white

Kitchen machines
1979–1984

With *Multiquick* a product idea that already existed on the market
was furnished with functional semantics. One distinguishing feature was the bent switch.

404

KM 210
1984 I Design Hartwig Kahlcke
Serie *Multipractic electronic* I No. 4261 /4262
white

UKW 1
1984 I Design: Hartwig Kahlcke
Kitchen scale No. 4243 to UK I No. 4261 /4262
white

Braun's first food processor, a compact kitchen machine developed
by French chefs, had the same universal motor as the *ZK 1* and
could be offered at an affordable price.

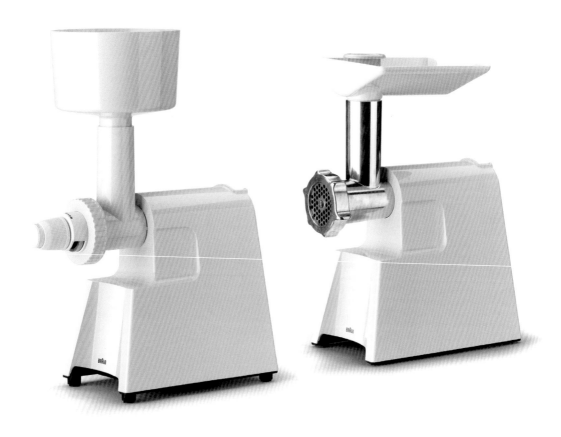

KGM 3/31
1986 | Design: Hartwig Kahlcke
grain mill | No.4239
white

KGZ 3/31
1982 | Design: Hartwig Kahlcke
meat grinder | No. 4242
white

Kitchen machines
1982–1993

Its smooth uninterrupted surfaces give this appliance an elegant look and facilitate cleaning. A new edition of the device was developed because, although meat grinders are less common in Western European households, they are used widely in other parts of the world.

K 1000

1993 | Design: Ludwig Littmann
Multisystem 1 bis 3 | No. 3210
white

A reinterpretation of the food processor that revived the market
for this item. Tested in an acoustics lab, this appliance has a quiet,
designed sound.

K 650
1996 | Design: Ludwig Littmann
CombiMax | No. 3205
white

MX 2050
2001 | Design: Ludwig Littmann / Misae Shiba
PowerBlend MX 2050 | No. 4184
white

Kitchen machines
1996–2001

The new standing mixer with 1.5-litre glass jug was geared particularly toward large markets such as Mexico and the USA. A plastic clutch minimizes the noise level.

K 3000

2000 | Design: Cornelia Seifert / Ludwig Littmann
Multisystem 3-in-1 | No. 3210
white / silver

This upgraded food processor can do three things: knead and
mix, chop and shred, mix and hack. These multiple talents made
this all-purpose machine a top-seller.

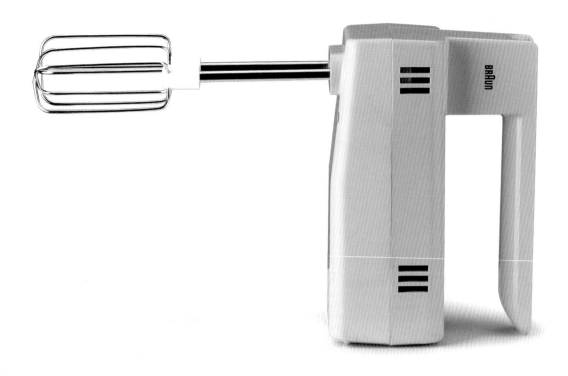

M 1/11

1960 | Design: Gerd Alfred Müller
Multiquirl | No. 4220/4221
light grey

Handmixers
1960–1968

Braun's first handmixer – a concept that, like so many kitchen appliances, came from the USA – had the typical uncluttered look, a narrow, open handle and parallel ventilation slits.

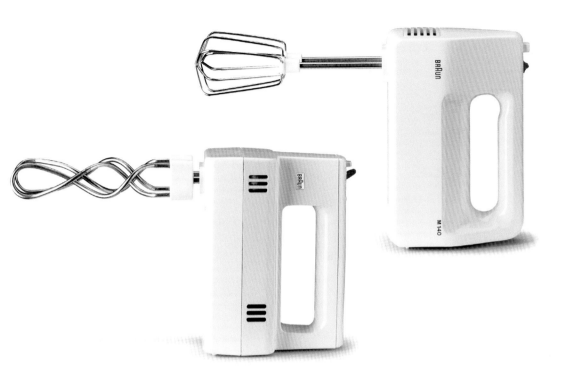

M 12
1963 | Design: Gerd Alfred Müller / Reinhold Weiss
Multiquirl | No. 4112
white

M 140
1968 | Design: Reinhold Weiss
Multiquirl | No. 4115
white

The handmixers that followed in the 1960s had a closed, and hence more stable, handle. The *M 140* also had an extra recess for a more secure grip.

M 800

1994 | Ludwig Littmann
Multimix duo / trio / quatro | No. 4262
white

Handmixers
1994

The new concept in the *M 800* was to position the motor directly above the mixing blades. This enables a higher degree of effectiveness. With the same amount of power, the motor could be made smaller and lighter.

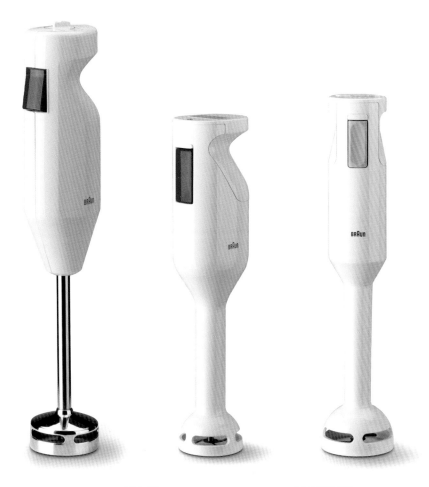

MR 6
1981 I Design: Ludwig Littmann
vario handblender I No. 4972
white / red

MR 30
1982 I Design: Ludwig Littmann
Stabmixer *junior* I No. 4172
white

MR 300 CA
1987/1993 I Design: Ludwig Littmann
compact handblender / *Multiquick 300*-Serie
No 4169 I white

In the progressive evolution of the handblender, a Swiss invention also known as a "pimer", the introduction of smaller, more powerful motors played a key role. A novelty: housing that extended downward to enclose the wand.

Handblenders
1981–1993

MR 555 MCA

1995 | Design: Ludwig Littmann
Multiquick control plus vario | No. 4189
white / black

MR 500 HC

1995 | Design: Ludwig Littmann
Multiquick control plus | No. 4187
white / anthracite

MR 5550

2001 | Design: Ludwig Littmann
Multiquick / Minipimer professional | No. 4191
white / grey

Handblenders
1995–2003

The advantages of a stable composite of hard and soft plastics –
a better grip and seal – were accompanied by an aesthetic trans-
formation: toward biomorphic forms and a more graphic presence.

MR 4000

2003 | Design: Ludwig Littmann
Multiquick Advantage | No. 4193
white / turquoise

MR 5550 MCA-V

2003 | Design: Ludwig Littmann
Multiquick Fresh System | No. 4191
white / blue

The *Fresh* System accessories include a stainless steel whisk for whipping cream and a dicer. Thanks to a vacuum pump system, food stored in *FreshWare* containers stays fresh longer.

MP 32
1965 | Design: Gerd Alfred Müller
Multipress | No. 4152
white

MP 50
1970 | Design: Jürgen Greubel
Multipress | No. 4154
white

Juicers, citrus presses
1965–1994

Braun's juice centrifuges likewise stand for unconditional practicality – a message underscored by the white surfaces that point up the contrasting logo. Users appreciate getting the most juice out of their fruit.

MPZ 1

1965 | Design: Robert Oberheim / Reinhold Weiss
Citruspresse | No. 4153
white

MPZ 22

1994 | Design: Dieter Rams / Jürgen Greubel
citromatic de luxe | No. 4979
white

Pressure from above triggers the juicing process – it's hard to
imagine greater ease of operation. The spout, out of which the juice
flows into a glass placed in the special recess, can be closed.

MPZ 4

1982 | Design: Ludwig Littmann
citromatic 2 | No. 4173
white

MPZ 7

1992 | Design Ludwig Littmann
citromatic 7 vario | No. 4161
white

Juicers, citrus presses
1982–2003

The *MPZ 4* citrus press has a double handle, which means the upper part can be lifted for pouring. The cord is wrapped around the base.

418

MPZ 9
2003 | Design: Ludwig Littmann / Sven Wuttig / Ingo Heyn
citromatic MPZ 9 | No. 4161
white

The *MPZ 9* citrus press unites the benefits of a transparent container with a curvy, emotional and ergonomic flow of line. The two-part
handle is teardrop-shaped.

MP 80

1988 | Design: Hartwig Kahlcke
Multipress Plus automatic | No. 4290
white

MP 75

1990 | Design: Ludwig Littmann
Multipress compact | No. 4235
white

Juicers, citrus presses
1988–1990

The juicers designed for constant use have an appealing closed look. Particularly in the USA, these devices are subject to high safety requirements. In the *MP 75* the lid and base are latched together.

HG 1
1962 | Design: Reinhold Weiss
combination grill
chrome / black

Braun's first and much-acclaimed grill had a glass window on the
rear side as well as on the front and was similar in structure to the
HT 1 toaster. The cover could be folded up, making the grill usable
as a rotisserie.

Grills
1962

421

HMT 1

1964 I Design: Reinhold Weiss / Dietrich Lubs
Multitherm I No. 4921
chrome-plated / black I (illus. top)

TT 10

1972 I Design: Florian Seiffert
thermos tray I No. 4005
aluminium / black I (illus. bottom)

**Electric skillets
Hotplates**
1964–1972

The basic idea behind this hotplate was to cast base and handles
from a single mould. The execution of the feet as runners also
meant additional heat protection. The successor model was flatter
and had open handles.

HT 2
1963 | Design: Reinhold Weiss
Automatictoaster | No. 4011
chrome / black | (illus. top)

HT 6
1980 | Design: Hartwig Kahlcke
toaster | No. 4037
grey / silver, brown / silver | (illus. bottom)

The second toaster, like its forerunner, *HT 1*, made the construction principle of nesting parts visible. The model *HT 6* was conspicuously asymmetrical and had rounded edges.

Toasters
1963–1980

HT 80/85

1991 I Design: Ludwig Littmann
Multitoast electronic-sensor toaster I No. 4108
white, red, black I (illus. top)

HT 450

2005 I Design: Ludwig Littmann
Multitoast HT 450 I No. 4120
black, white I (illus. bottom)

Toasters
1991–2005

In the two-slit *HT 450* (and the *HT 550* with its long single slit) the structural principle is evident on the outside. Noticeable here are the front and back sides that extend slightly beyond the ends, thicken toward the middle and exhibit a parallel curve above and

HT 600

2004 | Design: Ludwig Littmann
Impression HT 600 | No. 4118
metallic | (illus. top)

HT 550

2004 | Design: Ludwig Littmann
Multitoast HT 550 | No. 4119
black, white, anthracite | (illus. bottom)

below. A complex form is also displayed by the *Impression Line*
toaster *HT 600*. Characteristic for this model are the rounded
edges and the combination of plastic and stainless steel, as well as
the grey-and-silver colour scheme, which exudes an upscale aura.

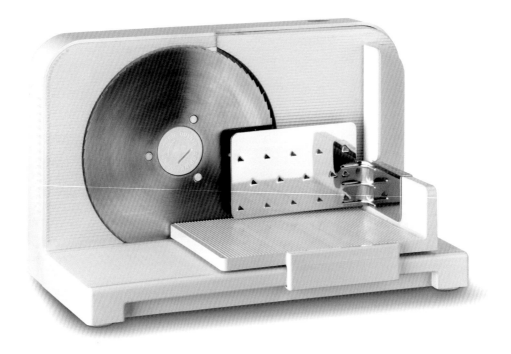

US 10

1973 | Design: Karl Dittert
electric | No. 4933
white

Universal slicers
1973

The combination of metal and the white plastic typical of household appliances gives the electric universal slicer a machine look.

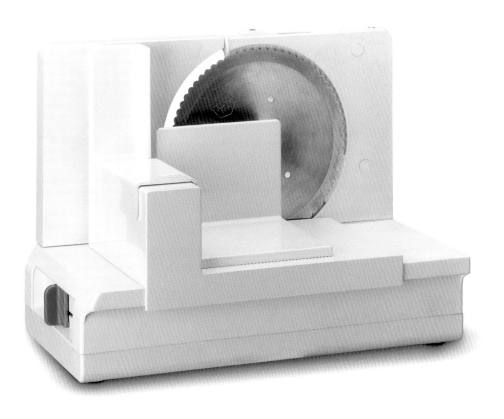

US 20

1973 | Design: Jürgen Greubel
electronic | No. 4926
white

This model could be folded up, and the thickness of the slices
adjusted infinitely through a sliding control.

EK 1
1978 | Design: Ludwig Littmann
electric knive
white

FS 10 Multigourmet
1996 | Design: Ludwig Littmann
No. 3216
white

Electric knives, steamers
1978–1996

The easy-to-operate steamer has a steaming basket (version *FS 20* has two stackable baskets) in which food can be separated by variable partitions.

428

HGS 10 / 20
1961 | manufactured in USA
tabletop dishwasher
white

The unusually compact dishwasher was equipped with sophisticated spray technology generated by a wandering water roller that
could be observed through the front pane.

Tabletop dishwasher
1961

429

WT 10

1974 | Design: Jürgen Greubel
drymatic clothes dryer | No. 4990
white

Clothes dryers

1974

This portable appliance could be hung on the wall or a door and is a prime example of the inventiveness of those years, as reflected in the many new products – even though some did not prove successful.

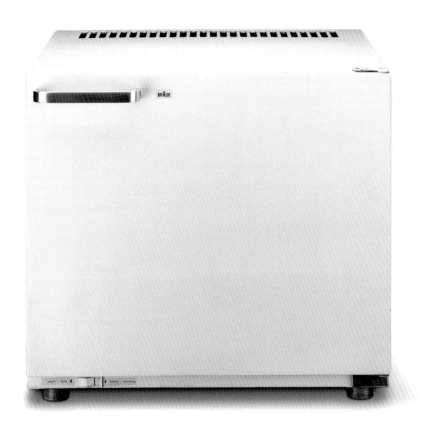

HTK 5
1964 | Design: Dieter Rams
freezer
white

The white box is as minimal as it gets. The parallel ventilation slits
are a typical Braun design element.

Freezer
1964

H 3/31
1962 | Design: Dieter Rams
heater with thermostat | No. 4513
white/grey

H 1/11
1959 | Design: Dieter Rams
heater with thermostat | No. 4305
white/grey

Heaters
1959–1965

The structure of the extremely small *H 1/11* heater, which caused
a sensation at the time of its launch, is similar to that of the *HT 1*
toaster: Two outer plastic parts frame the metal unit in the middle.

432

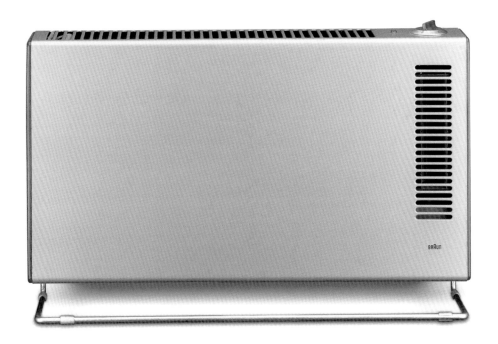

H 6
1965 I Design: Richard Fischer / Dieter Rams
convection heater I No. 4386
grey

The early heaters exhibit an architectural approach to product
design oriented on the repertoire of classic Modernism.

H 7
1967 | Reinhold Weiss / Dieter Rams
heater | No. 4517
grey, brown

H 5
1973 | Design: Jürgen Greubel
Novotherm | No. 4302
white / black, olive green / black, orange / black

Heaters
1967–1992

Equipped with an effective tangential blower, the model *H 7* puts its heating function on display through the cylindrical rear section. *H 5* resembles in structure and colours the contemporary compact hi-fi systems in the "8 degrees" series.

H 200
1992 | Design: Ludwig Littmann
heater
black / grey

H 30
1989 | Design: Ludwig Littmann
heater
black / grey

Two heaters with a simple structure and high graphic impact due to the combination of rectangle and concentric circles. While the *H 200* consists of three parts, the *H 30* is put together from two parts according to the pot-and-lid principle.

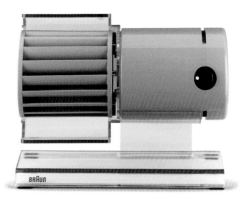

HL 1/11

1961 | Design: Reinhold Weiss
Multiwind | No. 4530
light grey, graphite

HL 70

1971 | Design: Reinhold Weiss / Jürgen Greubel
No. 4550/4551/4552
white, brown, yellow

Tabletop blowers
1961–1971

The version of the *HL 1/11* with screw-on base was also designed to be installed in the car. The innovative device with its tangential blower was produced again several years later in a slightly altered form.

ELF 1

1973 | Design: Jürgen Greubel
Air Control | No. 4451
black, white

The *ELF 1* electric air filter – a device for ridding the air of smoke, dust and allergens – has a facade of parallel ribs and was part of the "black wave" set off chiefly by the *D 300* slide projector three years earlier.

Air filters
1973

437

PV 4 vario 200
1984 | Design: Ludwig Littmann
Nr. 4374
white, green

Steam irons
1984–1989

The first iron Braun developed on its own has a few singular features: the gap between housing and sole, the parallel opening above it and the exaggerated tip, which prevents pulling when ironing synthetics.

438

PV 3 3000
1989 | Design: Ludwig Littmann
No. 4323 / 4324 / 4325 / 4347
white / black

The transparent tank cover below the handle (not easy to fabricate),
the heat-resistant material set off in a contrasting colour, and the flexible cords fed into the device via a ball were three new features.

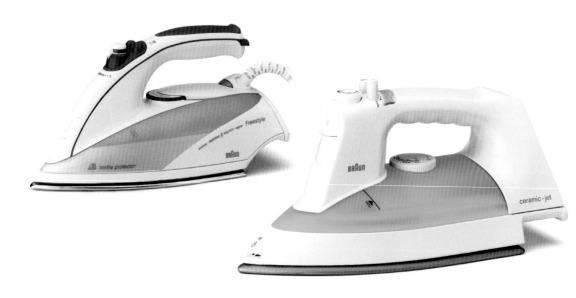

SI 6575

2001 | Design: Ludwig Littmann
FreeStyle Saphir | No. 4694
silver-metallic

PV 1205

1995 | Design: Jürgen Greubel / Ludwig Littmann
Ceramic-jet | No. 4394
white / green

Steam irons
1995–2004

The model *PV 1205* has a larger tank. A conceptual leap was made with the *FreeStyle*, whose open handle was only made possible by constructing the housing using tricky multi-component technology.

SI 9500

2004 | Design: Ludwig Littmann / Markus Orthey
FreeStyle Excel SI 9500 | No. 4677
blue

The round steam station with its large controls provides a steady
supply of steam. The steam penetrates the fabric under high pressure, significantly improving the ironing results.

HE 1/12
1961 | Design: Reinhold Weiss
No. 4911
chrome / black

WK 210
1999 | Design: Ludwig Littmann / Jürgen Greubel
AquaExpress | No. 3217
aqua, chameleon, vanilla, white

Water kettles
1961–2004

Braun's first electric water kettle has the simplest shape conceivable. The later model took on a more biomorphic form and had a more effective spout. The art of creating mottled, finely speckled surfaces is all about avoiding any unwanted "flow lines".

WK 300

1999 I Design: Ludwig Littmann / Jürgen Greubel
AquaExpress I No. 3219
titanium / black

WK 600

2004 I Design: Ludwig Littmann
Impression WK 600 I No. 3214
metallic

The "more emotional" forms of the new water kettles are combined with distinctive surfaces. These also include the classic colours of black and silver, which as ever connote quality and exclusiveness.

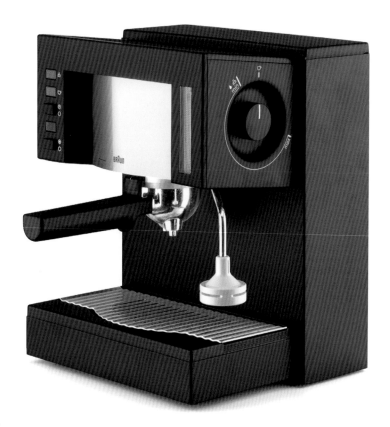

E 400 T

1991 | Design: Ludwig Littmann
Espresso Master professional | No. 3060
black / chrome

Espresso machines
1991–1995

The first espresso machines were so-called "OEM projects", i.e.
cooperations with external manufacturers. The cubic components
of this model were combined additively.

E 20

1994 | Design: Ludwig Littmann
Espresso Master | No. 3058
black

KFE 300

1995 | Design: Ludwig Littmann
Caféquattro | No. 3064
black

The elegant model *KFE 300* had a felicitous form. The narrow and quite squat machine had a housing made of textured ABS plastic as well as room to set cups on top.

KMM 1/121

1965 | Design: Reinhold Weiss
Aromatic coffee grinder with stone-mill
system No. 4398 | white/red, white/green

KMM 10

1975 | Design: Reinhold Weiss / Hartwig Kahlcke
Aromatic coffee grinder with stone-mill system | No.
4036
white, yellow

Coffee grinders
1965–1975

Grinders with the stone-mill system (which works more consistently) had a clear-cut structure. The later model was equipped with a timer and a larger container.

KSM 1/11

1967 | Design: Reinhold Weiss
Aromatic coffee grinder with hammer mechanism | No. 4024 /
4026
white, orange, red, yellow, green, chrome / black

The lid of the *KSM 1/11* wrote a further chapter in the history of
plastics at Braun. Its switching ridges made for cooler grinding.
This model also demonstrated the new, brighter colour concept
with formal perfection.

KMM 2

1969 | Design: Dieter Rams
Aromatic coffee grinder with stone-mill system | No.
4023
white, red, yellow

Coffee grinders
1969–1994

The first Braun coffee grinder with a stone-mill system had a window through which the filling level could be viewed. Its housing, with a pronounced bend underneath the filling container, came in three colours.

KSM 2

1979 | Design: Hartwig Kahlcke
Aromatic coffee grinder with hammer mechanism No. 4041 | white, yellow

KMM 30

1994 | Design: Ludwig Littmann / Jürgen Greubel
CaféSelect coffee / espresso grinder | No. 3045
white, black

In the last coffee grinder with its reverse-conical shape, the switch was a movable pestle that sank into the housing when pressed, a detail that meant improved safety. The cord could be wrapped around the base.

449

KF 21

1972 | Design: Florian Seiffert / Hartwig Kahlcke
Aromaster | No. 4051
white, yellow, orange

KF 30

1977 | Design: Hartwig Kahlcke
Aromat | No. 4052
white, yellow

Coffee machines

1972–1978

The Aromaster *KF 20* coffee machine was a milestone both in terms of design and sales figures. The pot for the *KF 21* was designed by Hartwig Kahlcke, who later created whole coffee machines.

450

KF 35

1978 | Design: Hartwig Kahlcke
Traditional / 2 | No. 4053
white, yellow

The various models were constructed of uniform parts, like building kits. In this simpler variation the switch was on the side. There
were also models with a filter drawer.

KF 40

1984 | Design: Hartwig Kahlcke
Aromaster 10 /plus, 10 /12 /plus, 12 | No. 4057 /63
white, red /grey, red /black, black

KF 70

1986 | Design: Hartwig Kahlcke
Aromaster special 10 | No. 4074 /4079
white

Coffee machines
1984–1994

The *KF 40 Aromaster* was mother to a whole generation of coffee machines, and not only those from Braun. It was also offered in a version with thermos (*KF 70*).

452

KF 80
1986 I Design: Hartwig Kahlcke
Aromaster control 12 I No. 4073/4091
white, black

KF 12
1994 I Ludwig Littmann
Aromaster 12 I No. 3075
white, black

The model *KF 80* had the proven swivelling filter, an electronic clock and capacity for twelve cups of coffee. *KF 12* was a smaller variation with a more delicate handle.

KF 180
1994 | Design: Roland Ullmann
AromaSelect | No. 3089 /3097 /3098
white, black

KF 170
1995 | Design: Roland Ullmann
AromaSelect thermoplus | No. 3102
white

Coffee machines
1994–2001

The double cone shape summons associations with the filter and lends the machine a more sculptural quality. The smaller lid makes for better closure, preserving the aroma.

KF 147

1999 I Design: Roland Ullmann / Ludwig Littmann
AromaSelect Millennium Edition I Nr . 3112
pearl titanium / black

KF 178

2001 I Design: Roland Ullmann / Ludwig Littmann / Dietrich Lubs
AromaSelect Juwel Edition Thermo I No. 3117
silver-blue / green

The *AromaSelect* series came in a wide range of versions and
colours. An optimally formed plastic spout (instead of glass) was
designed to avoid dripping and spillage.

KF 550

2002 | Design: Björn Kling
AromaPassion KF 550 | No. 3104
black / silver

KF 600

2004 | Design: Björn Kling
Impression KF 600 | No. 3106
metallic

Coffee machines
2002–2004

The *KF 550* has an automatic switch-off feature, as does the *KF 600*, which combines modern technology with historical overtones: the brushed stainless steel with its deluxe feel had a precedent in the *sixtant* electric shaver.

456

Product Lists

Product models and page numbers in boldface refer to illustrations.
Underlined page numbers refer to portraits of design milestones.

Entertainment Electronics

Tabletop radios and radio-phonograph combinations

Year	Type	Name	Colour	Designer	Page
1955	combi	radio-phonograph combi./portable radio	light grey	W. Wagenfeld	110
	TS-G	Tischsuper, RC 60	maple, walnut	H. Gugelot/H. Müller-Kühn	100
	G 11	Tischsuper, RC 60	maple	H. Gugelot	101
	SK 1	Kleinsuper, FM	light blue, pale green, graphite, light beige	A. Braun/Dr. F. Eichler	74
	SK 2	Kleinsuper, FM and MW	as SK 1	A. Braun/Dr. F. Eichler	
1956	G 11	Tischsuper, RC 61 A	maple	H. Gugelot	
	PK 1	radio-phonograph combination, RC 61	walnut	Thun Workshops	111
	SK 3	Kleinsuper, FM and MW	pale green, light beige	A. Braun/Dr. F. Eichler	
	SK 4	Phonosuper, FM and MW, record player	white/red elm	H. Gugelot, D. Rams	76
	TS 1	Tischsuper, RS 60	red elm, walnut	Thun Workshops	
	TS 2	Tischsuper, WKS-Möbel, RC 61	red elm, walnut	WKS/Braun Design Dept.	
1957	G 11	Tischsuper, RC 62–2	maple	H. Gugelot	
	SK 2	Kleinsuper, FM and MW	graphite, light grey	A. Braun/Dr. F. Eichler	
	SK 4/1	Phonosuper, FM and MW, record player	white/red elm	H. Gugelot/D. Rams	
	SK 4/1 A	Phonosuper, FM and MW, record player	white/red elm	H. Gugelot/D. Rams	
	TS 3	Tischsuper, RC 62-3	red elm, walnut	H. Hirche	
1958	G 11	Tischsuper, RC 7	maple	H. Gugelot	
	SK 2-US	Kleinsuper, FM and MW	graphite	A. Braun/Dr. F. Aichler	
	SK 4/2	Phonosuper, FM and MW, record player	white/red elm	H. Gugelot/D. Rams	
	SK 5	Phonosuper, FM, MW, LW, record player	white/red elm	H. Gugelot/D. Rams	
	TS 3	Stereo-Tischsuper, RC 8	white beech, walnut	H. Hirche	
1959	G 11	Stereo-Tischsuper, RC 88/RC 818	maple	H. Gugelot	
	SK 2/2	Kleinsuper, FM and MW	graphite, light grey	A. Braun/Dr. F. Eichler	
1960	SK 5 C	Phonosuper, FM, MW, SW, record player	white/red elm	H. Gugelot/D. Rams	
	SK 6	Stereo-Phonosuper, FM, MW, LW, record player	white/red elm	H. Gugelot/D. Rams	
	TS 3-81	Stereo-Tischsuper, RC 81	red elm, walnut	H. Hirche	
	TS 3 A	Stereo-Tischsuper, RC 81 U		H. Hirche	
1961	RT 20	Tischsuper, RC 31	beech/white, pearwood/graphite	D. Rams	103
	SK 25	Kleinsuper, FM and MW	graphite, light grey	A. Braun/Dr. F. Eichler	102
	SK 61	Stereo-Phonosuper, FM, MW, LW, record player	white/red elm	H. Gugelot/D. Rams	
	TS 31	Stereo-Tischsuper, RC 82, C	teak	H. Hirche	
1962	SK 61 C	Stereo-Phonosuper, FM, MW, SW, record player	white/red elm	H. Gugelot/D. Rams	
1963	SK 55	Phonosuper, FM, MW, LW, record player	white/ash	H. Gugelot/D. Rams	115

Music cabinets

Year	Type	Name	Colour	Designer	Page
1955	MS 1	music cabinet, RC 60	red elm, walnut	Thun Workshops	
	MS 2	music cabinet, RC 60, 10-disc record changer	red elm, walnut	Thun Workshops	
	PK-G (1)	radio-phonograph combination RC 60, maple stand	maple	H. Gugelot	
	PK-G (1)	radio-phonograph combination RC 60, steel stand	maple/anthracite	H. Gugelot	
	PK-G 2	radio-phonograph combination RC 60	maple	H. Gugelot	
1956	HM 1	music cabinet, RC 61	red elm, walnut	H. Hirche	123
	HM 2	music cabinet, RC 61, 10-disc record changer	red elm, walnut	H. Hirche	
	HM 3	music cabinet, RC 61, 10-disc record changer	red elm, walnut	H. Hirche	
	HM 4	music cabinet, RC 61, 10-disc record changer + reel-to-reel tape recorder	red elm, walnut	H. Hirche	
	MM 1	music cabinet, RC 60	red elm, walnut	Thun Workshops	
	MM 2	music cabinet, RC 60, 10-disc record changer	red elm, walnut	Thun Workshops	
	MM 3	music cabinet, RC 60, 10-disc record changer	red elm, walnut	Thun Workshops	

Year	Type	Name	Colour	Designer	Page
	MS 3	music cabinet, RC 61, 10-disc record changer	red elm, walnut	Thun Workshops	
	PK-G 3	radio-phonograph combination, RC 61, maple stand	maple	H. Gugelot	
	PK-G 4	radio-phonograph combination RC 61, 10-disc record changer, maple stand	maple	H. Gugelot	122
1957	HM 5	music cabinet, RC 61-1	teak	H. Hirche	
	HM 6	music cabinet, RC 62, 10-disc record changer	teak, walnut	H. Hirche	
	MM 4	music cabinet, RC 61-1, 10-disc record changer	red elm, walnut	Thun Workshops	122
	PK-G 5	radio-phonograph combination, RC 62, maple stand	maple	H. Gugelot	
1958	HM 5	music cabinet, RC 7	teak	H. Hirche	
	HM 5	stereo music cabinet, RC 8	teak, walnut	H. Hirche	
	HM 6	stereo music cab., RC 7/RC 8, 10-disc rec. changer	teak, walnut	H. Hirche	125
	HM 7	music cabinet, RC 7, 10-disc record changer	red elm, walnut	H. Hirche	
	MM 4	music cabinet RC 7	red elm, walnut	Thun Workshops	
	MM 4	stereo music cabinet, RC 8 A, 10-disc rec. changer	red elm, walnut	Thun Workshops	
	PK-G 5	radio-phonograph combination, RC 7, maple stand	maple	H. Gugelot	
	R 10	stereo music cabinet, RC 81	red elm, teak	H. Hirche	124
	HM 7	stereo music cabinet, RC 8	red elm, walnut	H. Hirche	
1959	HM 5	stereo music cabinet, RC 81 A	teak, walnut	H. Hirche	
	HM 6	stereo music cabinet, RC 81, 10-disc rec. changer	teak, walnut	H. Hirche	
	MM 4	stereo music cabinet, RC 81 A, 10-disc rec. changer	red elm, walnut	Thun Workshops	
	RB 10	storage cabinet (tape recorder cabinet)	red elm, teak	H. Hirche	124
	RL 10	box speaker	red elm, teak	H. Hirche	124
	HM 7	stereo music cabinet, RC 81	red elm, walnut	H. Hirche	
1960	PK-G 5	stereo combination, RC 8, maple stand	maple	H. Gugelot	
	PK-G 5	stereo combination, RC 81 B, maple stand	maple	H. Gugelot	
	R 10 W	stereo music cabinet, RC 81, 10-disc rec. changer	red elm, teak	H. Hirche	
	RS 11	stereo music cabinet, RC 82-C	red elm, teak, walnut	H. Hirche	
	R 22	stereo music cabinet, RC 82-C, 10-disc rec. changer	walnut, teak	H. Hirche	125
1961	MM 41	stereo music cabinet, RC 82 A, 10-disc rec. changer	teak	Thun Workshops	
	PK-G 51	stereo combination, RC 82 B, maple stand	maple	H. Gugelot	
	RS 12	stereo music cabinet, RC 9	teak, walnut	H. Hirche	
	R 23	stereo music cabinet, RC 9, 10-disc record changer	teak, walnut	H. Hirche	

Transistor and portable radios

Year	Type	Name	Colour	Designer	Page
1956	**exporter 2**	portable radio with NA 2 power base	grey-blue/-, English red/white	Ulm Acad. Des. (redes.)	106
1957	PC 3	portable record player	light & dark grey	D. Rams/W. Wagenfeld	
	transistor 1	portable radio S/M/L	light grey	D. Rams	
1958	PC 3 SV	portable record player, equipped for stereo	light & dark grey	D. Rams/W. Wagenfeld	
	T 3	transistor radio	light grey	D. Rams/Ulm Acad. Des.	
	transistor 2	portable radio M/L	light grey	D. Rams	
1959	KTH 1/2	earphones in aluminium case	graphite/chrome/aluminium	D. Rams	
	P 1	battery record player	light grey	D. Rams	
	TP1	transistor radio-phonograph, combines T 4 and P 1	light grey	D. Rams/Ulm Acad.	**82, 108**
	T 4	transistor radio	light grey	D. Rams	
	transistor k	portable radio S/M/L	light grey	D. Rams	
1960	PCK 4	portable stereo phonograph	light & dark grey	D. Rams	
	TP 2	transistor radio-phonograph, combines T 31 and P 1	light grey	D. Rams/Ulm Acad. Des.	
	T 22	portable radio F/S/M/L	light grey	D. Rams	104
	T 22-C	portable radio	light grey	D. Rams	
	T 23	portable radio 4 x S	light grey	D. Rams	
	T 24	portable radio S/M/L	grey-green	D. Rams	
	T 31	transistor radio	light grey	D. Rams/Ulm Acad. Des.	
1961	PCV 4	portable stereo amplifier-phonograph	graphite	D. Rams	

Year	Type	Name	Colour	Designer	Page
	T 52	portable radio F/M/L	light grey, blue-grey	D. Rams	**105**
1961	T 54	portable radio	blue-grey	D. Rams	
	T 220	portable radio F/S/M/L w/imitation leather cover	blue, black	D. Rams	
1962	**T 41**	transistor radio	light grey	D. Rams	**107**
	T 520	portable radio F/M/L	light grey, blue-grey, graphite	D. Rams	
	T 521	portable radio F/S/M	light grey, blue-grey, graphite	D. Rams	
	T 530	portable radio M/2 x S	light grey, blue-grey, graphite	D. Rams	
	T 540	portable radio S/M/L	light grey, blue-grey, graphite	D. Rams	
	TH	car mounting	alu.-coloured	D. Rams	
1963	T 221	portable radio F/M w/imitation leather cover	graphite	D. Rams	
	T 225	portable radio w/imitation leather cover	blue	D. Rams	
	T 510	portable radio F/M/L	light grey, blue-grey	D. Rams	
	T 580	Universal portable car radio F/M/L	white, graphite	D. Rams	
	T 1000	short-wave receiver	alu.-coloured/black, white dial	D. Rams	**86, 109**
1964	T 1000	short-wave receiver	alu.-coloured/black, black dial	D. Rams	
	TN 1000	mains adapter	dark grey	D. Rams	
1966	PK 1000	direction-finding antenna	black	D. Rams	
1968	PV 1000	direction-finding adapter	white	D. Rams	
	T 1000 CD	short-wave receiver	alu.-coloured/black, black dial	D. Rams	

Speaker units

Year	Type	Name	Colour	Designer	Page
1957	**L 1**	speaker for Atelier and SK 4	white/red elm	D. Rams	**114**
	L 3	speaker for studio 1	walnut/white/anthracite	G. Lander	**124**
1958	**L 2**	speaker mounted on runners	white/white beech, white/walnut	D. Rams	**126**
1959	**LE 1**	electrostatic speaker w/stand	light grey/graphite	D. Rams	**128**
	RL 10	box speaker	red elm/-, walnut/-, teak/anthracite	H. Hirche	
	L 01	additional speaker w/stand	white/alu.-col., graph. grey/chrome	D. Rams	**128**
	L 02	additional speaker	light grey/anthracite	D. Rams	**130**
1960	L 02 X	additional speaker w/control	light grey/anthracite	D. Rams	
	L 11	speaker for Atelier	white/red elm	D. Rams	
1961	L 12	speaker for Atelier	white/red elm	D. Rams	
	L 40	bookshelf speaker	white/-, graphite/-, walnut/alu.-coloured	D. Rams	**132**
	L 50	bass reflex speaker	white/alu.-coloured	D. Rams	
	L 60	bookshelf and floor-standing speaker	white/-, walnut/alu.-coloured	D. Rams	
	L 61	bookshelf and floor-standing speaker	white/-, graphite/-, walnut/alu.-coloured	D. Rams	
1962	L 20	bookshelf speaker	white/alu.-coloured	D. Rams	
	L 45	flat speaker	white/alu.-coloured	D. Rams	
	L 80	floor-standing speaker	white/-, walnut/fabric, perf.plate/white	D. Rams	
1963	L 25	flat speaker	white/-, graphite/alu.-coloured	D. Rams	
	L 46	flat speaker	white/-, graphite/-, walnut/alu.-coloured	D. Rams	
1964	L 40/1	bookshelf speaker	white/-, graphite/-, walnut/alu.-coloured	D. Rams	
	L 60-4	bookshelf and floor-standing speaker	white/-, graphite/-, walnut/alu.-coloured	D. Rams	
1965	L 700	floor-standing speaker	white/-, walnut/alu.-coloured	D. Rams	
	L 700-4	floor-standing speaker	white/-, walnut/alu.-coloured	D. Rams	
	L 1000	floor-standing speaker	white/alu.-coloured	D. Rams	**132**
	LS 75	PA column speaker	white/alu.-coloured	D. Rams	
	L 300	miniature speaker	white/alu.-coloured, black/black	D. Rams	
	L 450	flat speaker	white/-, graphite/alu.-coloured	D. Rams	
1966	L 800	floor-standing speaker	white/-, walnut/alu.-coloured	D. Rams	
	L 900	floor-standing speaker	white/-, walnut/alu.-coloured	D. Rams	
1967	EDL 2	PA disco speaker	white/alu.-coloured	D. Rams	
	L 250	bookshelf speaker	white/-, walnut/alu.-coloured	D. Rams	
	L 300/1	miniature speaker	white/alu.-coloured	D. Rams	

Year	Type	Name	Colour	Designer	Page
	L 450/1	flat speaker	white/-, graphite/alu.-coloured	D. Rams	
	L 460	speaker, round	white/alu.-coloured	A. Jacobsen	
	L 600	bookshelf speaker	white/-, walnut/alu.-coloured	D. Rams	
1968	ELR 1	PA line array speaker	white/alu.-coloured	D. Rams	
	L 250/1	additional speaker	white/-, walnut/alu.-coloured	D. Rams	
	L 400	bookshelf speaker	white/-, graphite/-, walnut/alu.-coloured	D. Rams	
	L 450-2	flat speaker	white/-, anthracite/-, walnut/alu.-coloured	D. Rams	
	L 910	studio/floor-standing speaker	white/-, walnut/alu.-coloured	D. Rams	
1969	L 300/2	miniature speaker	white/-, walnut/alu.-coloured	D. Rams	
	L 410	bookshelf speaker	white/-, graphite/-, walnut/alu.-coloured	D. Rams	
	L 470	flat speaker	white/-, graphite/-, walnut/alu.-coloured	D. Rams	
	L 610	bookshelf speaker	white/-, walnut/alu.-coloured	D. Rams	
	L 710	studio speaker	white/-, walnut/alu.-coloured, white/black	D. Rams	**94**, 138
	L 810	studio speaker	white/-, walnut/alu.-coloured	D. Rams	134
1970	EDL 3	PA disco speaker	white/alu.-coloured	D. Rams	
	EL 450	PA speaker	white/alu.-coloured	D. Rams	
	EL 250	PA speaker	white/alu.-coloured	D. Rams	
	L 310	flat speaker, small	white/-, walnut/alu.-coloured	D. Rams	
	L 500	bookshelf speaker	white/-, walnut/alu.-coloured	D. Rams	
	L 550	speaker, shallow	white/-, walnut/alu.-coloured	D. Rams	
1971	L 480	bookshelf speaker	white/-, anthracite/-, walnut/alu.-coloured	D. Rams	
	L 500/1	bookshelf speaker	white/-, black/-, walnut/alu.-coloured	D. Rams	
	L 550/1	flat speaker	white/-, walnut/alu.-coloured	D. Rams	
	L 620	bookshelf speaker	white/-, walnut/alu.-coloured	D. Rams	
	L 620/1	bookshelf speaker	white/-, black/-, walnut/alu.-coloured	D. Rams	
	LV 1020	powered speaker	white/-, walnut/alu.-coloured	D. Rams	
1972	**L 260**	shelf or wall speaker for cockpit 250/260	white/black	D. Rams	**151**
	L 420	bookshelf speaker	white/alu.-coloured	D. Rams	
	L 420/1	bookshelf speaker	white/-, black/-, walnut/alu.-coloured	D. Rams	
	L 480/1	bookshelf speaker, flat	white/-, black/-, walnut/alu.-coloured	D. Rams	
	L 485	flat speaker	white/-, black/-, walnut/alu.-coloured	D. Rams	
	L 555	flat speaker	white/-, walnut/alu.-coloured	D. Rams	
	L 810-1	floor-standing speaker	white/-, walnut/alu.-coloured	D. Rams	
1973	L 710/1	studio speaker	white/-, black/-, walnut/alu.-coloured	D. Rams	
	L 308	speaker 8°	white/black	D. Rams	**151**
	LV 720	powered speaker	white/-, black/-, walnut/alu.-coloured	D. Rams	
1974	L 425	bookshelf speaker	white/-, walnut/alu.-coloured	D. Rams	
	L 505	bookshelf speaker	white/-, black/-, walnut/alu.-coloured	D. Rams	
	L 625	bookshelf speaker	white/-, black/-, walnut/alu.-coloured	D. Rams	
1975	L 100	miniature speaker	black/black	D. Rams	
	L 320	bookshelf speaker	white/black, walnut/black	D. Rams	
	L 321	bookshelf speaker	white/-, walnut/alu.-coloured	D. Rams	
	L 322	bookshelf or wall speaker	white/black, walnut/black	D. Rams	
	L 530	bookshelf speaker	white/-, black/-, walnut/alu.-coloured	D. Rams	
	L 530 F	flat speaker	white/-, black/-, walnut/alu.-coloured	D. Rams	
	L 630	bookshelf speaker	white/-, black/-, walnut/alu.-coloured	D. Rams	
	L 715	studio speaker	white/-, black/-, walnut/alu.-coloured	D. Rams	
	L 730	bookshelf speaker	white/-, black/-, walnut/alu.-coloured	D. Rams	
	L 830	bookshelf and floor-standing speaker	white/-, black/-, walnut/alu.-coloured	D. Rams	
1976	L 200	bookshelf or wall speaker	white/alu.-coloured, black/black, brown/brown	D. Rams	
	L 2000	output compact studio speaker	white/alu.-coloured, black/black	D. Rams	
1977	L 300	bookshelf or wall speaker	white/alu.-coloured, black/black, brown/brown	D. Rams	
	L 350	bookshelf speaker	black/black	D. Rams	
	L 530 F	bookshelf or wall speaker	white/-, black/-, walnut/alu.-coloured, black/black	D. Rams	

Year	Type	Name	Colour	Designer	Page
1977	L 1030	floor-standing speaker	white/alu.-coloured, black/black	D. Rams	
	L 1030/4 US	floor-standing speaker	white/alu.-coloured, black/black, walnut/black	D. Rams	
1978	GSL 1030	floor-standing speaker	white/alu.-coloured, black/black	D. Rams	
	L 100 auto	car speaker	black/black	D. Rams/L. Littmann	
	L 1030	floor-standing speaker	walnut/black	D. Rams	
	L 1030/8	floor-standing speaker	black/black, walnut/black	D. Rams	
	LC 3	in concert, bookshelf speaker	black/black	D. Rams/P. Hartwein	
	SM 1002	studio mon., bookshelf speaker	white/-, black/-, walnut/alu.-coloured, black/black	D. Rams	
	SM 1003	studio mon., bookshelf speaker	white/-, black/-, walnut/alu.-coloured, black/black	D. Rams	
	SM 1004	studio mon., bookshelf speaker	white/-, black/-, walnut/alu.-coloured, black/black, walnut/brown	D. Rams	
	SM 1005	studio monitor, bookshelf or floor-standing speaker	white/-, black/-, walnut/alu.-coloured, black/black	D. Rams	**142**
1979	H 701	holophonie	black/black	P. Hartwein/P. Schneider	
	ic 50	in concert, booksh. and wall sp.	light grey, walnut/brown	D. Rams/P. Hartwein	
	ic 70	in concert, booksh. and wall sp.	black/black, walnut/brown	D. Rams/P. Hartwein	
	ic 90	in concert, booksh. and wall sp.	black/black, walnut/brown	D. Rams/P. Hartwein	
	LW1	bass speaker unit, tabletop speaker	black/-, walnut/-, oak/-, rosewood/black	D. Rams	
	SM 1006 TC	studio monitor, floor-standing sp.	black/black, walnut/black	D. Rams	
	SM 1002 S	studio monitor, square, bookshelf and wall speaker	white/-, black/-, walnut/alu.-coloured, black/black	D. Rams	
	SM 2150	studio monitor, floor-stand. sp.	alu.-coloured/-, black/-, grey/black	D. Rams/P. Hartwein	**144**
1980	BTB 50/70/90	Teleropa box speaker		D. Rams/P. Hartwein	
	ic 80	in concert	black/black, walnut/brown, brown/brown	D. Rams	
	ic 1002	in concert	walnut/black, walnut/brown	D. Rams/P. Hartwein	
	ic 1003	in concert	walnut/black, walnut/brown	D. Rams/P. Hartwein	
	ic 1004	in concert	walnut/black, walnut/brown	D. Rams/P. Hartwein	
	ic 1005	in concert	walnut/black, walnut/brown	D. Rams/P. Hartwein	
	L 8060 HE	bookshelf and wall speaker	black/black, walnut/brown	D. Rams/P. Hartwein	
	L 8070 HE	bookshelf and wall speaker	black/black, walnut/brown	D. Rams/P. Hartwein	
	L 8080 HE	bookshelf and wall speaker	black/black, walnut/brown	D. Rams/P. Hartwein	
	L 8100 HE	bookshelf, wall and floor-standing speaker	black/black, walnut/brown	D. Rams/P. Hartwein	
	LA sound	bass reflex speaker	black/black, walnut/brown	D. Rams/P. Hartwein	**144**
	SM 1001	studio mon., bookshelf speaker	black/black, white/alu.-coloured, walnut/alu.-coloured	P. Hartwein/P. Schneider	
	SM 1006	studio monitor, floor-stand. sp.	black/black, walnut/black	D. Rams	
1981	ic 60	in concert	black/black, walnut/brown	D. Rams/P. Hartwein	
	ic 100	in concert	black/black, walnut/brown	D. Rams	
	ic 1002	in concert	black/black	D. Rams/P. Hartwein	
	ic 1003	in concert	black/black	D. Rams/P. Hartwein	
	ic 1004	in concert	black/black	D. Rams/P. Hartwein	
	ic 1005	in concert	black/black	D. Rams/P. Hartwein	
1982	Bel 300 i	car speaker	black		
	LS 60	bookshelf speaker	black/black	P. Hartwein	
	LS 70	bookshelf speaker	black/black, white/white, walnut/black	P. Hartwein	**146**
	LS 80	bookshelf speaker	black/black, white/white, walnut/black	P. Hartwein	
	LS 100	bookshelf speaker	black/black, white/white, walnut/black	P. Hartwein	
	LS 120	bookshelf speaker	black/black, white/white, walnut/black	P. Hartwein	
	LS 150	bookshelf speaker	black/black	P. Hartwein	
1983	Bel 320 i	car speaker	black		

Year	Type	Name	Colour	Designer	Page
	LS 40	satellite speaker	black/black, white/white	P. Hartwein	**168**
	LS 130	floor-standing speaker	black/black, white/white	P. Hartwein	
	LS 150	bookshelf speaker	white/white	P. Hartwein	**171**
	LS 150 PA	powered floor-standing speaker	black/black, white/white	P. Hartwein	**148**
	SW 2	subwoofer	black/black, white/white	P. Hartwein	
1984	Bel 315 i	car speaker	black		
	LS 65	bookshelf speaker	black/black, white/white, walnut/black	P. Hartwein	
1985	CS 700	car speaker bass system	black		
1986	**LSV**	satellite speaker	black/black, white/white	P. Hartwein	**142**
1987	CM 5	CompactMonitor	black/black, white/white, grey/grey	P. Hartwein	
	CM 6	CompactMonitor	black/black, white/white, grey/grey	P. Hartwein	**148**
	CM 7	CompactMonitor	black/black, white/white, grey/grey	P. Hartwein	
	LS 150	bookshelf speaker	grey/grey	P. Hartwein	
	LS 150 PA	powered floor-standing speaker	grey	P. Hartwein	
	LS 200	floor-standing speaker	black/black, white/white, redwood	P. Hartwein	
	LTV	speaker for TV 3	black, crystal grey	P. Hartwein	
	S 10	car subwoofer	body		
1988	M 9	StandMonitor	black, crystal grey	P. Hartwein	
	M 90	StandMonitor	black, crystal grey	P. Hartwein	
1989	RM 5	RegalMonitor	black, white, crystal grey	P. Hartwein	
	RM 6	RegalMonitor	black, white, crystal grey	P. Hartwein	
	RM 7	RegalMonitor	black, white, crystal grey	P. Hartwein	
1990	M 10	StandMonitor	black, crystal grey, white, gloss black	P. Hartwein	
	M 12	StandMonitor	black, crystal grey, white, gloss black	P. Hartwein	
	M 15	StandMonitor	black, crystal grey, white, gloss black	P. Hartwein	

Headphones

1967	**KH 1000**	stereo headphones	black	R. Weiss	**172**
1968	**KH 100**	mono headph. for T 1000 CD	black	R. Weiss	**172**
1975	**KH 500**	stereo headphones	black	D. Rams	**172**

Speaker columns

1987		speaker columns for CM 5, CM 6, CM 7	black, crystal grey	P. Hartwein	

Receivers/pre-amplifiers

1972	CES 1020	receiver/pre-amplifier	anthr./black, anthr./alu.-coloured, black	D. Rams	
1980	AC 701	pre-amplifier	black	D. Rams/P. Hartwein	
1987	CC 4	receiver/pre-amplifier, atelier	black, crystal grey	P. Hartwein	

Receivers

1959	**CE 11**	receiver, studio 2	light grey/alu.-coloured	D. Rams	**84**, 129
	CE 12	receiver, studio 2	light grey/alu.-coloured	D. Rams	
1963	**CET 15**	receiver	light grey/alu.-coloured	D. Rams	130
1964	CE 16	receiver	light grey/alu.-coloured	D. Rams	
1965	CE 1000	receiver	anthracite/alu.-coloured	D. Rams	
1966	CE 500	receiver	anthracite/alu.-coloured	D. Rams	
	CE 500 K	receiver	anthracite/alu.-coloured	D. Rams	
1967	CE 250	receiver	anthracite/alu.-coloured	D. Rams	
1968	CE 1000/2	receiver	anthracite/alu.-coloured	D. Rams	

Year	Type	Name	Colour	Designer	Page
1969	CE 501	receiver	anthracite/alu.-coloured	D. Rams	
	CE 501/1	receiver	anthracite/alu.-coloured	D. Rams	
	CE 501/K	receiver	anthracite/alu.-coloured	D. Rams	
	CE 250/1	receiver	anthracite/alu.-coloured	D. Rams	
	CE 251	receiver	anthracite/alu.-coloured	D. Rams	136
1973	CE 1020	receiver	anthracite/alu.-coloured	D. Rams	
1977	CT 1020	receiver	anthracite/black	D. Rams	
1978	T 301	receiver	black, light grey	D. Rams/P. Hartwein	
	TS 501	receiver	black, light grey	D. Rams/P. Hartwein	143
1980	**T 1**	receiver, atelier 1	black, crystal grey	P. Hartwein	147
1982	**T 2**	receiver, atelier	black, crystal grey P. Hartwein		98, 149

Amplifiers

Year	Type	Name	Colour	Designer	Page
1959	**CV 11**	power amplifier, studio 2	light grey	D. Rams	84, 129
1961	**CSV 13**	amplifier	light grey/alu.-coloured	D. Rams	133
1962	CSV 130	amplifier	light grey	D. Rams	
	CSV 60	amplifier	light grey/alu.-coloured	D. Rams	133
	CSV 10	amplifier	light grey/alu.-coloured	D. Rams	
1965	CSV 1000	amplifier	anthracite/alu.-coloured	D. Rams	
1966	**CSV 12**	amplifier	light grey/alu.-coloured	D. Rams	131
	CSV 250	amplifier	anthracite/alu.-coloured	D. Rams	
1967	CSV 60-1	amplifier	light grey/-, anthr./alu.-coloured	D. Rams	
	CSV 500	amplifier	anthracite/alu.-coloured	D. Rams	135
1968	CSV 1000/1	amplifier	anthracite/alu.-coloured	D. Rams	
1969	CSV 250/1	amplifier	anthracite/alu.-coloured	D. Rams	
1970	**CSV 300**	amplifier	anthracite/alu.-coloured	D. Rams	137
	CSV 510	amplifier	anthracite/alu.-coloured	D. Rams	
1978	A 301	amplifier	light grey, black	D. Rams/P. Hartwein	
	A 501	amplifier	light grey, black	D. Rams/P. Hartwein	
143					
1980	AP 701	high-power amplifier	black	D. Rams/P. Hartwein	
	A 1	amplifier, atelier 1	black, crystal grey	P. Hartwein	147
1982	**A 2**	amplifier, atelier	black, crystal grey	P. Hartwein	98, 149
1987	PA 4	power amplifier, atelier	black, crystal grey	P. Hartwein	

Control units

Year	Type	Name	Colour	Designer	Page
1959	**CS 11**	control unit for record player, studio 2	light grey/alu.-coloured	D. Rams	84, 129
1961	**RCS 9**	control unit	light grey/alu.-coloured	D. Rams	127
1962	TS 40	control unit	light grey/alu.-coloured	D. Rams	
1964	TS 45	control unit	light grey/-, graphite/alu.-coloured	D. Rams	
1968	**regie 500**	control unit	anthracite/alu.-coloured	D. Rams	139
1969	regie 501	control unit	anthracite/alu.-coloured	D. Rams	
	regie 501 K	control unit	anthracite/alu.-coloured	D. Rams	
1972	**regie 510**	control unit	anthr./alu.-coloured, anthr./black	D. Rams	140
1973	**regie 308**	control unit, 8°	black/white	D. Rams	150
	regie 308 S	control unit, 8°	black/white	D. Rams	
1974	regie 308 F	control unit, 8°	black/white	D. Rams	
	regie 520	control unit	anthracite/black	D. Rams	
1975	regie 450	control unit	anthracite/black	D. Rams	
1976	**regie 350**	control unit	anthracite/black	D. Rams	141
	regie 450 S	control unit	anthracite/black	D. Rams	
	regie 450 E	control unit	anthracite/black	D. Rams	
	regie 550	control unit	black	D. Rams	

Year	Type	Name	Colour	Designer	Page
1977	regie 525	control unit	black	D. Rams	
	regie 526	control unit	black	D. Rams	
	regie 528	control unit	black	D. Rams	
	regie 530	control unit, digital	black	D. Rams	
1978	regie 540 E	control unit	light grey	D. Rams	
	regie 550 d	control unit, digital	black, light grey	D. Rams	
	RA 1	control unit, analog	light grey, black	D. Rams/P. Hartwein	**145**
	RS 1	control unit, synthesizer	light grey, black	D. Rams/P. Hartwein	**163**
1981	R 1	control unit, atelier 1	black, crystal grey	P. Hartwein	
1987	R 4	control unit, atelier	black, crystal grey	P. Hartwein	
1986	R 2	control unit, atelier	black, crystal grey	P. Hartwein	

Compact systems with record players

Year	Type	Name	Colour	Designer	Page
1957	**studio 1**	compact system, RC 62-5	grey	H. Gugelot/H. Lindinger	**113**
	atelier 1	compact system, RC 62	white/red elm	D. Rams	**112**
1958	atelier 1	compact stereo system, RC 7	white/red elm	D. Rams	
1959	atelier 1	compact stereo system, RC 8	white/red elm	D. Rams	
	atelier 1-81	compact stereo system, RC 81	white/red elm	D. Rams	
1961	atelier 11	compact stereo system, RC 82	white/red elm	D. Rams	
	atelier 2	compact system, RC 9	white/red elm	D. Rams	
1962	atelier 3	compact system, RC 9	white/alu.-coloured	D. Rams	
	audio 1	compact system	white/-, graphite/alu.-coloured	D. Rams	
	audio 1 M	compact system	white/-, graphite/alu.-coloured	D. Rams	
1963	TC 20	compact system	white/graphite	D. Rams	
1964	**audio 2**	TC 45, compact system	white/-, graphite/alu.-coloured	D. Rams	**116**
1965	audio2/3	compact system	white/-, anthracite/alu.-coloured	D. Rams	
1967	audio 250	compact system	white/-, anthracite/alu.-coloured	D. Rams	
1969	audio 300	compact system	white/-, anthracite/alu.-coloured	D. Rams	
1970	**cockpit**	250 S, compact system	black/light grey	D. Rams	**117**
	cockpit	250 SK, compact system	black/light grey, black/red	D. Rams	
1971	audio 310	compact system	white/-, anthracite/alu.-coloured	D. Rams	
	cockpit	250 W, compact system	black/light grey	D. Rams	
	cockpit	250 WK, compact system	black/light grey	D. Rams	
1972	cockpit	260 S, compact system	black/white	D. Rams	
	cockpit	260 SK, compact system	black/white, black/red	D. Rams	
1973	**audio 308**	compact system, 8°	black	D. Rams	**96**, **118**
	audio 400	compact system	black	D. Rams	**119**
1975	audio 308 S	compact system, 8°	black, black/alu.-coloured	D. Rams	
	audio 400 S	compact system	black	D. Rams	
1977	**C 4000**	audio system	anthracite/black	D. Rams	**121**
	P 4000	audio system	anthracite/black	D. Rams	
	PC 4000	audio system	anthracite/black	D. Rams	**120**

Record players

Year	Type	Name	Colour	Designer	Page
1955	G 12	record player, Valvo-Chassis, 3-tourig	maple	H. Gugelot	
1956	G 12	record player, PC-3-Chassis, 3-tourig	maple	H. Gugelot/W. Wagenfeld	
	PC 3	record player	grey/white	W. Wagenfeld/D.Rams/ G. A. Müller	**152**
1957	G 12	4-speed record player, PC 3 body	maple	H. Gugelot/W. Wagenfeld	
	G 12 V	4-speed record player, PC 3 body	maple	H. Gugelot/W. Wagenfeld	**153**
1958	G 12 SV	record player, equipped for stereo	maple	H. Gugelot/W. Wagenfeld	
1959	**PC 3-SV**	record player, equipped for stereo	white/graphite	W. Wagenfeld/D. Rams/G. A. Müller	**154**

Year	Type	Name	Colour	Designer	Page
1961	PCS 4	record player	white/graphite	D. Rams/G. A. Müller	
1962	PC 5	record player	light grey	D. Rams	
	PCS 5 A	record player	light grey, graphite	D. Rams	
	PCS 45	record player	light grey	D. Rams	
	PCS 51	record player	light grey	D. Rams	
	PCS 52	record player	light grey, graphite	D. Rams	
	PCS 5	record player	light grey, graphite	D. Rams	**133, 155**
1963	**PS 2**	record player	white/graphite	D. Rams	**154**
	PCS 5-37	record player	light grey, graphite	D. Rams	
	PCS 46	record player	light grey	D. Rams	
1965	PCS 52-E	record player	light grey, graphite	D. Rams	
	PS 400	record player	white, graphite	D. Rams	
	PS 1000/1000 AS	record player	anthracite	D. Rams	**90**
1967	PS 402	record player	white	D. Rams	
1968	PS 410	record player	white, graphite	D. Rams	
	PS 500/500 E	record player	black/black, anthr./alu.-coloured	D. Rams	**135, 155**
1969	PS 420	record player	white, anthracite	D. Rams	
	PS 600	record player	white, black, walnut	D. Rams	
1971	PS 430	record player	white, anthracite	D. Rams	
1973	PS 350	record player	black	D. Rams/R. Oberheim	
	PS 450	record player	black	D. Rams/R. Oberheim	
	PS 358/458	record player, 8°	black/white	D. Rams/R. Oberheim	**156**
1976	**PS 550**	record player	black, grey	D. Rams/R. Oberheim	**143**
1977	PS 550 S	record player	black, grey	D. Rams/R. Oberheim	
	PDS 550	record player	black, grey	D. Rams/R. Oberheim	**157**
1978	**PC 1**	integral studio system, record player and cassette recorder	black, grey	D. Rams/P. Hartwein	**145**
1979	PC 1 A	record player and cassette recorder	black, grey	D. Rams/P. Hartwein	
1980	**P 1**	record player, atelier 1	black, crystal grey	P. Hartwein	**147**
1981	P 501	record player	black	D. Rams/P. Hartwein	
	P 701	record player	black	D. Rams/R. Oberheim	
1982	P 2	record player, atelier	black	P. Hartwein	
	P 3	record player, atelier	black, crystal grey	P. Hartwein	
1984	**P 4**	record player, atelier	black, crystal grey	P. Hartwein	**98, 149**

Reel-to-reel tape recorders

Year	Type	Name	Colour	Designer	Page
1965	**TG 60**	reel-to-reel tape recorder	white/-, graphite/alu.-coloured	D. Rams	**92**
1967	TG 502/502-4	reel-to-reel tape recorder	white/-, anthr./alu.-coloured	D. Rams	
	TG 504	reel-to-reel tape recorder	white/-, anthr./alu.-coloured	D. Rams	**158**
	TGF 1	remote control	anthracite	D. Rams	
1968	TG 550	reel-to-reel tape recorder	anthracite/alu.-coloured	D. Rams	
	TGF 2	remote control	white	D. Rams	
1970	TD 1000	cover, TG 1000	anthracite	D. Rams	
	TG 1000	reel-to-reel tape recorder	anthr./anthr., -/alu.-coloured	D. Rams	**159**
	TGF 3	remote control, TG 1000	anthracite	D. Rams	
1972	TG 1000/4	reel-to-reel tape recorder	anthr./anthr., -/alu.-coloured	D. Rams	
1974	TG 1020	reel-to-reel tape recorder	anthr./anthr., -/alu.-coloured	D. Rams	
	TG 1020/4	reel-to-reel tape recorder	anthr./anthr., -/alu.-coloured	D. Rams	

Cassette recorders

Year	Type	Name	Colour	Designer	Page
1975	**TGC 450**	cassette recorder	anthracite	D. Rams	**160**
1978	**C 301**	cassette recorder	black, grey	D. Rams/P. Hartwein	**143, 160**

Year	Type	Name	Colour	Designer	Page
1979	C 301 M	cassette recorder	black, grey	D. Rams/P. Hartwein	
1980	**C 1**	cassette recorder, atelier 1	black, crystal grey	P. Hartwein	**147, 161**
1982	**C 2**	cassette recorder, atelier	black, crystal grey	P. Hartwein	**98**, 149
1983	C 3	cassette recorder, atelier	black, crystal grey	P. Hartwein	
1987	C 4	cassette recorder, atelier	black, crystal grey	P. Hartwein	
1988	C 23	cassette recorder, atelier	black, crystal grey	P. Hartwein	

CD players

Year	Type	Name	Colour	Designer	Page
1985	**CD 3**	atelier	black, crystal grey	P. Hartwein	**162**
1986	**CD 4**	atelier	black, crystal grey	P. Hartwein	**162**
1988	CD 2	atelier	black, crystal grey	P. Hartwein	
	CD 5	atelier	black, crystal grey	P. Hartwein	
1989	CD 23	atelier	black, crystal grey	P. Hartwein	

Quadro hi-fi systems

Year	Type	Name	Colour	Designer	Page
1973	CE 1020	receiver	anthracite	D. Rams	
	CSQ 1020	pre-amplifier w/SQ decoder	anthracite	D. Rams	
	PSQ 500	record player	anthracite	D. Rams	
1974	CD-4	demodulator	anthracite	D. Rams	
	QF 1020	remote control unit	anthracite	D. Rams	

Television sets

Year	Type	Name	Colour	Designer	Page
1955	FS 1	tabletop set	walnut, red elm		
	FS 2	tabletop set w/stand	walnut, red elm		
	FS-G	tabletop set	maple, red elm	H. Gugelot	**164**
	FS-G	stand	maple, red elm	H. Gugelot	
1956	FS 2/12	floor-mounted set	walnut, red elm		
	FS 2/13	floor-mounted set	walnut, red elm		
	HFK	television-music cabinet	walnut, red elm	H. Hirche	
1957	HFS	television cabinet	walnut, red elm	H. Hirche	
1958	**FS 3**	tabletop set (accessory tubular steel stand)	walnut, red elm		**164**
	FS 4	tabletop set (accessory tubular steel stand)	walnut, red elm, teak	H. Hirche	
	HFS 1	television cabinet	walnut, red elm, teak	H. Hirche	
	HF 1	tabletop set (accessory tubular steel stand)	dark grey/light grey	H. Hirche	**80**, 166
1959	**HFS 2**	television cabinet	walnut, red elm, teak	H. Hirche	**165**
1961	FS 5	tabletop set (accessory tubular steel stand)	walnut, red elm, teak	H. Hirche	
1962	FS 51	tabletop set (accessory tubular steel stand)	walnut, red elm, teak	H. Hirche	
1963	FS 6	tabletop set (accessory tubular steel stand)	white/walnut, -/red elm, -/teak	H. Hirche	
1964	**FS 60**	tabletop set (accessory tubular steel stand)	white/walnut, -/red elm, -/teak	H. Hirche/D. Rams	166
	FS 80	floor-mounted set w/pedestal stand	light grey	D. Rams	167
1966	FS 80/1	floor-mounted set w/pedestal stand	light grey	D. Rams	
	FS 600	tabletop set	light grey, anthracite/walnut	D. Rams	
1967	**FS 1000**	tabletop set, colour	light grey	D. Rams	167
1969	FS 1010	tabletop set, colour	light grey	D. Rams	
1986	RC 1	remote control, atelier	black, crystal grey	P. Hartwein	
	TV 3	tabletop set, colour, atelier	black, crystal grey	P. Hartwein	**168, 169**

Video cassette recorder

Year	Type	Name	Colour	Designer	Page
1988	VC 4	video cassette recorder, atelier	black, crystal grey	P. Hartwein	

Hi-fi PA systems

Year	Type	Name	Colour	Designer	Page
1963	PCS 5	record player chassis	alu.-coloured	D. Rams	
1965	LS 75	PA column speaker	white/alu.-coloured	D. Rams	
1967	DSM 1	disco mixing console	alu.-coloured	D. Rams	
	DSV 2	PA high-power amplifier	alu.-coloured	D. Rams	
	EDL 2	PA disco speaker	white/alu.-coloured	D. Rams	
	EKF 1	PA mains and control unit	alu.-coloured	D. Rams	
	ELF 1	PA ventilator unit	alu.-coloured	D. Rams	
	EMM 68-2	PA microphone mixer	alu.-coloured	D. Rams	
	EPL 1	PA record player drawer (not incl. record player)	alu.-coloured	D. Rams	
	ETE 500	PA tuner	alu.-coloured	D. Rams	
	ETG 60	PA reel-to-reel tape recorder	alu.-coloured	D. Rams	
	ETG 402/4	PA reel-to-reel tape recorder	alu.-coloured	D. Rams	
	ETG 502/4	PA reel-to-reel tape recorder	alu.-coloured	D. Rams	
	EVL 500-1	PA high-power amplifier	alu.-coloured	D. Rams	
	EVS 400	PA control amplifier	alu.-coloured	D. Rams	
	EVV 600	PA high-power amplifier	alu.-coloured	D. Rams	
	EVV 600	PA integrated amplifier	alu.-coloured	D. Rams	
	EGZ	PA main equipment rack	alu.-coloured	D. Rams	
	MP 1	stereo mixing console	alu.-coloured	D. Rams	
	SP 1	control console	alu.-coloured	D. Rams	
1968	DSM 1/1	disco mixing console	alu.-coloured	D. Rams	
	ELR 1	PA line array speaker	white/alu.-coloured	D. Rams	
1969	ETE 50	PA tuner	alu.-coloured	D. Rams	
1970	EDL 3	PA disco speaker	white/alu.-coloured	D. Rams	
	EL 250	PA speaker	white/alu.-coloured	D. Rams	
	EL 450	PA speaker	white/alu.-coloured	D. Rams	
1971	DSM 2	disco mixing console	alu.-coloured	D. Rams	

Stands, system cabinets

Year	Type	Name	Colour	Designer	Page
1967	system stand	metal base separate, 33.5 cm /36 cm deep (FS)	alu.-coloured	D. Rams	
	system stand	connecting plates: 80/75/66/53/50/45/ 43/40/28.5 cm wide	anthracite	D. Rams	
	system stand	record compartment 42 cm wide	light grey	D. Rams	
	stand	for FS 600	anthracite/alu.-coloured	D. Rams	
1968	**stand**	for FS 1000/1010	anthracite/alu.-coloured	D. Rams	**167**
1977	GT 500/501	audio tower rack	black	P. Hartwein	
		Systemwagen 1	black, white	P. Hartwein	
1978	**GS 1/2**	appliance stand for vert. and horiz. format	black, white	P. Hartwein	**170**
		Systemwagen 2	black, white	P. Hartwein	
1982	**AF 1**	pedestal stand, atelier	black, crystal grey	P. Hartwein/D. Rams	**98, 170**
1984	**GS 3/4/5/6**	appliance cabinet, atelier	black, crystal grey, white	P. Hartwein	**169, 171**
1989	RB 1	rollboard, atelier	black, crystal grey	P. Hartwein	

Braun Lectron

Year	Type	Name	Colour	Designer	Page
1967	Lectron	Mini-system, Expanded mini-system, Basic system, Expanded system 1/2/3, Basic and expanded system 1, System 300	white	D. Rams/J. Greubel	
	Lectron	Radio experiment set, Intercom experiment set	white	D. Rams/J. Greubel	

Year	Type	Name	Colour	Designer	Page
1969	Lectron	Pupils' practice system 1100/1101/1102/ 1200/1300, Demonstration system 3101/3201, Laboratory system – special/basic/expanded 1	white	D. Rams/J. Greubel	
	Lectron	Book laboratory	white	D. Rams/J. Greubel	

Photography and Film

Flash units

Year	Type	Name	Colour	Designer	Page
1958	**EF 1**	hobby standard	light grey	D. Rams	**184**
	EF 2/NC	hobby special	light grey	D. Rams	
1959	**F 60/30**	hobby	light grey	D. Rams	**185**
	ZL 5	additional flash wand	light grey	D. Rams	
1960	F 22	hobby	light grey	D. Rams	
1961	F 20	hobby	light grey	D. Rams	
	F 80	hobby professional	grey	R. Fischer	
1962	FZ 1	photo cell	light grey	D. Rams	
	F 21	hobby	light grey	D. Rams	**185**
	F 65	hobby	light grey, anthr.	D. Rams	
1963	**F 25**	hobby	grey	D. Rams	**186**
	F 26	hobby	grey	D. Rams	
1964	**EF 300**	hobby	grey	D. Rams	**187**
	F 40	hobby	grey	D. Rams	
1965	F 200	hobby	grey	D. Rams	
	F 260	hobby	grey	D. Rams	
	F 800	professional	grey	R. Fischer	
1966	**F 100**	hobby	light grey	D. Rams	**186**
	F 270	hobby	grey	D. Rams	
	F 650	hobby	grey	D. Rams	
	F 1000	studio flash system	black/alu.-coloured	D. Rams	
1968	F 110	hobby	grey	D. Rams	
	F 210	hobby	grey	D. Rams	
	F 700	professional	grey	D. Rams	
1969	F 220	hobby	grey	D. Rams	
	F 280	hobby	grey	D. Rams	
	F 290	hobby	grey	D. Rams	
	F 655	hobby	grey	D. Rams	**187**
	F 655 LS	hobby-mat	grey	D. Rams	
1970	F 240 LS	hobby-mat	black	D. Rams	
	F 111	hobby	black	D. Rams	**188**
	F 410 LS	hobby-mat	black	D. Rams	
1971	F 16 B	hobby	black	D. Rams	
	F 18 LS	hobby-mat	black	D. Rams	
	F 245 LSR	hobby-mat	black	D. Rams	
1972	40 VCR	2000 vario computer	black	R. Oberheim	
	F 022	2000 vario computer	black	R. Oberheim	<u>180</u>, **188**
	F 17	hobby	black	D. Rams	
	F 027	2000 vario computer	black	R. Oberheim	
1974	17 B	hobby	black	R. Oberheim	
	17 BC	hobby	black	R. Oberheim	
	23 B	hobby	black	R. Oberheim	**188**
	23 BC	hobby	black	R. Oberheim	
	28 BC	hobby	black	R. Oberheim	
	28 BVC	vario computer	black	R. Oberheim	

Year	Type	Name	Colour	Designer	Page
1974	42 VCR	vario computer	black	R. Oberheim	
	F 900	professional	black	R. Oberheim	**189**
1976	280 BVC	vario computer	black	R. Oberheim	
	280 BC	vario	black	R. Oberheim	
	380 BVC	vario computer	black	R. Oberheim	**189**
	400 VC	vario computer	black	R. Oberheim	
	460 VCS	vario computer	black	R. Oberheim	
1977	34 VC	vario computer	black	R. Oberheim	
	42 VC	vario computer	black	R. Oberheim	
	F 910	professional	black	R. Oberheim	
1978	170 B	hobby	black	R. Oberheim	
	170 BC	hobby	black	R. Oberheim	
	200 B	hobby	black	R. Oberheim	
	200 BC	hobby	black	R. Oberheim	
	230 BP	hobby	black	R. Oberheim	
	260 B	hobby	black	R. Oberheim	
	260 BC	hobby	black	R. Oberheim	
	260 C	hobby	black	R. Oberheim	
	270 BK	hobby	black	R. Oberheim	
	310 BC	vario	black	R. Oberheim	
	370 BVC	vario computer	black	R. Oberheim	
	410 VC	vario computer	black	R. Oberheim	
	420 BVC	vario computer	black	R. Oberheim	
	440 VC	vario computer	black	R. Oberheim	
	500 VC	vario computer	black	R. Oberheim	
	900	vario control	black	R. Oberheim	
1980	320 BVC/SCA	vario distance	black	R. Oberheim	
	340 SCA/M SCA	vario zoom	black	R. Oberheim	
1981		macro flash	black	R. Oberheim	
1982	28 M	Ultrablitz	black	R. Oberheim	
	32 M	Ultrablitz	black	R. Oberheim	
	34 M	Ultrablitz	black	R. Oberheim	
	400 M	logic	black	R. Oberheim	
1983	38 M	Ultrablitz logic	black	R. Oberheim	
1989	SCA 1	vario control	black	R. Oberheim	

Nizo film cameras

Year	Type	Name	Colour	Designer	Page
1963	**FA 3**	spring mech. Variogon 1.8/9–30 mm	black/alu.-coloured	D. Rams/R. Fischer/	**190**
		Angénieux Zoom 1.8/7.5–35 mm		R. Oberheim	
1964	**EA 1**	electric Variogon 1.8/9–30 mm	black/alu.-coloured	D. Rams/R. Fischer	**190**
1965	**S 8**	Variogon 1.8/8–40 mm	alu.-coloured	R. Oberheim	**176**
	S 8 M	Variogon 1.8/10–35 mm	alu.-coloured	R. Oberheim	
1966	S 8 E	Variogon 1.8/10–35 mm	alu.-coloured	R. Oberheim	
	S 8 L	Variogon 1.8/8–40 mm	alu.-coloured	R. Oberheim	
	S 8 T	Variogon 1.8/7–56 mm	alu.-coloured	R. Oberheim	**191**
1967	S 8 S	Variogon (Export)	alu.-coloured	R. Oberheim	
1968	S 36	Variogon 1.8/9–36 mm	alu.-coloured	R. Oberheim	
	S 40	Variogon 1.8/8–40 mm	alu.-coloured	R. Oberheim	
	S 55	Variogon 1.8/7–56 mm	alu.-coloured	R. Oberheim	
	S 56	Variogon 1.8/7–56 mm	alu.-coloured	R. Oberheim	**191**
	S 80	Variogon 1.8/10–80 mm	alu.-coloured	R. Oberheim	
	spezial	Variogon 1.8/7–56 mm	alu.-coloured	R. Oberheim	
1969	S 48	Variogon 1.8/8–48 mm	alu.-coloured	R. Oberheim	

Year	Type	Name	Colour	Designer	Page
1970	S 30	Variogon 1.8/10–30 mm	alu.-coloured	R. Oberheim	
	S 480	Variogon 1.8/8–48 mm	alu.-coloured	R. Oberheim	
	S 560	Variogon 1.8/7–56 mm	alu.-coloured	R. Oberheim	
	S 800	Variogon 1.8/7–80 mm	alu.-coloured	R. Oberheim	
	S 800 set	Variogon 1.8/7–80 mm	black	R. Oberheim	**192**
1972	S 1	Variogon 1.8/10–30 mm	black	R. Oberheim	
	S 2	Variogon 1.8/8–40 mm	black	R. Oberheim	
	S 48-2	Variogon 1.8/8–48 mm	alu.-coloured	R. Oberheim	
1973	**spezial 136**	Variogon 1.8/9–36 mm	alu.-coloured	R. Oberheim	**193**
	spezial 148	Variogon 1.8/8–48 mm	alu.-coloured	R. Oberheim	
1974	136 XL	Variogon 1.8/9–36 mm	alu.-coloured	R. Oberheim	
	148 XL	Variogon 1.8/8–48 mm	alu.-coloured	R. Oberheim	
	156	Variogon 1.8/7–56 mm	alu.-coloured	R. Oberheim	
	156 XL	Variogon 1.8/7–56 mm	alu.-coloured	R. Oberheim	
	481	Variogon 1.8/8–48 mm	alu.-coloured	R. Oberheim	
	561	Variogon 1.8/7–56 mm	alu.-coloured	R. Oberheim	
	801	Variogon 1.8/7–80 mm	black	R. Oberheim	
	801 set	Variogon 1.8/7–80 mm	alu.-coloured	R. Oberheim	
	professional	Variogon macro 1.8/7–80 mm	alu.-coloured	R. Oberheim	**195**
1975	106 XL	Variogon 1.8/8–48 mm	black	R. Oberheim	
	125	Variogon 1.8/9–36 mm	black	R. Oberheim	
	126	Variogon 1.8/7–48 mm	black	R. Oberheim	
	128	Variogon 1.8/7–56 mm	black	R. Oberheim	
1976	116	Nizogon 1.8/8–48 mm	black	R. Oberheim	
	148 macro	Variogon macro 1.8/8–48 mm	alu.-coloured	R. Oberheim	
	156 macro	Variogon macro 1.8/7–56 mm	alu.-coloured, black	R. Oberheim	
	206 XL	Variogon macro 1.8/7–56 mm	black	R. Oberheim	
	481 macro	Variogon macro 1.7/8–48 mm	alu.-coloured	R. Oberheim	
	561 macro	Variogon macro 1.7/7–56 mm	alu.-coloured	R. Oberheim	
	801 macro	Variogon macro 1.7/7–80 mm	alu.-coloured	R. Oberheim	
	801 macro set	Variogon macro 1.7/7–80 mm	black	R. Oberheim	
	1048 sound	Macro-Variogon 1.8/8–48 mm	alu.-coloured	P. Schneider	
	2056 sound	Macro-Variogon 1.4/7–56 mm	alu.-coloured	P. Schneider	**194**
1978	3048 sound	Macro-Variogon 1.8/8–48 mm	black	P. Schneider	
	3056 sound	Macro-Variogon 1.4/7–56 mm	black	P. Schneider	
	4056	Macro-Variogon 1.4/7–56 mm	black	P. Schneider	
	4080	Macro-Variogon 1.4/7–80 mm	black	P. Schneider	
1979	integral 5	Macro-Variogon 1.2/8–40 mm	black	P. Schneider	
	integral 6	Macro-Variogon 1.2/7.5–45 mm	black	P. Schneider	
	integral 6 S	Macro-Variogon 1.2/7.5–45 mm	black/alu.-coloured	P. Schneider	
	integral 7	Macro-Variogon 1.2/7–50 mm	black	P. Schneider	<u>**182**</u>, **195**
1980	6056	Macro-Variogon 1.4/7–56 mm	black	P. Schneider	
	6080	Macro-Variogon 1.4/7–80 mm	black	P. Schneider	
1981	integral 10	Macro-Variogon 1.4/7–70 mm	black	P. Schneider	

Film projectors

Year	Type	Name	Colour	Designer	Page
1964	FP 1	Nizo film projector	light grey	D. Rams/R. Oberheim	
1965	**FP 1 S**	Nizo film projector	light grey	D. Rams/R. Oberheim	**196**
1966	FP 3 S	film projector	alu.-coloured	R. Oberheim	
1969	FP 5	film projector	alu.-coloured	R. Oberheim	
1971	FP 7	film projector	black	R. Oberheim	
	FP 25	film projector	black	R. Oberheim	
	FP 30	film projector	alu.-coloured	R. Oberheim	**197**

Year	Type	Name	Colour	Designer	Page
1973	FP 35	film projector	black	R. Oberheim	
	FP 35 S	film projector	black	R. Oberheim	
	Synton FP	sound synchronizing unit	black	R. Oberheim	
1974	FP 8	film projector	black/alu.-coloured	R. Oberheim	
1976	100	Visacustic multiplay, sound projector	black	P. Hartwein	
	1000	Visacustic stereo, sound projector	black	P. Hartwein	198
1977		Visacustic control unit	black	P. Hartwein	
1979	2000	Visacustic digital, sound projector	black	P. Hartwein	

Film accessories

Year	Type	Name	Colour	Designer	Page
1964	FF 1	film light	grey/alu.-coloured	R. Fischer	
1968	**FK 1**	film splicer	grey/alu.-coloured	R. Oberheim	199
	SB 1	film viewer	grey/alu.-coloured, black	R. Oberheim	
1972	FK 2	film splicer	black	P. Schneider	
1975	**ST 3**	shoulder tripod	black	P. Hartwein	192
1977	**FK 4**	film splicer	black	P. Schneider	199
	SB 2	film viewer	black	R. Oberheim	
1978	**1000**	Nizolux film light	black	R. Oberheim	206
	1000 G	Nizolux w/fan	black	R. Oberheim	

Slide projectors

Year	Type	Name	Colour	Designer	Page
1956	**PA 1**	automatic projector	light grey	D. Rams	200
1957	PA 2	automatic projector	light grey	D. Rams	
1961	D 40	automatic projector	light grey/alu.-coloured	D. Rams	
1962	D 5	Combiscope	light grey	D. Rams	
	D 10	small projector	light grey	D. Rams	202
	D 20	automatic low-voltage projector	light grey, graphite	D. Rams	202
1963	**D 6**	Combiscope	light grey	D. Rams	201
1964	D 21	automatic slide projector	light grey	D. Rams/R. Oberheim	
1965	D 45	automatic slide projector	alu.-coloured	D. Rams/R. Oberheim	
1966	**D 25**	automatic slide projector	light grey/dark grey	R. Oberheim	203
	D 47	automatic slide projector	alu.-coloured	D. Rams/R. Oberheim	
1967	D 15	semi-automatic slide projector	light grey/dark grey	R. Oberheim	
	D 46/46 J	automatic slide projector	alu.-coloured	D. Rams	
1968	D 35	automatic slide projector	alu.-coloured/grey	R. Oberheim	
1970	D 7	slide viewer and projector	grey	R. Oberheim	
	D 46/MV	Multivision special projector	alu.-coloured	P. Hartwein	
	D 300	automatic slide projector	black	R. Oberheim	**178**, 204
	PG	Multivision programme projector	anthracite		
1974	D 300 AF	automatic slide projector w/autofocus	black	R. Oberheim	
	PG 100	programme computer	black	P. Hartwein	
	Tandem	Professional	black	P. Hartwein	205
	Tandem	Variotuner	black	P. Hartwein	
	Tandem	projector	black	P. Hartwein	
	Tandem	remote control w/timer	black	P. Hartwein	

Photo camera

Year	Type	Name	Colour	Designer	Page
1968	**Nizo 1000**	pocket camera	black/alu.-coloured	R. Oberheim	206

472

Year	Type	Name	No.	Colour	Designer	Page

Clocks and Pocket Calculators

Desktop and alarm clocks

Year	Type	Name	No.	Colour	Designer	Page
1971	**phase 1**	battery and mains	4915–4917/4928	pearl white, red, olive green, trans.	D. Rams/D.Lubs	**224**
1972	**phase 2**	battery and mains, date or signal	4924/4925	black, red, yellow	D. Lubs	**224**
	phase 3	analog clock, mains	4927	black, white	D. Lubs	
1975	**AB 20/20 tb**	exact quartz/travel	4963	black	D. Rams/D. Lubs	**226**
	functional	Digital DN 18	4958	velour nickel-plated	D. Lubs	**225**
	functional	Digital DN 42	4815	black	D. Lubs	<u>**210**</u>
	digital compact	Digital DN 19	4937	white	D. Lubs	**224**
	AB 20 exact	quartz color	4963	grey, green, red, brown	D. Rams/D. Lubs	
1976	**DN 40**	electronic	4967	black, red, white	D. Rams/D. Lubs	**225**
1978	**AB 21/s**	signal quartz	4821/4836	black, red, white	D. Rams/D. Lubs	**226**
1979	**DN 50**	visotronic	4850	black	L. Littmann	**227**
	phase 4	analog clock, mains	4842	black, white	D. Lubs	
1980	**AB 11**	megamatic quartz	4834	black, white	D. Lubs	**228**
	DN 30	digital alarm	4832	black, white	D. Lubs	
1982	AB 20 sl	sensormat quartz	4838	black	D. Lubs	
	AB 22	quartz	4849	black, white	D. Rams/D. Lubs	
	AB 3/31 t/ts	compact quartz	4857/4829	black,white, brown, grey, light grey, blue	D. Lubs	
	AB 30	alarm quartz	4847	black, white, black/white	D. Lubs	**228**
	AB 310 ts	alarm quartz	4858	black	D. Lubs	
	AB 44	quartz	4851	black, white	D. Lubs	
1983	AB 3 (a)	compact quartz	4750	black, white, brown	D. Lubs	
	AB 30 s	quartz	4853	black/silver	D. Lubs	
	DN 30 s	digital alarm	4808	black, white	D. Lubs	
	DN 54	visotronic 4	4807	black	L. Littmann	
1984	**AB 2**	quartz	4761	black, white, yellow, green, other	J. Greubel/D. Rams	**229**
	AB 30 vs	voice control	4763	black	D. Lubs	
	AB 45 vsl	voice control	4762	black	D. Lubs	
1985	AB 30 sl	quartz	4768	black	D. Lubs	
	AB 46/24h	quartz	4765	black	D. Lubs	
	AB 312 vsl	voice control	4760	black	D. Lubs	<u>**218**</u>, **230**
	AB 312 sl	quartz	4759	black, white	D. Lubs	
	KT timer	timer	4859	white	D. Lubs	
1986	AB 30 vs	Version SMD	4763	black	D. Lubs	
1987	**AB 1**	quartz	4746	black, white	D. Lubs	**230**
	AB 4	quartz	4749	black, white	D. Lubs	
	AB 35 rs	reflex control	4751	black	D. Lubs	
	AB 50 rsl	reflex control	4775	black	D. Lubs	
1988	AB 35	quartz	4761	black	D. Lubs	
	AB 50 l/sl	quartz	4772/4774	black	D. Lubs	
	AB 312 s	quartz	4770	black	D. Lubs	
	KTC/KC	comb. quartz clock + timer	4863/4859	white	D. Lubs	**229**
1990	AB 5	quartz	4748	black, white	D. Lubs	
	AB 313	quartz	4785	black	D. Lubs	
	AB 313 rsl	reflex control	4783	black	D. Lubs	
	AB 313 sl	quartz	4784	black, white	D. Lubs	
	AB 313 vsl	voice control	4786	black	D. Lubs	
1991	**DB 10 sl**	digital	3876	grey/green, grey	D. Lubs	<u>**220**</u>, **231**

Year	Type	Name	No.	Colour	Designer	Page
1991	DB 10 fsl	time control digital radio-contr. clock	3877	black	D. Lubs	
1992	AB 7	quartz	4744	black, white, brown	D. Lubs	
	AB 40 sl	quartz	4742	black, white	D. Lubs	
	AB 40 vsl	voice control	4745	black	D. Lubs	230
1993	**AB 6**	quartz	4747	black	D. Lubs	233
	DAB 80 fsl	time control radio-contr. clock	3863	black	D. Lubs	232
	DAB 80 sl	electronic	3860	black	D. Lubs	
	DB 10 sl	digital	3876	black	D. Lubs	
1994	AB 1 A	quartz	3855	black, white	D. Lubs	
	AB 60 fsl	time control radio-contr. clock	3850	black	D. Lubs	232
1995	AB 60 rsl	reflex control	3851	black	D. Lubs	
	AB 314	basic quartz	3872	black	D. Lubs	
	AB 314 fsl	time control travel alarm clock, radio-contr.	3868	black	D. Lubs	
	AB 314 sl	quartz	3864	black, white	D. Lubs	233
	AB 314 rsl	reflex control infra red	3866	black	D. Lubs	
	AB 314 vm	voice memo	3867	black	D. Lubs	
1996	AB 55 fsl	time control radio-contr. clock	3856	black	D. Lubs	
	AB 55 rf	time control reflex	3858	black	D. Lubs	
	AB 55 vf	time control voice radio-contr. clock	3857	black	D. Lubs	
	AB 314 vsl	voice control	3865	black	D. Lubs	
	DB 12 fsl	time control temperature	3875	black	D. Lubs	231
1999	ABW 31	Classic Millennium Edition	4861	silver	D. Lubs	
	DB 12 fsl	time control temperature, Millennium Edition	3875	silver	D. Lubs	
	AB 5	quartz, Millennium Edition	4748	silver	D. Lubs	
2001	AB 1	quartz	4746	silver	D. Lubs	
	AB 1	quartz	4746	dark blue-metallic	D. Lubs	
2005	AB 25	quartz advance	3831	silver	P. Hartwein	
	AB 4	quartz	3830	silver	P. Hartwein	
	AB 5A	quartz classic	3829	silver	P. Hartwein	

Clock radios

Year	Type	Name	No.	Colour	Designer	Page
1978	**ABR 21**	signal radio	4826	black, white	D. Rams/D. Lubs	**214**, 234
	ABR 21	fm signal radio	4840	white	D. Rams/D. Lubs	
1981	**ABR 11**	megamatic radio	4846	black	D. Rams/D. Lubs	234
1990	**ABR 313 sl**	radio alarm quartz	4779	black	D. Lubs	234
1996	**ABR 314 df**	digital radio time control	3869	black	D. Lubs	235
1999	**ABR 314 df**	digital radio time control, Millennium Edition	3869	silver	D. Lubs	235

Wall clocks

Year	Type	Name	No.	Colour	Designer	Page
1979	**ABW 21**	domo quartz fix + flex	4833	black, white	D. Lubs	236
1980	ABW 22	domo quartz 2 fix + flex	4837	black, white	D. Lubs	
	ABW 21 d	domodesk quartz desktop version	4833	black, white	D. Lubs	236
	ABW 21 set	domoset quartz clock w/barometer	4855	black	D. Lubs	236
1981	**ABW 41**	domodisque	4839	black	D. Lubs	**216**, 237
1982	**ABK 30**	quartz	4861	white/-,yellow/-,blue/-,red/-, brown/white, black/black	D. Lubs	237
	ABW 30	quartz	4861	as ABK 30	D. Lubs	
1985	ABK 40	wall clock	4823	white, black	D. Lubs	
	ABK 20	wall clock	4780	red, white, blue, black, brown	D. Lubs	238
	ABW 20	wall clock	4780	red, white, blue, black, brown	D. Lubs	
	ABK 31	wall clock	4781	white/white, red/grey, brown/brown	D. Lubs	238
1987	**ABW 21**	quartz	4782	grey/blue/transparent	D. Lubs	239

Year	Type	Name	No.	Colour	Designer	Page
1988	**ABW 35**	quartz	4778	grey/transparent	D. Lubs	**239**
1999	ABW 31	Edition	4861	silver	D. Lubs	

Wristwatches

Year	Type	Name	No.	Colour	Designer	Page
1977	**DW 20**	quartz LCD digital	4812	chrome, black	D. Rams/D. Lubs	**240**
1978	**DW 30**	quartz LCD digital	4814	chrome (black not sold)	D. Rams/D. Lubs	<u>212</u>
1989	**AW 10**	quartz analog	4789	chrome, black	D. Lubs	**240**
1990	AW 20	quartz analog w/numerals	3802	chrome, black	D. Lubs	
1991	**AW 50**	quartz analog	3805	platinum	D. Lubs	**240**
1992	AW 50	quartz analog	3805	titanium ceramic	D. Lubs	
1994	AW 15	quartz analog	3801	chrome, black	D. Lubs	
	AW 20	quartz analog w/o numerals	3802	chrome, black	D. Lubs	
	AW 30	quartz analog	3803	chrome, black	D. Lubs	
1995	AW 60 S	Chronodate	3806	stainless steel	D. Lubs	
	AW 60 T	Chronodate	3806	titanium ceramic	D. Lubs	**241**
1998	AW 21	quartz analog (polished)	3804	silver/black	D. Lubs	
1999	AW 70	Chronodate Millennium Edition	3806	silver/black	D. Lubs	
2001	AW 75	Chronodate titanium	3806	titanium/black	D. Lubs	
2003	AW 12	quartz	3811	silver/blue	P. Hartwein	
	AW 22	quartz	3812	silver/black	P. Hartwein	**241**
	AW 24	quartz	3814	black/blue	P. Hartwein	**241**
	AW 55	quartz	3815	silver	P. Hartwein	

Pocket calculators

Year	Type	Name	No.	Colour	Designer	Page
1975	**ET 11**	control	4954	black	D. Rams/D. Lubs	**242**
1976	**ET 22**	control	4955	black	D. Rams/D. Lubs	**242**
1977	ET 23	control	4955	black	D. Rams/D. Lubs	
	ET 33	control LCD (slim LCD)	4993	black	D. Rams/D. Lubs/ L. Littmann	<u>222</u>, 242
1978	**ET 44**	control LCD	4994	black	D. Rams/D. Lubs	**243**
1981	ET 55	control LCD	4835	black	D. Rams/D. Lubs	
1983	ET 55	control LCD	4835	white	D. Rams/D. Lubs	
1987	ET 66	control	4776	black	D. Rams/D. Lubs	
	ETS 77	control solar	4777	black	D. Lubs/D. Rams	**243**
	ST 1	solar card	4856	black	D. Lubs	**244**
1991	**ET 88**	world traveller	4877	black	D. Lubs	**244**
1995	ET 90	protocol	4769	black	D. Lubs	
2002	ET 100	business control	4831	black	D. Lubs	

Lighters and Flashlights

Table lighters

Year	Type	Name	No.	Colour	Designer	Page
1966	**TFG 1**	permanent	6826/601	plastic, black, grid pattern	R. Weiss	**254**
	TFG 1	permanent	6826/603	oxford leather, grained	R. Weiss	
	TFG 1	permanent	6826/607	polished chrome, grid pattern	R. Weiss	
	TFG 1	permanent	6826/608	silver-plated, grid pattern	R. Weiss	
	TFG 1	permanent	6826/609	gold-plated, grid pattern	R. Weiss	
	TFG 1	permanent	6826/610	silver, 925 Str	R. Weiss	
	TFG 1	permanent	6826/611	14-carat gold	R. Weiss	
1966	TFG 1	permanent	6826/612	18-carat gold	R. Weiss	
	TFG 1	permanent	6826/700	acrylic	R. Weiss	

Year	Type	Name	No.	Colour	Designer	Page
	TFG 1	permanent	6826/700	morocco leather, smooth, silver-plated edge	R. Weiss	
	TFG 1	permanent	6826/700	oxford leather, grained, platinum-plated edge	R. Weiss	
	TFG 1	permanent	6826/700	morocco leather, smooth	R. Weiss	
1968	**T 2/TFG 2**	cylindric	6822/272	metal – silver-plated, longitudinal grooves	D. Rams	**248**, 255
	T 2/TFG 2	cylindric	6822/708	metal – silver-plated, smooth	D. Rams	
	T 2/TFG 2	cylindric	6822/712	plastic – red	D. Rams	
	T 2/TFG 2	cylindric	6822/713	plastic – blue	D. Rams	
	T 2/TFG 2	cylindric	6822/715	plastic – black, black top	D. Rams	
	T 2/TFG 2	cylindric	6822/716	plastic – black, chrome-plated top	D. Rams	
	T 2/TFG 2	cylindric	6822/717	plastic – orange	D. Rams	
	T 2/TFG 2	cylindric	6822/718	metal – chrome-plated, ring texture	D. Rams	
	T 2/TFG 2	cylindric	6822/730	acrylic	D. Rams	
	T 2/TFG 2	cylindric	6822/302	metal – chrome-plated, polished	D. Rams	
	T 2/TFG 2	cylindric	6822/303	metal – chrome-plated, longitud. grooves	D. Rams	
	T 2/TFG 2	cylindric	6822/304	metal – black, ring texture	D. Rams	
	T 2/TFG 2	cylindric	6822/305	metal – silver-plated, grid pattern	D. Rams	
1970	**T 3**	domino, battery ignition	6740/700	plastic – red	D. Rams	**250**, 256
	T 3	domino, battery ignition	6740/701	plastic – yellow	D. Rams	
	T 3	domino, battery ignition	6740/702	plastic – blue	D. Rams	
	T 3	domino, battery ignition	6740/703	plastic – white	D. Rams	
1976	domino	w/piezo ignition	6834/301	plastic – black, matte	D. Rams	
	domino	w/piezo ignition	6834/302	plastic – red	D. Rams	
	domino	w/piezo ignition	6834/303	plastic – yellow	D. Rams	
	domino	w/piezo ignition	6834/304	plastic – green	D. Rams	
	domino set	w/3 ashtrays	6855/301	plastic – black, matte	D. Rams	
	domino set	w/3 ashtrays	6855/302	plastic – red	D. Rams	
	domino set	w/3 ashtrays	6855/303	plastic – yellow	D. Rams	
	domino set	w/3 ashtrays	6855/304	plastic – green	D. Rams	

Pocket lighters

Year	Type	Name	No.	Colour	Designer	Page
1971	**F 1**	mactron	6902/703	metal – chrome/black, grid pattern	D. Rams	**257**
	F 1	mactron	6902/237	metal – chrome, grid pattern	D. Rams	
	F 1	mactron	6902/237	metal – chrome, silver-plated, grid pattern	D. Rams	
	mach 2		6991/302	metal – black chrome-plated, grid pattern	D. Rams/F. Seiffert	**257**
	mach 2		6991/303	metal – velour chrome-plated, grid pattern	D. Rams/F. Seiffert	
	mach 2		6991/305	metal – silver-plated, rhodium-plated	D. Rams/F. Seiffert	
	mach 2		6991/307	plastic – black/chrome	D. Rams/F. Seiffert	
	mach 2		6991/311	metal – velour/black chrome-plated, smooth	D. Rams/F. Seiffert	
	mach 2		6991/312	metal – velour chrome-plated, smooth	D. Rams/F. Seiffert	
	mach 2		6991/313	metal – black chrome-plated, smooth	D. Rams/F. Seiffert	
	mach 2		6991/314	metal – gold-plated, grid pattern	D. Rams/F. Seiffert	
	mach 2		6991/314	metal – velour/black chrome-plated, grid pattern	D. Rams/F. Seiffert	
1972	**electric**	(mach 2 slim)	6060/301	metal – black, smooth	Gugelot Institute	**257**
	electric	(mach 2 slim)	6060/302	metal – chrome, smooth/brushed	Gugelot Institute	
	electric	(mach 2 slim)	6060/303	metal – black, longitud. grooves	Gugelot Institute	
	electric	(mach 2 slim)	6060/304	metal – chrome, longitud. grooves	Gugelot Institute	
1973	**T 4**	studio	6809/110	plastic – black, black button	Gugelot Institute	**258**
	T 4	studio	6809/111	plastic – black, orange button	Gugelot Institute	
	T 4	studio	6809/112	plastic – black, brown button	Gugelot Institute	
	T 4	studio	6809/113	plastic – black, green button	Gugelot Institute	
1974	centric		6817/331	black anodized	J. Greubel	
	centric		6817/332	light anodized	J. Greubel	
	centric		6817/333	black, longitud. grooves, w/border	J. Greubel	

Year	Type	Name	No.	Colour	Designer	Page
	centric		6817/334	chrome, longitud. grooves, w/border	J. Greubel	
	centric		6817/335	polished chrome	J. Greubel	
	centric		6817/336	chrome, transv. stripe pattern, w/border	J. Greubel	
	centric		6817/337	black, full-length longitud. stripe pattern	J. Greubel	
	centric		6817/338	chrome, grid pattern, w/border	J. Greubel	258
	energetic	solar	6933/001	metal – chrome, smooth (not sold)	D. Rams	
	weekend		6813/062	orange	D. Rams	
	weekend		6813/062	black	D. Rams	258
	weekend		6813/063	green	D. Rams	
	weekend		6813/063	black	D. Rams	
	weekend		6813/064	brown	D. Rams	
	weekend		6813/064	black	D. Rams	
	weekend		6813/033	black	D. Rams	
	weekend		6813/302	black	D. Rams	
	weekend		6813/302	chrome	D. Rams	
	weekend		6813/303	black, grid pattern	D. Rams	
	weekend		6813/303	black	D. Rams	
	weekend		6813/304	black, line pattern	D. Rams	
	weekend		6813/304	black	D. Rams	
1975	**dino**		6110/302	plastic – black	Busse Design (redesign)	259
	DERBY[1]			black	D. Rams	
	SMOKI[1]			blue, black, yellow, red, orange, brown, chrome-plated, striped guilloche	D. Rams	
1976	linear		6880/301	metal – chrome/black, grid pattern	D. Rams	
	linear		6880/302	metal – chrome, grid pattern	D. Rams	
	linear		6880/303	metal – chrome, stripe pattern	D. Rams	
	linear		6880/304	metal – polished chrome	D. Rams	
1977	contour		6848/301	chrome, matte	Gugelot Institute	
	contour		6848/302	black, matte	Gugelot Institute	
	contour		6848/305	chrome, line pattern, terminated by transv. line	Gugelot Institute	
	contour		6848/306	black, line pattern	Gugelot Institute	
	contour		6848/307	chrome, grid pattern	Gugelot Institute	
	contour		6848/308	chrome, black grip surface	Gugelot Institute	
	contour		6848/309	chrome, line pattern	Gugelot Institute	
	contour		6848/310	chrome, grid patern, black depressions	Gugelot Institute	
	duo		6070/302	black, smooth	Busse Design	259
	duo		6070/302	steel, smooth	Busse Design	
	duo		6070/303	black, grooved	Busse Design	
	duo		6070/303	steel, smooth	Busse Design	
	duo		6070/304	black, smooth	Busse Design	
	duo		6070/304	steel, gerillt	Busse Design	
	duo		6070/305	black, smooth	Busse Design	
	duo		6070/305	black, smooth	Busse Design	
	duo		6070/310	black, grooved	Busse Design	
	duo		6070/310	black, smooth	Busse Design	
	duo plus	w/fluid canister	6070/320	black, smooth	Busse Design	
	duo plus	w/fluid canister	6070/320	black, smooth	Busse Design	
1980	**dymatic**		6120/301	chrome, matte	D. Rams	259
	dymatic		6120/302	black	D. Rams	
	dymatic		6120/303	chrome, grooved, gloss	D. Rams	
1981	club		6135/700	chrome, gloss	D. Rams	
	club		6135/701	chrome, matte	D. Rams	
	club		6135/702	black, matte	D. Rams	
	club		6135/703	stainless steel, brushed	D. Rams	

Year	Type	Name	No.	Colour	Designer	Page

Wand lighters

Year	Type	Name	No.	Colour	Designer	Page
1977	CG 1	wand lighter for kitchen[1]		white, blue, red, orange	L. Littmann	
1981	**variabel**	wand lighter	6130/700	brushed chrome	D. Rams	**260**
	variabel	wand lighter	6130/700	brushed stainless steel	D. Rams	
1985	BG 1	wand lighter for kitchen[1]		white, blue, red	D. Rams	

Flashlights

Year	Type	Name	No.	Colour	Designer	Page
1964	**manulux DT 1**	dynamo flashlight	826	dark olive, black	H. Gugelot/H. Sukopp	**261**
1970	**diskus**	battery-powered flashlight	904	black, yellow, orange, white	H. Gugelot	**262**
	manulux NC	rechargeable flashlight	5903	black	R. Weiss/D. Rams	**252, 261**

Electric Shavers

Year	Type	Name	No.	Colour	Designer	Page
1955	300 special DL 3			white/chrome/brown		
	300 special DL 3			white/brown/red		**282**
	300 special DL 3			white/chrome/red		
1957	**combi DL 5**	Typee 1, type A	5249	white	D. Rams/G. A. Müller	**282**
1958	S 60	Standard 1		white/chr. w/o hair trimmer	G. A. Müller	
1960	**S 60**	Standard 2		white/chr. w/o hair trimmer	G. A. Müller	**283**
	SM 3		5300	white w/type plate	G. A. Müller	
	SM 3		5300	white, anthracite	G. A. Müller	**283**
1962	**S 62**	Standard 3	5620	white/olive w/hair trimmer	G. A. Müller	**284**
	sixtant SM 31		5310	black/brushed matte finish	G. A. Müller/H. Gugelot	**268**
1963	combi 2		5220	white/grey, white/dark olive	R. Fischer	
	commander SM 5	mains, rech. batt.	5500	dark grey	R. Fischer	**284**
	special SM 2		5220	white/grey, white/dark olive	R. Fischer	
	special SM 22		5220	white/grey, white/dark olive	R. Fischer	
1965	S 63	Standard	5630	light grey/grey w/hair trimmer	G. A. Müller	
	stab B 1	battery	5960	light grey	R. Fischer	
	stab B 1	battery	5961	dark olive	R. Fischer	
1966	**stab B 2**	battery	5962–5965	light grey, blue, yellow, red	R. Fischer	**285**
	parat	BT SM 53, mains	5224	olive/chrome	D. Rams/R. Fischer	
1967	shaving mirror		5001	black, white, red-orange	F. Seiffert	
	sixtant BN	mains, rech. batt.	5511	black	R. Fischer	**286**
	sixtant NC	rech. battery	5510	black	R. Fischer	
1968	**stab B 3**	battery	5970	aluminium	R. Fischer	**285**
	sixtant S	Service	5330	black/silver	R. Fischer	
	sixtant S	Service	5333	black/black	R. Fischer	
	parat BT SM 53	battery 6/12 V, battery 12/24 V	5230	olive/chrome	D. Rams/R. Fischer	**284**
1969	**stab B 11**	battery	5969	aluminium	R. Fischer	**285**
	sixtant S automatic BN 2	rech. battery	5512	black	R. Fischer	
	special 202 SM 24		5240	white/chrome	D. Rams/R. Fischer	
1970	cassett	battery	5536–5538	red, yellow, black	F. Seiffert	**287**
	sixtant 6006		5340	black	R. Fischer	**286**
1971	**rallye/sixtant color**		5321–5323	red/-, yellow/-, black/black	F. Seiffert	**287**
	sixtant 6006 automatic	rech. battery	5515	black	R. Fischer/F. Seiffert	
	synchron S	mains[1]		black	D. Rams	
1972	cassett standard	battery	5529	black	F. Seiffert	
	garant		5250	black	R. Fischer	
	Intercontinental	rech. battery	5550	black/chrome	F. Seiffert/R. Oberheim	**287**
1973	sixtant S 50/60 Hz		5352	black	R. Fischer	

Year	Type	Name	No.	Colour	Designer	Page
	sixtant 6007		5346	black	D. Rams/R. Fischer	
	sixtant 8008		5380	black	D. Rams/F. Seiffert	
	sixtant 8008		5383	brown	D. Rams/F. Seiffert/	**288**
					R. Oberheim	
	Special	mains[1]		black	D. Rams	
	synchron plus		5381	black	D. Rams/F. Seiffert/	
					R. Oberheim/P. Hartwein	
	vario-set		5450	creamy white (not sold)	H. Kahlcke	**288**
1974	marcant		5260	black/black, red/red	R. Oberheim	
1976	**micron**		5410	black, textured surface	R. Ullmann	**288**
	micron L		5410	black, smooth	R. Ullmann	
1977	**intercity**	rech. battery	5545	black	R. Ullmann	**289**
	marcant S		5260	black/chrome	R. Oberheim	
	sprint	battery	5543	black	R. Ullmann	
1978	marcant S		5260	red/chrome	R. Oberheim	
	sixtant 2002/synchron standard		5209	dark blue, grey	R. Ullmann	**289**
1979	micron plus/2000	mains	5420	black, grip bumps	R. Ullmann	
	micron plus/2000	mains	5422	2 plastics	R. Ullmann	
	sixtant 4004/compact S		5372	smooth/chrome,	D. Rams/R. Oberheim/	**289**
				ribbed/black	R. Ullmann	
1980	micron plus exclusive	mains	3423	black, grip bumps	R. Ullmann	
	micron plus de luxe/2000 metal	mains	5421/	stainless steel	R. Ullmann	
			5426			
1981	sixtant 2003		5211	dark blue, black	R. Ullmann	
	synchron start/S (as 2003)		5212	black	R. Ullmann	
1982	**micron plus universal**	mains, rech. batt.	5561	stainless steel	R. Ullmann	<u>**272**</u>, 290
1983	micron 1000 universal	mains, rech. batt.	5563	black	R. Ullmann	
	sixtant (compact) two way	mains, rech. batt.	5553	black	R. Ullmann	
1984	**pocket**	battery	5526	black	R. Ullmann	**290**
	sixtant 2004		5213	black/chrome,	R. Ullmann	**290**
				black/black		
	sixtant 5005		5372	white	R. Ullmann	
	sixtant (compact) battery	battery	5522	black	R. Ullmann	
1985	micron vario 2 electronic/3025 electronic	mains	5419	black	R. Ullmann	
	micron vario 3 universal L/3525 universal L	mains, rech. batt.	5567	grey/chrome-plated	R. Ullmann	
	micron vario 3 universal/3512 universal	mains, rech. batt.	5564	black	R. Ullmann	<u>**274**</u>, 291
	micron vario 3/L/3012	mains	5424	black	R. Ullmann	
1986	**linear 245**	mains	5235	black/red, grey, green	R. Ullmann	**291**
	linear rechargeable/linear 275	rech. battery	5365	grey/black, grey/red	R. Ullmann	**291**
	linear two way universal/linear 276 universal	mains, rech. batt.	5266	grey/red, grey/yellow	R. Ullmann	
	micron S universal/2505/2514/2515	mains, rech. batt.	5556	black	R. Ullmann	**292**
1988	3509 universal	mains, rech. batt.	5569	black, grey	R. Ullmann	
	3010	mains	5469	black	R. Ullmann	
	3510 universal	mains, rech. batt.	5569	black, grey	R. Ullmann	
	micron vario 3 universal cc/3550 cc	mains, rech. batt.	5470	grey/chrome-plated	R. Ullmann	
1989	808	mains	5428	black	R. Ullmann	
	2005	mains	5428	black	R. Ullmann	
	2014	mains	5428	black	R. Ullmann	
	2015	mains	5428	black	R. Ullmann	
	2050	mains	5428	black	R. Ullmann	
	linear 260 universal	mains, rech. batt.	5533	grey/black, grey/red, bl./bl.	R. Ullmann	
	linear 270 universal	mains, rech. batt.	5533	grey/black, black/black	R. Ullmann	
	linear 278 universal	mains, rech. batt.	5533	grey/black, grey/red, bl./bl.	R. Ullmann	

Year	Type	Name	No.	Colour	Designer	Page
1989	micron S	mains	5428	black	R. Ullmann	
	micron SL	mains	5428	black	R. Ullmann	
1990	**Flex control 4515/4520 universal**	mains, rech. batt.	5585/5509	black	R. Ullmann	**292**
	Flex control 4525 universal	mains, rech. batt.	5586	grey/chrome-plated	R. Ullmann	
	pocket	battery	5523	black	R. Ullmann	
	pocket de luxe	battery	5524	black	R. Ullmann	
	pocket de luxe traveller	battery	5525	black	R. Ullmann	
1991	**Flex control 4550 universal cc**	mains, rech. batt.	5580	grey/chrome-plated	R. Ullmann	**292**
1992	**action line**	mains	5479	black	R. Ullmann	**293**
	action line universal	mains, rech. batt.	5579	black	R. Ullman	
	Flex control 4510 universal	mains, rech. batt.	5584/5528	black	R. Ullmann	
	Flex control 4015	mains	5434/5538	black	R. Ullmann	
	sixtant 2006	mains	5235	black	R. Ullmann	
	vario 3009	mains	5469	black	R. Ullmann	
1993	Flex control 4505 universal	mains, rech. batt.	5501	black	R. Ullmann	
	Flex control 4010	mains	5437	black	R. Ullmann	**293**
	sixtant 2006 universal	mains, rech. batt.	5533	black	R. Ullmann	
1994	1008/1012	mains	5462	grey	R. Ullmann	
	1508/1512 universal	mains, rech. batt.	5597	grey	R. Ullmann	
	2040/2035	mains	5461	black	R. Ullmann	
	2540 universal	mains, rech. batt.	5596	black	R. Ullmann	**293**
	Flex control 4005	mains	5403	black	R. Ullmann	
	Flex control 4504 universal	mains, rech. batt.	5502	grey	R. Ullmann	
	Flex Integral 5510 universal	mains, rech. batt.	5506	black	R. Ullmann	
	Flex Integral 5015	mains	5507	black	R. Ullmann	
	Flex Integral 5515 universal	mains, rech. batt.	5505	black	R. Ullmann	
	Flex Integral 5525 universal	mains, rech. batt.	5503	grey/matte chrome-plated	R. Ullmann	
	Flex Integral 5550 universal	mains, rech. batt.	5504	grey/matte chrome-plated	R. Ullmann	**276**
	micron plus universal	mains, rech. batt.	5561	platinum finish	R. Ullmann	
	Classic-Platin Edition					
1995	2060	2000, mains	5459	met. black/anthracite met.	R. Ullmann	
	2560 universal	2000, mains, rech. batt.	5596	black/anthracite met.	R. Ullmann	**294**
	5005	Flex Integral 5005	5468	black	R. Ullmann	
	Flex Integral 3 universal BG		5315	black/anthracite	R. Ullmann	
	Flex control 4501	rechargeable	5471	grey/anthracite	R. Ullmann	
	Flex control 4501	rechargeable	5471	black	R. Ullmann	
	Flex Integral 5314	universal	5466	black	R. Ullmann	
	Flex Integral universal 5316	universal	5465	metallic	R. Ullmann	
	Flex Integral 5414		5476	black	R. Ullmann	
	Flex Integral 5415		5477	black	R. Ullmann	
	pocket 8 h		5519/5520	grey	R. Ullmann	
	Traveller (1h)	pocket RC	5518	black	R. Ullmann	
1996	2540 S	Shave & Shape	5596	black	R. Ullmann	
	3008	micron vario 3008	5419	black	R. Ullmann	
	3011	micron vario 3011	5419	black, grip bumps	R. Ullmann	
	3508	micron vario 3508 universal	5569	black	R. Ullmann	
	3511	micron vario 3511 universal	5564	black, grip bumps	R. Ullmann	
	5315	Flex Integral 5315 universal	5465	black/anthracite	R. Ullmann	
	5414	Flex Integral 5414	5476	black	R. Ullmann	
	5414	Flex Integral 5414 Color-Selection	5476	red, met. green, met. blue	R. Ullmann	
	5415	Flex Integral 5415	5477	black	R. Ullmann	
	5415	Flex Integral 5414 Colour-Selection	5477	red, metallic blue	R. Ullmann	
	battery 4000	Flex control	5473	black	R. Ullmann	
	battery 5000	Flex Integral	5483	black/silver	R. Ullmann	

Year	Type	Name	No.	Colour	Designer	Page
	Flex Integral 5416	universal	5478	grey/chrome-plated	R. Ullmann	
	Flex Integral 3 GT		5313	grey/anthracite	R. Ullmann	
1997	1013	Braun 1000	5462	dark grey	R. Ullmann	
	1507		5597	dark grey	R. Ullmann	
	5414	Flex Integral 5414 Color-Selection	5476	yellow, black, red, met. green, met. blue	R. Ullmann	
	5415	Flex Integral 5415 Colour-Selection	5477	yellow, black, red, met. blue	R. Ullmann	
	5416	Flex Integral 5416 universal	5478	grey/matte chrome-plated	R. Ullmann	
	6015	Flex Integral ultra speed 6015	5707	anthracite	R. Ullmann	
	6510	Flex Integral ultra speed 6510	5706	anthracite	R. Ullmann	
	6515	Flex Integral ultra speed 6515	5705	anthracite	R. Ullmann	
	6525	Flex Integral ultra speed 6525	5703	matte chrome-plated	R. Ullmann	295
	6550	Flex Integral ultra speed 6550	5704	matte chrome-plated	R. Ullmann	
	Flex control 4500	rechargeable 4500	5472	black	R. Ullmann	
	Pocket Twist		5614	dark grey	R. Ullmann	
	Pocket Twist plus		5615	dark grey	R. Ullmann	
1998	1008		5462	black	R. Ullmann	
	1508		5597	black	R. Ullmann	
	3520	micron vario 3520	5564	black/silver	R. Ullmann	
	5010	Flex Integral 5010	5474	black	R. Ullmann	
	5010	Flex Integral 5010 – Japan	5475	black	R. Ullmann	
	5520	Flex Integral 5520	5505	matte chrome-plated	R. Ullmann	
	6550	Flex Integral Ultra Speed 6550	5704	24-carat gold	R. Ullmann	
	Flex Integral 5414	special edition World Cup '98	5476	black/white	R. Ullmann	
	micron vario 3020		5419	black/silver	R. Ullmann	
1999	370 PTP	Pocket Twist plus 370	5615	black/matte chrome-plated	R. Ullmann	
	370 PTP TB	Pocket Twist plus 370 Transparent	5615	transparent blue	R. Ullmann/C. Seifert	295
	375 PTP	Pocket Twist plus 375	5615	black/matte chrome-plated	R. Ullmann	295
	2540 S TB	Shave & Shape	5596	transparent blue	R. Ullmann/C. Seifert	296
	5414	Flex Integral 5414 Color-Selection	5476	milano blue, milano gold	R. Ullmann	
	6518	Flex Integral ultra speed 6518 Millennium Edition	5705	titanium-coated	R. Ullmann	
	6520	Flex Integral ultra speed 6520	5705	matte chrome-plated	R. Ullmann	
	7570	Syncro System 7570 Clean&Charge	5491	matte chrome-plated/black	R. Ullmann	
	IF 3615	InterFace IF 3615	5629	silver	R. Ullmann/P. Vu	
2000	6012	Flex Integral ultra speed 6012	5707	black	R. Ullmann	
	6512	Flex Integral ultra speed 6512	5706	black	R. Ullmann	296
	6522	Flex Integral ultra speed 6522	5703	matte chrome-plated	R. Ullmann	
	7015	Syncro 7015	5495	black	R. Ullmann	
	7505	Syncro 7505	5494	black	R. Ullmann	
	7515	Syncro 7515	5493	grey/metallic	R. Ullmann	
	7520	Syncro System 7520 Clean&Charge	5493	grey/metallic	R. Ullmann	
	7540	Syncro 7540	5492	matte chrome-plated/black	R. Ullmann	
	7630	Syncro System Logic 7630	5493	silver/blue	R. Ullmann	
	7680	Syncro System Logic 7680	5491	champagne	R. Ullmann	298, 299
	Clean&Charge	Clean&Charge	5301	black	R. Ullmann	299
	CCR 3	cleaning cartridge	5331		R. Ullmann	
	IF 3105	InterFace IF 3105	5447	blue	R. Ullmann/P. Vu	
	IF 3612	InterFace IF 3612	5629	black	R. Ullmann/P. Vu	
	IF 3615	InterFace IF 3615	5629	silver	R. Ullmann/P. Vu	
	4615	TwinControl	4615	silver	B. Kling/P. Vu	296
2001	370 PTP TB	E.Razor Pocket	5615	transparent black	R. Ullmann	
	2540 S TB	E.Razor Shave & Shape	5596	transparent black	R. Ullmann	
	5414	Flex Integral 5414	5476	silver	R. Ullmann	294
	5414	Flex Integral 5414 Vision	5476	burgundy	R. Ullmann	

Year	Type	Name	No.	Colour	Designer	Page
2001	5441cc	Flex Integral System 5441cc	5485	black/silver	R. Ullmann	
	5600	Flex XP 5600	5719	black	R. Ullmann	
	5614	Flex XP 5614	5723	silver/blue	R. Ullmann	
	7505 SI	Syncro 7505	5494	matte chrome-plated	R. Ullmann	
	7510	Syncro System 7510	5494	black	R. Ullmann	
	7516	Syncro System 7516	5494	matte chr.-plated/black	R. Ullmann	298
	IF 3614	InterFace IF 3614	5629	blue-metallic	R. Ullmann/P. Vu	
2002	**5612**	Flex XP 5612	5720	silver/black	R. Ullmann	297
	ECO	Flex XP ECO	5721		R. Ullmann	
	6620	FreeGlider 6620	5708	black	R. Ullmann	
	6680	**FreeGlider 6680**	5710	silver/blue	R. Ullmann	297
2003	6610	FreeGlider 6610	5708	silver/black	R. Ullmann	
	8595	Activator 8595	5643	silver	R. Ullmann	**278**, 298
	8595	Activator 8595	5645	silver, grey	R. Ullmann	299
	IF 3710	InterFace 3710	5449	black	R. Ullmann	
	IF 3770	InterFace 3770	5634	transparent blue	R. Ullmann	
	IF 3775	InterFace 3775	5635	silver-blue	R. Ullmann	
2004	**2675**	cruZer³ 2675	5732	silver/black	R. Ullmann/Concept: O. Grabes/D. Wykes	297
	2865	cruZer³ 2865	5733	silver/black	R. Ullmann/Concept: O. Grabes/D. Wykes	
	4715	TriControl 4715	5717	black	R. Ullmann	
	4740	TriControl 1740	5714	black/dark blue	R. Ullmann	
	4745	TriControl 4745	5714	grey	R. Ullmann	
	4775	TriControl 4775	5713	silver	R. Ullmann	
	5410	Flex Integral 5410	5474	black	R. Ullmann	
	5412	Flex Integral 5412	5474	silver	R. Ullmann/P. Vu	
	5443	Flex Integral 5443	5476	black	R. Ullmann/P. Vu	
	5446	Flex Integral 5446	5476	silver	R. Ullmann/P. Vu	
	5691	Flex XP System 5691	5732	silver/blue	R.Ullmann/P. Hartwein/ J. Greubel	
	5715	Flex XP II 5715	5726	blue/metallic	R. Ullmann	
	5770	Flex XP II 5770	5724	silver/blue	R. Ullmann	
	5775	Flex XP II 5775	5724	chrome	R. Ullmann	
	5790	Flex XP II System 5790	5732	silver/black	R. Ullmann	
	6680	FreeGlider 6680	5710	black/silver	R. Ullmann	
	7490	Synchro System 7493	5494	black/grey	R. Ullmann	
	7504	Synchro 7504	5494	black	R. Ullmann	
	8583	Activator 8583	5645	silver	R. Ullmann	
	8588	Activator 8588	5644	silver	R. Ullmann	

Beard and hair trimmers

Year	Type	Name	No.	Colour	Designer	Page
1986	**exact universal/5 universal**	mains, rech. batt.		black	R. Ullmann	**300**
1989	exact battery	battery	5594	grey	R. Ullmann	
1992	exact 6 memory universal	mains, rech. batt.	5281	black	R. Ullmann	
1993	exact 6 battery	battery	5521	black	R. Ullmann	
1999	EP 100	Exact Power EP 100	5601	blue	B. Kling/R. Ullmann	
2000	EP 20	Exact Power EP 20	5602	petrol	B. Kling/R. Ullmann	
	EP 20 AllStyle	AllStyle	5602	transparent black	B. Kling/R. Ullmann	
	EP 80	Exact Power EP 80	5601	silver/blue	B. Kling/R. Ullmann	
2001	**HC 20**	hair perfect	5606	blue/light green	B. Kling	**300**
	HC 50	hair perfect	5605	blue/bordeaux	B. Kling	
2004	EP 20 E.Razor	EP 20 E-Razor AllStyle	5602	transparent black	B. Kling	

Year	Type	Name	No.	Colour	Designer	Page
2005	**EP 15**	Exact Power EP 15	5602	black/light grey	B. Kling/R. Ullmann/B. Wilson	**300**
	HC 20	hair perfect	5606	blue/grey/brown	B. Kling/B. Wilson	
	EP 100	Exact Power EP 100	5601	silver/grey/blue	B. Kling/R. Ullmann/B. Wilson	**300**

Body Care Appliances

Epilators and lady shavers

Year	Type	Name	No.	Colour	Designer	Page
1971	**ladyshaver**		5650	white, orange	F. Seiffert	**318**
1972	**BM 12/BL 12**	underarmshaver, battery	5967	orange	F. Seiffert	**318**
	BM 12/BL 12	underarmshaver, battery	5971	red	F. Seiffert	
	BM 12/BL 12	underarmshaver, battery	5972	yellow	F. Seiffert	
1979	Lady Braun elegance		5660	white, green, red with case	R. Ullmann	
1981	Lady Braun elegance	2 batteries	5546	white	R. Ullmann	
1982	**Lady Braun elegance exclusive**	mains, rech. batt.	5565	red-transparent with case	R. Ullmann	**318**
1985	CC 1/M	wax hair remover/epilette[1]		white	D. Rams	
	Lady Braun elegance 2		5667	white	R. Ullmann	**319**
	Lady Braun elegance 3		5666	white, aubergine	R. Ullmann	
1987	CC 2	wax hair remover/epilette[1]		white, vanilla	L. Littmann	
1988	Lady Braun style rech.	rech. battery	5576	white	R. Ullmann	
	Lady Braun style	mains	5577	white	R. Ullmann	**319**
	Lady Braun style battery	battery	5568	white	R. Ullmann	
1989	**EE 1**	Silk-épil, mains	5285	white	Serge Brun	**314**
1990	Lady Braun style universal	mains, rech. batt.	5575	white	R. Ullmann	
	EE 2/EE 20	Silk-épil cosmetic, mains	5284	white	Serge Brun	
	EE 3	Silk-épil, mains, rech. batt.	5282	white	Serge Brun	
1991	automatic EE 4/duo/ plus automatic EE 40	Silk-épil, mains	5283/5290/ 5270	white	Serge Brun	
1992	duo/plus EE 10	Silk-épil, mains	5291/5271	white	Serge Brun	
	duo/plus EE 30	Silk-épil rech. mains, rech. batt.	5292/5272	white	Serge Brun	**314**
1993	**cosmetic EF 20**	Silk-épil, battery	5293	white	P. Schneider/P. Eckart	**315**
1995	cosmetic EF 25	Silk-épil, mains, cosmetic	5294	white	P. Schneider/P. Eckart	
	EE 100	Silk-épil select, mains	5296	white	P. Schneider	
	ER 100	Silk-épil select body system	5296	white	P. Schneider	
	EE 110	Silk-épil comfort	5306	white/yellow	P. Schneider	
	ER 220	Silk-épil comfort body system	5306	white/yellow	P. Schneider	
	EE 300	Silk-épil select rechargeable	5298	white	P. Schneider	**315**
	EE 330	Silk-épil comfort rechargeable	5308	white/yellow	P. Schneider	
	select rechargeable	Silk-épil mains, rech. batt.	5298	white	P. Schneider	
	transformer for Silk-épil	4.2 V and 12 V			B. Kling/P. Schneider	
1997	**EE 90**	Silk-épil comfort	5306	white/yellow	P. Schneider	**315**
	EE 111	Silk-épil comfort	5306	white/pink	P. Schneider	
1998	EE 1070	Silk-épil SuperSoft	5303	white/green	P. Schneider/J. Greubel	
	ER 1270	Silk-épil SuperSoft body system	5304	white/green	P. Schneider/J. Greubel	
	EE 1570	Silk-épil SuperSoft rechargeable	5305	white/mint	P. Schneider/J. Greubel	
1999	EE 1170	Silk-épil SuperSoft Plus	5303	white/mint	P. Schneider/J. Greubel	
	EE 1670	Silk-épil SuperSoft Plus rech.	5305	white/mint	P. Schneider/J. Greubel	
	ER 92	Silk-épil comfort body system	5306	white/yellow	P. Schneider	
	ER 1373	Silk-épil SuperSoft Plus body sys.	5304	white/lilac	P. Schneider/J. Greubel	
2000	**EE 1020**	Silk-épil SuperSoft	5303	sunshine	P. Schneider/J. Greubel	**316**
	EE 1170	Silk-épil SuperSoft Plus	5303	aqua	P. Schneider/J. Greubel	
	EE 1670	Silk-épil SuperSoft Plus rech.	5305	aqua	P. Schneider/J. Greubel	

Year	Type	Name	No.	Colour	Designer	Page
2000	ER 1373	Silk-épil SuperSoft Plus body system	5304	alabaster	P. Schneider/J. Greubel	
	Lady style	Lady style	5577	aqua	R. Ullmann/C. Seifert	
	Lady style	Lady style battery	5568	botanica	R. Ullmann/C. Seifert	
	Lady style	Lady style universal	5575	white, alabaster	R. Ullmann/C. Seifert	
2001	EE 1040	Silk-épil SuperSoft	5303	mint	P. Schneider	
	EE 1180 S	Silk-épil Sensitive Skin	5303	botanica	P. Schneider/J. Greubel/C. Seifert	
	ER 1383 S	Silk-épil Sensitive Skin	5304	alabaster	P. Schneider/J. Greubel/C. Seifert	
2002	2170	Silk-épil eversoft Solo	5316	yellow/silver	P. Schneider/J. Greubel	316
	2270	Silk-épil eversoft Easy Start Solo	5316	lilac/metallic	P. Schneider/J. Greubel/C. Seifert	
	2370	Silk-épil eversoft Body System	5316	violet/metallic	P. Schneider/J. Greubel	
	2470	Silk-épil eversoft Easy Start	5316	lilac/metallic	P. Schneider/J. Greubel/C. Seifert	**308**
2003	2170	Silk-épil eversoft Solo	5316	vanilla	P. Schneider/J. Greubel/C. Seifert	
	2270	Silk-épil eversoft Easy Start Solo	5316	lavender	P. Schneider/J. Greubel/C. Seifert	
	2370	Silk-épil eversoft Body System	5316	aubergine	P. Schneider/J. Greubel/C. Seifert	
	2470	Silk-épil eversoft Easy Start Body System	5316	lavender	P. Schneider/J. Greubel/C. Seifert	
	ER 1250	Silk-épil SuperSoft Body System	5304	alabaster	P. Schneider/J. Greubel/C. Seifert	
2004	**3270**	Silk-épil SoftPerfection Easy Start	5318	amethyst, silver	P. Schneider/J. Greubel/ C. Seifert/B. Kling	**317**
	3370	Silk-épil SoftPerfection Body System	5319	aquamarine	P. Schneider/J. Greubel/ C. Seifert/B. Kling	
	3470	Silk-épil SoftPerfection Easy Start Body System	5319	amethyst, silver	P. Schneider/J. Greubel/ C. Seifert/B. Kling	
2005	2130	Silk-épil eversoft Solo	5316	vanilla	P. Schneider/J. Greubel/B. Kling	
	2170 DX	Silk-épil eversoft Deluxe Solo	5366	rose quartz	P. Schneider/J. Greubel/B. Kling	
	2270 DX	Silk-épil eversoft Deluxe Easy Start Solo	5366	amethyst	P. Schneider/J. Greubel/B. Kling	
	2330	Silk-épil eversoft Body System	5357	lavender	P. Schneider/J. Greubel/B. Kling B. Kling	
	LS 5100	Silk&Soft BodyShave LS 5100 battery	5327	pearl	B. Kling	
	LS 5300	Silk&Soft BodyShave LS 5300 mains	5329	pearl	B. Kling	
	LS 5500	Silk&Soft BodyShave LS 5500 rech. battery/mains	5328	transl. blue/silver transl. white/silver	B. Kling	319

Hair dryers

Year	Type	Name	No.	Colour	Designer	Page
1964	**HLD 2/20/21**	hair dryer	4410	black, white	R. Weiss	**320**
	HLD 23/231	hair dryer	4414	black, white	R. Weiss	**320**
1970	**HLD 4**	hair dryer	4416	red, blue, yellow	D. Rams	**321**
1971	**HLD 6/61**	hair dryer	4418	white, orange	J. Greubel	**322**
1972	HLD 3/31	Coiffeur/Set	4425	black, white	R. Weiss	
	HLD 5/50/51	hairstyling set/Man styler	4402/ 4406	orange, brown, black, white	R. Weiss/J. Greubel/ H. U. Haase	**323**
1975	HLD 80/58/518	hairstyling set/Man styler	4423	orange, red, black	R. Weiss/J. Greubel/H. U. Haase	
	HLD 1000/ PG 1000	Braun 1000	4407	white	J. Greubel	**324**
1976	**HLD 550**	hair dryer	4422	orange	H. U. Haase	**324**
1978	SD 800	hairstyling set	4423	red	R. Weiss/J. Greubel	
	SD 800-3	hairstyling set	4423	red	R. Weiss/J. Greubel	
	SDE 850	hairstyling set Protector	4470	white	R. Weiss/J. Greubel	
	SDE 850-3	hairstyling set Protector	4470	white	R. Weiss/J. Greubel	
	PGC 1000	super compact	4456	white/grey	H. U. Haase	**304**
	PGE 1200	Protector electronic sensor hairdryer	4455	white	H. U. Haase	**325**
1979	PGA 1000	travelair/international	4503	white, brown	R. Oberheim/H. U. Haase	
	PGD	travelair/international	4503	white, brown	R. Oberheim/H. U. Haase	
1980	PG 800	hair dryer[1]		green	D. Rams	

Year	Type	Name	No.	Colour	Designer	Page
1981	P 1500	compact	4516	beige	R. Oberheim	
	PE 1500	Protector electronic	4518	white	R. Oberheim	
1982	PG 1000	hair dryer		white	D. Rams	
	PGA/PGD/PGM/	travelcombi/international/travelair/		brown, white	H. U. Haase	
	PGI 1200	mobil 1200				
	PGS 1000	softstyler	4502	green	R. Oberheim/H. U. Haase	
	PGS/PGC 1200	softstyler/super compact	4457	green, white	H. U. Haase	326
	PSK/PK 1200/B	silencio1200/vario plus/plus cool	4479/4548	white, black, blue	R. Oberheim	325
	PS 1200	silencio 1200 vario	4547	beige, blue	R. Oberheim	
1983	IA	Bügelvorsatz	4459	white	R. Oberheim	
	PG 700	hair dryer w/hinged handle[1]		white	D. Rams	
	PST 1000	hair dryer[1]		white	D. Rams	
	Z/ZM/ZA/**BP 1000**	travelair mini/mobil mini/		brown, aubergine,	R. Oberheim	327
		international mini/compact1000		blue, white		
1985	P 1200	silencio 1200	4528	blue	R. Oberheim	
	P 1600	silencio 1600	4533	grey	R. Oberheim	
	PD/PM/PA/	silencio/travelair/mobil/international/		white, grey,	R. Oberheim	
	PI 1200/1250 sil	travelcombi		dark blue		
	PE 1600	silencio 1600 electronic	4532	white, black	R. Oberheim	
1986	PDC 1200	silencio 1200/service set/warm air pillow	4525	white/transparent	R. Oberheim	
1988	**P 1000**	silencio 1000	4588	grey, blue, violet	R. Oberheim	326
	P 1100	silencio 1100	4604	red	R. Oberheim	
	PC 1200/1250	silencio 1200/1250	4549	blue	R. Oberheim	327
	Pro 1500	silencio professional	4591	white	R. Oberheim	
	PX 1200	silencio 1200	4583	white, black	R. Oberheim	
1989	PF 1600	professional studio 12	4601	white	R. Oberheim	
	PFV 1600	professional control	4600	black	R. Oberheim	
1990	DF 3/4	Finger Diffuser	4583/4600	white, black	R. Oberheim	
1991	**HL 1800**	Control 1800 high-line	4493	white/black	R. Oberheim/J. Greubel	328
	HL 2000	Control 2000 high-line	4494	black	R. Oberheim/J. Greubel	
	TD/TC/TY/	silencio/international/mobil/		grey, black,	R. Oberheim	
	TM/TV/TI 1250	travelair/travelcombi		blue, white		
1992	**C 1500 E/P**	Professional Power Salon Master	3503	white	R. Oberheim	328
	DFB 5/6	soft diffusor	4583/4600	black	R. Oberheim	
	DFB 7	soft diffusor plus	4583	black	R. Oberheim	
	DFW 5	soft diffusor	4583	white	R. Oberheim	
1993	PX 1600	silencio 1600	3509	white, black	R. Oberheim	
	PXE 1600	silencio electronic	3510	white, matte black	R. Oberheim	
	SVW 1	supervolume	3510	white	R. Oberheim/C. Seifert	
	SVB 1/2	supervolume	4605	black	R. Oberheim/C. Seifert	
1995	HS 1	volume shaper	3571	grey-violet/lilac	R. Oberheim/C. Seifert	
	HS 2	control shaper	3572	blue/black	R. Oberheim/C. Seifert	
	HS 3	style shaper	3585	grey-violet/lilac	R. Oberheim/C. Seifert	
	PFV 1600 SVB4	supervolume twist 1600 control	4600	black	R. Oberheim	
	PF 1600 SVB4	supervolume twist 1600	4601	black	R. Oberheim	
	PX 1200 SVB3	supervolume twist 1200	4583	black	R. Oberheim	
	PX 1200 SVW1	supervolume 1200	4583	white	R. Oberheim	
	TA 1250	travel silencio 1250 international	4497	black	R. Oberheim	
	DFB 3	diffuser attachment	4583	black	R. Oberheim	
	DFB 4	diffuser attachment	4600	black	R. Oberheim	
	DFW 3	diffuser attachment	4583	white	R. Oberheim	
	DFW 4	diffuser attachment	4601	white	R. Oberheim	
1996	PX 1200 SVL 3	supervolume twist	4583	white/grey	R. Oberheim	
1997	**P 1000 SVB 1**	supervolume 1000	4588	black	C. Seifert	

Year	Type	Name	No.	Colour	Designer	Page
1998	CP 1600 AA1	Sensation	3512	black/dark blue	B.Kling/J.Greubel	
	CPC 1600	Création cool	3514	black/dark green	B.Kling/J.Greubel	
	CPC 1600 DFB6	Création cool diffusor duo	3514	black/dark green	B.Kling/J.Greubel	
	CPS 1800 AA1	Sensation	3513	black/magenta	B.Kling/J.Greubel	
	CPSC 1800	Création cool select	3521	black/magenta	B.Kling/J.Greubel	
	PRSC 1800	Professional 1800	3522	black/grey/chrome	B. Kling/J. Greubel	**306, 329**
	PRSC 1800 DFB 5	Professional 1800 diffusor duo	3522	black/grey/chrome	B. Kling/J. Greubel	
1999	**A 1000**	cosmo 1000	3533	aqua	J. Greubel/C. Seifert/T. Winkler	**329**
	B 1200	Swing 1200	3516	black	T. Winkler	
	CPC 1600	Création cool Millennium Edition	3514	crystal black, cryst. blue	B.Kling/J.Greubel	
	PX 1200	Silencio 1200 Millennium Edition	4583	crystal black (matte), crystal blue (matte)	R. Oberheim	
2000	ATD 1000	cosmo travel	3534	black	J. Greubel/M. Shiba/T. Winkler	
	B 1200 DFB 5	Swing Diffusor 1200	3516	black	T. Winkler	
	B 1200 SVB 1	Swing Supervolume 1200	3516	black	T. Winkler	
	BC 1400	Swing cool	3519	metallic	T. Winkler	**330**
	PRSC 1800	Professional Style Mystic Gold	3522	mystic gold	B. Kling/J. Greubel	
2001	A 1000 Plus	cosmo 1000 platinum	3533	metallic	J. Greubel/C. Seifert/T. Winkler	
	ATD 1000 A	cosmo travel platinum	3534	metallic	J. Greubel/M. Shiba/T. Winkler	
	BC 1400 V2	Volume & more	3519	metallic	T. Winkler/C. Seifert	
	CP 1600	Création CP 1600	3511	blue	D. Lubs	
	CP 1600	Création Colour Edition Clivia	2671/2672	orange, green, lilac	J. Greubel/B. Kling/C. Seifert	**331**
	CPSC 1800 V3	Volume & more	3521	silver-metallic	B. Kling/J. Greubel/C. Seifert	
	PRSC 1800	Professional Style silver dust	3522	silver-metallic	B. Kling/J. Greubel/C. Seifert	
2002	A 1000	cosmo 1000	3533	silver-metallic	T. Winkler/D. P. Vu	
	ATD 1000 A	cosmo Travel platinum	3534	grey-metallic	T. Winkler/D. P. Vu	
	B 1200	Swing 1200	3516	pearl green	T. Werner/D. P. Vu	
	CP 1600	CP Braun Création	3511	sunshine	D. Lubs	
	CP 1600	Création CP 1600	3511	black, green-met.	D. Lubs	
	CPC 1600	Création cool CPC 1600	3514	blue-metallic	D. Lubs	
	CPC 1600 DF	Création cool diffusor duo	3514	blue-metallic	D. Lubs	
	CPSC 1800	Création cool select CPSC 1800	3521	silver-metallic	J. Greubel/B. Kling/C. Seifert	
	PRO 2000	FuturPro 2000 solo Pro 2000	3537	pearl-metallic	D. Lubs	**332**
	PRO 2000 DF	FuturPro 2000 diffusor	3537	silver/blue	D. Lubs	
2004	PRO 2000 Ion	FuturPro IonCare solo	3539	ocean-blow	P. Vu/D. Lubs	
	PRO 2000 Ion DF	FuturPro IonCare diffusor	3539	ocean-blow	P. Vu/D. Lubs	**332**
2005	C 1600	creation2 C 1600	3540	green-metallic	P. Vu	
	C 1800	creation2 C 1800	3541	violet-metallic	P. Vu	
	C 1800 DF	creation2 C 1800 DF	3541	violet-metallic	P. Vu	
	C 1800 Ion DF	creation2 IonCare C 1800 DF	3542	silver-blue	P. Vu	**333**
	e-Go Sport	e-Go Sport	3544	dark blue	P. Vu	
	e-Go Travel	e-Go Travel	3544	silver	P. Vu	

Roundstylers

Year	Type	Name	No.	Colour	Designer	Page
1977	**RS 60/65**	roundstyler set	4429	orange	H. U. Haase	**334**
	RS 61/66	roundstyler set	4427	orange	H. U. Haase	
1978	**RS 68**	roundstyler hood set	4449	red	H. U. Haase	**334**
1979	RS 67	roundstyler	4472	orange	H. U. Haase/R. Oberheim	
	RS 67 K/63 K/62 K	roundstyler cool curl	4473	white, beige, aubergine	H. U. Haase/R. Oberheim	
	RSE 70/71	roundstyler hood set	4448/4453	white	R. Oberheim/H. U. Haase/ R. Ullmann	
1982	**RSK 1005/1003**	cool curl roundstyler set	4522	white, black	R. Oberheim	**335**
	RSE 1003/1005	Protector roundstyler set	4523	white	R. Oberheim	

Year	Type	Name	No.	Colour	Designer	Page
1991	RS 62 W	roundstyler cool curl	4473	white	R. Oberheim	
1998	BS 1	Straight & Shape	3566	lilac	C. Seifert	

Hood dryers

Year	Type	Name	No.	Colour	Designer	Page
1971	HLH 1/3	Astronette	4986	orange	J. Greubel	
1974	HLH 2	Astronette	4987	black	J. Greubel	
1975	HLH 10	Super-Luftkissen hood hair dryer	4991	red	J. Greubel	
	HLH 11B	hood hair dryer/Astronette[1]		orange	D. Rams	
1977	HLH 15	Luftkissen styler	4435	red	J. Greubel	
1982	HLH 20	Gemini dual motor floating hood	4436	white	R. Oberheim	
1984	HLH 18	Uno floating hood	4544	white	R. Oberheim	
1992	SH 2	silencio balance	4594	white	R. Oberheim	
2001	HLH 18	Classic		aqua	D. Lubs	
	HLH 20	Elegance		vanilla	D. Lubs	

Air stylers/ curling irons

Year	Type	Name	No.	Colour	Designer	Page
1975	**DLS 10**	Quick curl	4441	orange	H. U. Haase	**336**
1976	DLS 20	Curl control	4442	red	H. U. Haase	
1977	DLS 12	Quick curl	4443	orange	H. U. Haase	
1979	**LS 35**	quick style	4504	white	M. S. Cousins	**336**
1982	LS 36	quick style	4526	white	R. Oberheim	
	LS 40/41	quick style duo/set		white	R. Oberheim	
	GC 2	independent styler	4506	white	R. Oberheim	**336**
1984	GC 1	independent curler	4509	white	R. Oberheim/J. Greubel	
	GC 40	independent combi	4559	white	R. Oberheim	
	LS 38	slim style	4543	white	R. Oberheim	
	LS 40 R	quick style combi	4428	white	R. Oberheim	
1985	LS 30/30 R	quick style compact	4565	white/black	R. Oberheim	
1986	AS 1/AS 2	silencio air styler/duo styler	4574	blue, white	R. Oberheim	
1988	GCC 3/50	gas curler/combi	4507	white	R. Oberheim	
	GCC 4	universelle gas styler	4539	white	R. Oberheim	
	LS 34	easy style	4570	red/grey, red/black	R. Oberheim	
1989	AS 11/12/13	silencio plus/duo plus/travel	4584/4484	white/grey, white	R. Oberheim	
1990	**FZ 10**	ZZ-look	4495	white/grey	R. Oberheim	**337**
	LS 33	curly style	4569	white	R. Oberheim	
1991	AS 8	silencio air styler	4483	blue	R. Oberheim	
	TC 22/TCC 30	tricurl/3-in-1 curl	4563	white, red/black	R. Oberheim	
	TC 23/TCB 10	trend style/trend curl	4482	black	R. Oberheim	
1992	AS 22	air styler vario	3520	black	R. Oberheim	
	AS 400/R	silencio air styler ultra	4485	white/grey	R. Oberheim	**337**
	GCS 5/70	gas curler slim	4560	black	R. Oberheim	
	GCS 6	gas curler slim	4498	black	R. Oberheim	
	TCC 20 A	2-in-1-curl	4486	white/grey	R. Oberheim	
	TCC 40/A	4-in-1-curl	3563	white/grey	R. Oberheim	**337**
	TCS 12	fashion curl	3570	white/grey	R. Oberheim	
	TCT 11	fashion curl	3562	white/grey	R. Oberheim	
1995	AS 400 BC	Big Curls ultra	4485	white/grey	C. Seifert	
1996	GCC 8	Big Curls independent	3586	white	C. Seifert	
	GCC 90	Big Curls independent	3587	white	C. Seifert	
1998	**BS 1**	Straight & Shape	3588	lilac	C. Seifert	**339**
	AS 400 duo	Volume Curls Duo	4485	white/blue	C. Seifert	
	AS 400 Set	Volume Curls Set	4485	white/blue	C. Seifert	

Year	Type	Name	No.	Colour	Designer	Page
2000	AS 200	Curls & Style	3580	lilac/light	R. Oberheim/C. Seifert	
	AS 400 BC&S	Maxi Curls & Style	4485	lavender/metallic	C. Seifert	
	AS 400 V&S	Volume & Style	4485	lavender/metallic	C. Seifert	
	AS 1000	power styler professional	4522	black/chrome	R. Oberheim/C. Seifert	**338**
	C 20	New Cordless Styler	3589	metallic blue/light blue	Till Winkler	
	C 20 S	New Cordless Styler	3589	metallic lilac/sky-blue	Till Winkler	
	C 100 S	New Cordless Styler	3589	anthracite/black	T. Winkler	
2001	C 20	Independent Curls & Waves	3589	lilac-metallic	T. Winkler	
2002	C 20	Independent Curls & Waves	3589	light green/lime-green	T. Winkler	
	C 20 S	Independent Steam	3589	stonewashed-blue	T. Winkler	
	C 200 S	New Cordless Styler	3589	rose/lilac	Till Winkler	
2003	**ASS 1000 Pro**	Steam & Style ASS 1000 Pro	3536	silver/lavender	L. Littmann	**338**
	C Club	New Cordless Styler	3589	rose	Till Winkler	
2004	C 20 S	Independent Steam	3589	lilac-metallic, violet	T. Winkler	
	C 30 S	Cordless Keramik Steam C 30 S	3589	ocean-blue, light blue	T. Winkler	
	C Pro S	Cordless Steam Styler	3589	silver	T. Winkler	**338**
	Club	New Cordless Styler	3589	pink-transparent	Till Winkler	
2005	C 20	Cordless Keramik C 20	3589	aqua-green	T. Winkler	
	ES 1	professional ceramic hair straightener	3543	black	P. Vu	**339**

Cosmetic/ body care

Year	Type	Name	No.	Colour	Designer	Page
1964	**HUV 1**	Cosmolux	4395	white/alu.-coloured	D. Rams/R. Weiss/	**340**
					D. Lubs	
1968	HB 1	cosmetic set	4430	black	R. Oberheim	
	HBM	manicure set	4984	alu.-coloured	R. Oberheim	
	HW 1	personal scale	4960	alu.-coloured/black	D. Rams	**340**
1970	HML 1	measuring stick	4437	alu.-coloured	R. Oberheim	
1974	**EPK 1**	Swing-hair, detangler comb only	4431	orange	J. Greubel	**323**
1975	SL 1	cosmetic mirror[1]		white	D. Rams	
1980	BC 1	Lady Braun beauty care	4505	white	R. Ullmann	

Infrared ear thermometers

Year	Type	Name	No.	Colour	Designer	Page
1996	pro 1	ThermoScan pro 1	6006	white	ThermoScan	
	pro LT	ThermoScan pro LT	6007	grey	ThermoScan	
1998	IRT 2020	ThermoScan Instant Thermometer	6015	white	ThermoScan (frog design)	
	IRT 3020	ThermoScan IRT 3020	6012	white/grey	B. Kling/D. Lubs/T. Winkler	
	IRT 3520	ThermoScan plus IRT 3520	6013	white	B. Kling/D. Lubs/T. Winkler	**342**
1999	**IRT Pro 3000**	ThermoScan IRT Pro 3000	6014	metallic silver/grey	B. Kling/D. Lubs/T. Winkler	**310, 342**
2004	IRT 4020	ThermoScan IRT 4020	6023	white/mint	J. Greubel/L. Littmann	
	IRT 4520	ThermoScan IRT 4520	6022	white/blue	J. Greubel/L. Littmann	
	IRT Pro 4000	ThermoScan IRT Pro 4000	6021	silver	J. Greubel/L. Littmann	**342**
2005	IRT 2000	ThermoScan compact	6026	white/mint	P. Vu	

Blood pressure monitors

Year	Type	Name	No.	Colour	Designer	Page
1998	BP 1000	VitalScan	6050	white/grey	B. Kling/D. Lubs	
	BP 1500	VitalScan plus	6052	white/grey	B. Kling/D. Lubs	**341**
2000	BP 2005	PrecisionSensor	6057	white	D. Lubs	
	BP 2510	PrecisionSensor	6954	white	D. Lubs	**341**
	BP 2510 UG	PrecisionSensor 2510 UG	6954	white	D. Lubs	
2001	BP 2550	PrecisionSensor	6053	dark blue	D. Lubs	
	BP 2590	PrecisionSensor	6059	silver	D. Lubs	

Year	Type	Name	No.	Colour	Designer	Page
2002	BP 1600	VitalScan Plus BP 1600	6057	white	P. Hartwein	
	BP 1650	VitalScan Plus BP 1650	6057	anthracite	P. Hartwein	**341**
2004	BP 2510 UG	SensorControl BP 2510 UG	6054	white	P. Hartwein	
2005	BP 3510	SensorControl EasyClick BP 3510	6083	blue	P. Hartwein	
	BP 3560 Pharmacy	SensorControl EasyClick BP 3560 Pharmacy	6085	silver	P. Hartwein	**341**

Oral Care Appliances

Year	Type	Name	No.	Colour	Designer	Page
1963	**mayadent**			white	W. Zimmermann	**346**, **358**
1978	zb 1/d 1	electric toothbrush w/rech. battery	4801	white, black	R. Oberheim/R. Weiss	
1979	**md 1**	dental oral irrigator	4802	white, black	R. Oberheim	358
1980	DC 1	instant denture cleaner	4090	white	L. Littmann	
	md 2	aquaplus oral irrigator	4946	white	R. Oberheim	359
	zb 1t/d 1t	travel set w/rech. bat., el. toothbrush	4801	black	R. Oberheim	359
1984	**d 3/3t/31**	Dental/Timer, toothbrush and travel set	4804	white	P. Hartwein	361
1984	d 3a	toothbrush w/adapter	4804	white	P. Hartwein	
	md 3/30	Dental oral irrigator	4803	white	P. Hartwein	360
	OC 3/30/301	Dental Center/Timer, toothbrush and oral irrigator	4803	white	P. Hartwein	**348**, 360
1991	D 5025/5525/5011	Plak Control/timer/basic	4726	white	P. Hartwein	
	md 5000	Plak Control oral irrigator	4723	white	P. Hartwein	
	OC 5025/ 5525/5545	Plak Control Center	4723	white	P. Hartwein	361
1992	D 5525 T	Plak Control Travel timer	4725	white	P. Hartwein	
1994	D 5025 S/5525S/X/5545 S	Plak Control/timer set/family timer	4730	white/blue	P. Hartwein	
	D 5525 TS	Plak Control Travel timer/set	4725	white/blue	P. Hartwein	
	D 7011	Plak Control Solo	4728	white/blue	P. Hartwein	
	D 7022/7522	Plak Control/duo timer	4727	white/blue	P. Hartwein	**352**
	MD 5000 S	Plak Control oral irrigator	4723	white/blue	P. Hartwein	
	OC 5025 S/5525 S/5545 S	Plak Control Center	4723	white/blue	P. Hartwein	
1995	D 7025 Z	Plak Control	4726	white/blue	P. Hartwein	
	D 7521 K	Plak Control children	4726	white/blue	P. Hartwein	
	D 7521 K	Plak Control Kids	4728	blue/turquoise	P. Hartwein	362
	D 7525 Z	Plak Control timer	4726	white/blue	P. Hartwein	
	D 7525	Plak Control timer	4728	white/blue	P. Hartwein	
1996	D 7025	Plak Control	4728	white/blue	P. Hartwein	
	D 7511	Plak Control solo timer	4728	white/blue	P. Hartwein	
	D 9011	Oral-B Plak Control Ultra Solo	4713	white/mint	P. Hartwein	
	D 9022	Plak Control Ultra duo	4713	white/mint	P. Hartwein	
	D 9025	Oral-B Plak Control Ultra	4713	white/mint	P. Hartwein	
	D 9525	Plak Control Ultra timer	4713	white/mint	P. Hartwein	
	D 9525 T	Oral-B Plak Control Ultra Travel timer	4713	white/mint	P. Hartwein	
	D 9511	Plak Control Ultra timer	4713	white/mint	P. Hartwein	
	D 9522	Plak Control Ultra duo timer	4727	white/mint	P. Hartwein	
	IC 2522	Interclean Ultra System	3725	white/mint	P. Hartwein	362
	ID 2000	Interclean Body	3725	white/mint	P. Hartwein	
	ID 2025	Interclean Tower	3725	white/mint	P. Hartwein	362
	ID 2021	Interclean Solo	3725	white/mint	P. Hartwein	
	ID 2025 T	Interclean deluxe	3725	white/mint	P. Hartwein	
	MD 31	oral irrigator	4803	white/blue	P. Hartwein	363
	MD 9000	Oral Irrigator	4723	white/mint	P. Hartwein	
	OC 5545 TS	Plak Control Center timer	4723	white/blue	P. Hartwein	
	OC 9025	Oral-B Plak Control Ultra Center	4714	white/mint	P. Hartwein	

Year	Type	Name	No.	Colour	Designer	Page
1996	**OC 9525**	Plak Control Ultra Center timer	4714	white/mint	P. Hartwein	**363**
	OC 9545 T	Plak Control Ultra Center timer	4723	white/mint	P. Hartwein	
1997	D 7511	Plak Control solo timer		white/blue	P. Hartwein	
	D 9011	Plak Control Ultra solo	4713	white/mint	P. Hartwein	
	D 9025	Plak Control Ultra	4713	white/mint	P. Hartwein	
	OC 9025	Plak Control Ultra Center	4714	white/mint	P. Hartwein	
1998	D 6011	Plak Control solo	4728	white/blue	P. Hartwein	
	D 9025 Z	Plak Control Ultra	4713	white/mint	P. Hartwein	
	D 9500	Plak Control Ultra timer	4713	white/mint	P. Hartwein	
	D 9525 Z	Plak Control Ultra timer	4713	white/mint	P. Hartwein	
	D 15.525	Plak Control 3D standard	4729	white/silver-grey	P. Hartwein	
	D 15.525 X	Plak Control 3D deluxe	4729	white/silver-grey	P. Hartwein	
1999	D 15.511	Plak Control 3D solo	4729	white/silver-grey	P. Hartwein	
	MD 15	OxyJet	4715	white/silver-grey	P. Hartwein	
	OC 15.525	OxyJet 3D Center	4715	white/silver-grey/cyan	P. Hartwein	**364**
	OC 15.545 X	OxyJet 3D Center deluxe	4715	white/silver-grey	P. Hartwein	
2000	D 8011	Plak Control	4731	white/mint	P. Hartwein	
	D 10.511	children's toothbrush	4733	d.&l. lilac, blue/yellow	P. Hartwein/T. Winkler	**365**
2001	D 2	batt.-powered toothbrush for children		green/blue/red	B. Kling	
	D 4010	Plak Control batt.-powered toothbrush	4739	white/green	B. Kling/P. Vu	**366**
	D 15.513 T	Plak Control 3D travel	4729	white/silver-grey	P. Hartwein	
	D 17.511	3D Excel solo	4736	white/blue	B. Kling/P. Vu	
	D 17.525	3D Excel standard	4736	white/blue	B. Kling/P. Vu	**366**
	D 17.525 X	3D Excel deluxe	4736	white/blue	B. Kling/P. Vu	
	D 2010	AdvancePower Kids batt.-powered toothbrush	4721	light blue/orange/red	B. Kling	**365**
2002	**D 4510**	AdvancePower batt.-powered toothbrush	4740	white/blue	P. Vu	**366**
	D 8525	Oral-B Plak Control timer D 8525	4731	white/mint	P. Vu	
2003	D 17.500	Oral-B Professional Care 7000 handpiece	4736	blue/white	B. Kling/P. Hartwein/P. Vu	
	D 17.511	Oral-B Professional Care 7000	4736	blue/white	B. Kling/P. Vu	
	D 17.525	Oral-B Professional Care 7500	4736	blue/white	B. Kling/P. Vu	
	D 17.525 X	Oral-B Professional Care 7500 dlx	4736	blue/white	B. Kling/P. Vu	
	MD 15 A	Oral-B Professional Care 5500 oral irrigator	3718	white/blue	P. Hartwein/B. Kling	
	MD 17	OxyJet	3719	blue/white	B. Kling	
	OC 15.525 A	Oral-B Professional Care 550 Center	3718	white/blue	P. Hartwein/B. Kling	
	OC 17.525	Oral-B Professional Care 7500 Center	3719	blue/white	B. Kling/P. Hartwein	
	OC 17.545	Oral-B Professional Care 7500 dlx Center	3719	blue/white	B. Kling/P. Hartwein	
2004	D 15.511 XL	Oral-B Professional Care 5000 XL	4729	blue/white	B. Kling/P. Hartwein	
	D 17.525 XL	Oral-B Professional Care 5500 XL	4729	blue/white	B. Kling	**367**
	D 18.565	Oral-B Professional Care 8500	3728	silver/white	B. Kling/M. Orthey	
	D 18.585 X	Oral-B Professional Care 8500 DLX	3728	silver/white	B. Kling/M. Orthey	
	S 18.525.2	Oral-B Sonic Complete	4717	blue/white	P. Vu	**367**
	S 18.535.3	Oral-B Sonic Complete DLX	4717	blue/white	P. Vu	
2005	MD 18	Oral-B Professional Care 8500 Oxy-Jet	3719	silver/white	B. Kling/P. Hartwein	
	OC 18.585 X	Oral-B Professional Care 8500 DLX OxyJet Center	3719	silver/white	B. Kling/P. Hartwein	

Toothbrushes

Year	Type	Name		Colour	Designer	Page
1987	**Oral-B Plus**	toothbrush			P. Schneider/J. Greubel	
	Oral-B Plus	interdental handle	interdental cleaner		P. Schneider/J. Greubel	
1988	Oral-B Angular	toothbrush	1-component material		P. Schneider/J. Greubel	
1989	Oral-B	floss holder	interdental cleaner		P. Schneider/J. Greubel	
	Oral-B Indicator	toothbrush	indicator bristles		P. Schneider/J. Greubel	
	Oral-B Angular Indicator	toothbrush	indicator bristles		P. Schneider/J. Greubel	

Year	Type	Name	No./Colour/Material	Designer	Page
1990	**Oral-B Plus travel**	travel toothbrush		P. Schneider/J. Greubel	**368**
1991	**Oral-B Advantage**	toothbrush	1-component material	P. Schneider/J. Greubel	**369**
1994	**Oral-B Advantage**	toothbrush	2-component material	P. Schneider/J. Greubel	**369**
	Oral-B Advantage Plus	toothbrush	2-component material/new head	P. Schneider/J. Greubel	
1996	**Oral-B CrossAction**	toothbrush	2-component material	P. Schneider/J. Greubel	**354**
2002	**Oral-B New Indicator**	toothbrush	2-component material/transp./opaque	T. Winkler/P. Vu	370
2003	Oral-B Indicator Interdental Set	interdental cleaner	2-component material/transp./opaque	T. Winkler	
	Oral-B Advantage Next Generation	toothbrush	2-component material	B. Kling	370
	Oral-B CrossAction Vitalizer	toothbrush	3-component material/new head	P. Schneider/J. Greubel/	369
				T. Winkler	
	Oral-B New Classic	toothbrush	2-component material	B. Kling	370
	Oral-B CrossAction Power	batt.-pow. tothbrush		Till Winkler	370
2004	Oral-B Kolibri	interdental cleaner	battery-powered	Till Winkler	
	Oral-B Advantage Artica	toothbrush	3-component material/transp./new head	B. Kling	

Household Appliances

Kitchen machines

Year	Type	Name	No./Colour/Material	Designer	Page
1957	**KM 3/31**	food processor, basic model	4203/4206	white/blue	G. A. Müller	**376**, 402
		attachments:				
		shredder 1 and 2		white/blue		
		mixing attachment		transparent		
		meat grinder		white/blue		
		citrus press		transparent		
		coffee grinder		transparent		
		cookbook				
1964	**KM 32/B/321**	food processor, basic model	4122/4123	white/green	G. A. Müller/R. Oberheim	403
		attachments:				
	KS 32	shredder for KM 32/B/321	4613	white/green	G. A. Müller/R. Oberheim	
	KX 32	mixing attachment for KM 32/B/321	4614	transparent	G. A. Müller/R. Oberheim	
	KGZ 2	meat grinder for KM 32/B/321	4610	white/green	G. A. Müller/R. Oberheim	
	KMZ 2	citrus press for KM 32/B/321	4612	transparent	G. A. Müller/R. Oberheim	
	MXK 3	coffee grinder for KM 32/B/321	4615	transparent	G. A. Müller/R. Oberheim	
1965	**KM 2**	Multiwerk, basic model	4130	white	D. Rams/R. Fischer	403
		attachments:				
	KMZ 2	citrus press for KM 2		white	D. Rams/R. Fischer	
	KMK 2	stone-mill coffee grinder for KM 2	4620	white	D. Rams/R. Fischer	
1982	MC 1Vario	food processor[1]		white	H. Kahlcke	
1983	UK 1/9/19/11/90/ 95/100/110/120	Multipractic series	4243/4259	white	H. Kahlcke	
1984	**KM 20/200/210/ 250/40/400/410/430**	Multipractic electronic series	4261/4262	white	H. Kahlcke	405
		attachments:				
	UKZ 1/4	citrus press no. 4243 for UK	4261/4262	transparent	H. Kahlcke	
	UKRT 2/4	whipping attachment no. 4261 for UK	4261/4262	white	H. Kahlcke	
	UKT 2	whipped-cream pot no. 4558 for UK	4261/4262	white	H. Kahlcke	
	UKE 1/4/R 5	juicer no. 4289 for UK	4262	white	H. Kahlcke	
	UKM 1/10	grain mill no. 4237 for UK	4262	white	H. Kahlcke	
	UKW 1	kitchen scale no. 4243 for UK	4261/4262	white	H. Kahlcke	405
	UKC 4	chopping attachment for UK	4261/4262	white	H. Kahlcke	
1985	KS 33	shredder for KM 32/B/321	4247	white/green	H. Kahlcke	

Year	Type	Name	No.	Colour	Designer	Page
1986	**KGM 3/31**	grain mill	4239	white	H. Kahlcke	**406**
1990	MC 100	food processor[1]		white	H. Kahlcke	
	MC 200	food processor[1]		white	H. Kahlcke	
1993	K 850	Multisystem 1	3210	white	L. Littmann	
	K 1000	Multisystem 1 to 3	3210	white	L. Littmann	**407**
	KC 1	System 3 expansion set	3210	transparent	L. Littmann	
	KER 1	juicer for K 1000	3210	grey	L. Littmann	
	KU 2	System 2 expansion set	3210	transparent	L. Littmann	
1994	KPC 1	citrus press	3210	transparent	L. Littmann	
1996	K 600	CombiMax 600	3205	white	L. Littmann	
	K 650	CombiMax	3205	white	L. Littmann	**408**
	K 700	CombiMax 700	3202	white	L. Littmann	
	K 750	CombiMax 750	3202	white	L. Littmann	
	PJ 600	CombiMax	3200	white/transparent	L. Littmann	
	SJ 600	juicer attachment	3200	grey/transparent	L. Littmann	

Mixers/ food processors

Year	Type	Name	No.	Colour	Designer	Page
1958	MX 3/31	Multimix	4213/4215	white/blue	G. A. Müller	
1962	KGZ 2	meat grinder for MX 32/32 B	4610	white	G. A. Müller	
	KMZ 2	citrus press for MX 32/32 B	4612	transparent	G. A. Müller	
	KS 32	shredder for MX 32/32 B	4613	white/green	G. A. Müller	
	MX 32/32 B	Multimix	4142	white/green	G. A. Müller	**402**
	MXK 3	coffee grinder for MX 32/32 B	4615	transparent	G. A. Müller	
1967	MX 111	Multimix toy version	4946	white		
1979	**ZK1/2/5-9/100-500**	Multiquick series	4249/4250	white	H. Kahlcke	**404**
		attachments:				
	ZK 3	mixing attachment	4250	transparent	H. Kahlcke	
	ZK 4	shredder	4250	white	H. Kahlcke	
1982	**KGZ 3/31**	meat grinder	4242	white	H. Kahlcke	**392, 406**
1983	**MC 1/2**	Multiquick compact/electronic	4171	white	H. Kahlcke	**404**
1985	KS 33	shredder for MX 32/32 B	4247	white/green	H. Kahlcke	
1995	G 1100 K	Power Plus 1100 meat grinder	4195	white/green	L. Littmann/H. Kahlcke	
2000	M 700	Multimix	4643	vanilla	L. Littmann	
	K 3000	Multisystem 3-in-1	3210	white/silver	C. Seifert/L. Littmann	**409**
2001	G 1300 K	Power Plus 1300 meat grinder	4195	white	L. Littmann/H. Kahlcke	
	MX 2000	PowerBlend MX 2000	4184	white	L. Littmann	
	MX 2050	PowerBlend MX 2050	4184	white	L. Littmann	**408**

Handmixers/ handblenders

Year	Type	Name	No.	Colour	Designer	Page
1960	**M 1/11**	Multiquirl	4220/4221	light grey	G. A. Müller	**410**
1963	**M 12/121/125**	Multiquirl	4112	white	G. A. Müller/R. Weiss	**411**
1966	MR 2	itc handblender	4942	white	R. Garnich	
1968	**M 140**	Multiquirl	4115	white	R. Weiss	**411**
	MS 140	shredder	4618	white	R. Weiss	
	MZ 140	citrus press	4622	white	R. Weiss	
	MZ 142	Turbomesser	4263	grey	R. Weiss	
1973	MR 4	Minipimer[1]		white	D. Rams	
1978	MR 5	handblender[1]		white	D. Rams	
1979	MR 62	handblender[1]		white	L. Littmann	
1981	**MR 6**	vario handblender	4972	white/red	L. Littmann	**413**
1982	**MR 30**	junior handblender	4172	white	L. Littmann	**413**
	MR 72	handblender[1]		white	L. Littmann	

Year	Type	Name	No.	Colour	Designer	Page
1985	MR 7	vario handblender	4166	white	L. Littmann	
	MR 74	handblender[1]		white	L. Littmann	
1986	MR 73	handblender[1]		white	L. Littmann	
1987	**MR 300/CA/ HC/M/305**	compact handblender/ Multiquick 300 series	4169	white	L. Littmann	**413**
1989	MR 700	Vario-Set handblender	4181	white	L. Littmann	
1991	MR 730	handblender[1]		white	L. Littmann	
	MR 743	handblender[1]		white	L. Littmann	
1992	MR 350/HC	Multiquick 350 series	4164	white	L. Littmann	
1994	CA-M	chopping attachment	4642	white	L. Littmann	
	HA-M	handblender attachment	4642	white	L. Littmann	
	M 700	Multimix	4643	white	L. Littmann	
	M 800/810/820/ 830/870/880	Multimix duo/trio/quatro	4262	white	L. Littmann	**412**
1995	CA 5	handblender[1]		white	L. Littmann	
	MR 500	Multiquick 500	4187	white	L. Littmann	
	MR 500 CA	Multiquick/Minipimer control plus	4187	white/anthracite	L. Littmann	
	MR 500 HC	Multiquick control plus	4187	white/anthracite	L. Littmann	**394, 414**
	MR 500 M	Multiquick 500 M	4189	white	L. Littmann	
	MR 500 MCA	Multiquick	4189	white	L. Littmann	
	MR 505	Multiquick/Minipimer control plus	4187	white/anthracite	L. Littmann	
	MR 505 M	Multiquick/Minipimer control plus	4187	white/anthracite	L. Littmann	
	MR 550	Multiquick	4189	white	L. Littmann	
	MR 550 CA	Multiquick control plus vario	4189	white/black	L. Littmann	
	MR 550 M	Multiquick/Minipimer control plus vario	4189	white/black	L. Littmann	
	MR 555 CA	Multiquick 555 CA	4189	white	L. Littmann	
	MR 555 MCA	Multiquick/Minipimer control plus vario	4189	white/black	L. Littmann	**414**
1997	MR 400	handblender[1]		white, yellow, light blue, dark lilac	L. Littmann	
1998	MR 350 CA	Multiquick 350 CA	4164	white	L. Littmann	
	MR 400	Multiquick 400		white	L. Littmann	
	MR 400 CA	Multiquick 400 CA	4185	white	L. Littmann	
	MR 400 HC	Multiquick	4185	white	L. Littmann	
	MR 404	Multiquick 404	4185	yellow, blue	L. Littmann	
	MR 405	Multiquick 405	4185	white	L. Littmann	
	MR 430	Multiquick 430	4185	white	L. Littmann	
	MR 430 CA	Multiquick 430 CA	4185	white	L. Littmann	
	MR 430 HC	Multiquick	4185	white	L. Littmann	
1999	MR 404	Multiquick	4185	vanilla, aqua, chameleon	L. Littmann	
	MR 440 HC	Multiquick Baby Set	4185	chameleon	L. Littmann	
2000	M 700	Multimix	4683	vanilla	L. Littmann	
2001	**MR 5000/5550**	Multiquick/Minipimer professional	4191	white/grey	L. Littmann	**400, 414**
	MR 5550 BCHC	Multiquick/Minipimer professional	4191	white/grey	L. Littmann	
	MR 5550 CA	Multiquick/Minipimer professional	4191	white/grey	L. Littmann	
	MR 5550 M	Multiquick professional	4191	white	L. Littmann	
	MR 5550 MCA	Multiquick/Minipimer professional	4191	white/grey	L. Littmann	
	MR 5550 MBCHC	Multiquick professional	4191	white	L. Littmann	
2002	MR 404	Multiquick MR 404	4179	atlantic, sahara	L. Littmann/C. Seiffert	
2003	**MR 4000**	Multiquick Advantage	4193	white/turquoise	L. Littmann	**415**
	MR 4000 HC	Multiquick Advantage	4193	white/blue	L. Littmann	
	MR 4050 HC	Multiquick Advantage	4193	white/blue	L. Littmann	
2004	CT 600	FreshWare containers	4194	transparent	L. Littmann	
	CT 900	FreshWare containers	4194	transparent	L. Littmann	
	CT 1200	FreshWare containers	4194	transparent	L. Littmann	
	CT 3100	FreshWare containers	4194	transparent	L. Littmann	

Year	Type	Name	No.	Colour	Designer	Page
2004	MR 4050 HC-V	Multiquick Fresh System	4193	white/blue	L. Littmann	
	MR 5550 MCA-V	Multiquick Fresh System	4191	white/blue	L. Littmann	415
2005	MR 5000 FS	Multiquick Fresh Set	4194	white/blue, transp.	L. Littmann	

Juicers/ citrus presses

Year	Type	Name	No.	Colour	Designer	Page
1957	MP 3/31	Multipress	4203/4206	white	G. A. Müller	
1965	**MP 32**	Multipress	4152	white	G. A. Müller	416
	MPZ 1	Citruspresse	4153	white	R. Oberheim/R. Weiss	417
1970	**MP 50**	Multipress	4154	white	J. Greubel	416
1972	MPZ 2/21/22	citromatic/de luxe	4155/4979	white	D. Rams/J. Greubel	
1982	**MPZ 4**	citromatic 2	4173	white	L. Littmann	418
	MPZ 4	citromatic[1] citrus press		white	L. Littmann	
1983	MP 70	juicer[1]		white	L. Littmann	
1985	MR 63	citromatic[1] citrus press		white	D. Rams	
	MPZ 5	citromatic 3	4173	white	L. Littmann	
1988	**MP 80**	Multipress Plus automatic	4290	white	H. Kahlcke	420
1990	**MP 75**	Multipress compact	4235	white	L. Littmann	420
1992	MPZ 6	citromatic 6 compact	4161	white	L. Littmann	
	MPZ 7	citromatic 7 vario	4161	white	L. Littmann	418
1994	**MPZ 22**	citromatic/de luxe	4979	white	D. Rams/J. Greubel	384, 417
2003	**MPZ 9**	citromatic MPZ 9	4161	white	L. Littmann/S. Wuttig/I. Heyn	419

Grills

Year	Type	Name	No.	Colour	Designer	Page
1962	**HG 1**	combination grill	HG 1	chrome/black	R. Weiss	421
1970	HTG 1	tabletop grill	4001	aluminium/black	J. Greubel	
1971	**HAT 51**	Imbisstoaster Lunchquick	4014	aluminium/black	J. Greubel	
	HTG 2	Multigrill	4002	aluminium/black	J. Greubel	

Hotplates

Year	Type	Name	No.	Colour	Designer	Page
1972	**TT 10**	thermos tray	4005	aluminium/black	F. Seiffert	422
	TT 20	thermos tray	4005	aluminium/black	F. Seiffert	
	TT 30	thermos tray	4005	aluminium/black	F. Seiffert	

Water kettles

Year	Type	Name	No.	Colour	Designer	Page
1961	**HE 1/12**	water kettle	4911	chrome/black	R. Weiss	442
1999	**WK 210**	AquaExpress	3217	aqua, chameleon, vanilla, white	J. Greubel/L. Littmann	442
	WK 300	AquaExpress	3219	titanium, black	J. Greubel/L. Littmann	443
2001	WK 308	AquaExpress Juwel Edition	3219	silver-blue, silver-green	J. Greubel/L. Littmann/ D. Lubs	
2002	WK 210	AquaExpress WK 210	3217	atlantic, sahara	J. Greubel/L. Littmann/ C. Seiffert	
	WK 300	AquaExpress WK 300	3219	black/silver	L. Littmann	
2004	**WK 600**	Impression WK 600	3214	metallic	L. Littmann	443

Toasters

Year	Type	Name	No.	Colour	Designer	Page
1961	HT 1	toaster	4270	chrome/black	R. Weiss	
1963	**HT 2**	Automatictoaster	4011	chrome/black	R. Weiss	423

Year	Type	Name	No.	Colour	Designer	Page
1980	**HT 6**	toaster	4037	grey/silver, brown/silver	H. Kahlcke	**423**
	HT 50/55/56/57	infrarot electronic sensor	4104	white, red, black	H. Kahlcke	
	HT 40/45/46/47	electronic toaster	4102	white, red, black	H. Kahlcke	
1991	HT 70/75	Multitoast electronic-sensor	4107	white, red, black	L. Littmann	
	HT 80/85	Multitoast electronic-sensor	4108	white, red, black	L. Littmann	**424**
	HT 90/95	Multitoast infrared-sensor toaster	4109	white, red, black	L. Littmann	
1992	HT 180	Multitoast 180 toast + sandwich	4105	white	L. Littmann	
1994	HT 165	Multitoast 165 toast + sandwich	4105	white	L. Littmann	
2004	**HT 550**	MultiToast HT 550	4119	black, white, anthracite	L. Littmann	**425**
	HT 600	Impression HT 600	4118	metallic	L. Littmann	**425**
2005	**HT 450**	MultiToast HT 450	4120	black, white	L. Littmann	**424**

Coffee machines

Year	Type	Name	No.	Colour	Designer	Page
1972	**KF 20**	Aromaster	4050	white, yellow, orange, red, dark red, olive	F. Seiffert	**386**
1973	KTT	tea infuser	4050	black	F. Seiffert	
1976	**KF 21**	Aromaster	4051	white, yellow, orange	F. Seiffert/H. Kahlcke	450
1977	**KF 30**	Aromat	4052	white, yellow	H. Kahlcke	450
1978	**KF 35**	Traditional/2	4053	white, yellow	H. Kahlcke	451
1984	KF 40/45/60/65	Aromaster 10/plus 10/12/plus 12	4057/63	white, red/grey, red/black, black	H. Kahlcke	**390**, 452
	KF 50/55	Aromaster thermo 10	4058	white	H. Kahlcke	
	TF 1	tea filter	4057	transparent	H. Kahlcke	
1986	**KF 70/75**	Aromaster special 10/de luxe 10	4074/4079	white	H. Kahlcke	452
	KF 80/82/83	Aromaster control 12	4073/4091	white, black	H. Kahlcke	453
	KF 90/92	Aromaster control 10 s	4082/4097	white	H. Kahlcke	
1988	KF 22/26/32/36/ 8/10/8-plus/10-plus	Aromaster compact	4083	white, red/black, black	H. Kahlcke	
	KF 72/76	Aromaster 10/special de luxe	4094/4096	white	H. Kahlcke	
1989	KF 42/41 T/46/62/66	Aromaster 10/combi/plus/12/plus	4088/4093	white, red/grey, red/black, black	H. Kahlcke	
1990	KF 43T/43/ 47/63/67	Aromaster 43 combi/43/47, plus/63/63, 47/63/67 plus	4087/4069/ 4076/4077	white, red/black, black	H. Kahlcke/L. Littmann	
1991	KF 85	Aromaster 85 sensor control	3092	white, black	H. Kahlcke/L. Littmann	
1992	KF 74	Aromaster 74	3090	white	H. Kahlcke/L. Littmann	
1994	**KF 12**	Aromaster 12	3075	white, black	L. Littmann	453
	KF 140/145/ 150/155	AromaSelect 10/12	3093/3094/ 3095	white, red, black	R. Ullmann	
	KF 180/185/160	AromaSelect	3089/3097/ 3098	white, black	R. Ullmann	**454**
1995	KF 130	AromaSelect PureAqua	3111	white	R. Ullmann/L. Littmann	
	KF 130	AromaSelect PureAqua	3122	black	R. Ullmann/L. Littmann	
	KF 140	AromaSelect PureAqua 10	3066	white, black	R. Ullmann	
	KF 145	AromaSelect PureAqua 10	3067	white, black, red	R. Ullmann	
	KF 150	AromaSelect PureAqua 12	3068	white	R. Ullmann	
	KF 155	AromaSelect PureAqua 12/18	3069	white, black	R. Ullmann	
	KF 155	AromaSelect PureAqua 12/18	3069/3114	white	R. Ullmann	
	KF 170	AromaSelect thermoplus	3102	white	R. Ullmann	454
	KF 170	AromaSelect PureAqua 8/12	3072/3117	white	R. Ullmann	
	KF 185	AromaSelect PureAqua 12/18	3071/3116	white, black	R. Ullmann	
	KFT 150	AromaSelect PureAqua 12/18	3120	white	R. Ullmann	
	TF 2	AromaSelect tea filter	3120	white	R. Ullmann	
1997	KF 16	Aromaster pure aqua	3076	white	L. Littmann	

Year	Type	Name	No.	Colour	Designer	Page
1997	KF 37	Aromaster 37 compact	3085	white, black	H. Kahlcke	
	KFT 16	Aromaster PureAqua	3076	white	L. Littmann	
1998	KF 140	AromaSelect PureAqua	3111	blue, yellow	R. Ullmann/L. Littmann	
	KF 145	AromaSelect PureAqua	3112	blue, yellow	R. Ullmann/L. Littmann	
	KF 147	AromaSelect Pearl-Black Collection	3112	pearl-blue, green/black	R. Ullmann/L. Littmann	
1999	KF 130	AromaSelect PureAqua	3122	vanilla, aqua, chameleon	L. Littmann	
	KF 147	AromaSelect Millennium Edition	3112	pearl titanium/black	R. Ullmann/L. Littmann	**455**
	KF 177	AromaSelect Pearl-Black Collection	3117	pearl blue, pearl green	R. Ullmann/L. Littmann	
	KF 177	AromaSelect Pearl-Black Collection Millennium Edition	3117	pearl titanium/black	R. Ullmann/L. Littmann	
	KF 190	AromaSelect PureAqua Cappuccino	3123	titanium/black	L. Littmann/P. Vu	
2000	KF 37	Aromaster 37 compact	3085	vanilla	H. Kahlcke	
2001	KF 148	AromaSelect Juwel Edition	3112	silver-blue/silver-green	R. Ullmann/L. Littmann/D. Lubs	
	KF 178	AromaSelect Juwel Edition Thermo	3117	silver-blue/silver-green	R. Ullmann/L. Littmann/D. Lubs	**455**
2002	KF 130	Aroma Select KF 130	3122	sahara, atlantic	L. Littmann/C. Seiffert	
	KF 500	AromaPassion KF 500	3104	white/grey	B. Kling	
	KF 510	AromaPassion KF 510	3104	white/silver	B. Kling	
	KF 550	AromaPassion KF 550	3104	black/silver	B. Kling	**456**
	KF 580 E	AromaPassion time control KF 580 E	3105	black/silver	B. Kling	
2003	KF 540	AromaPassion	3104	black/silver	B. Kling	
2004	**KF 600**	Impression KF 600	3106	metallic	B. Kling	**456**

Espresso machines

Year	Type	Name	No.	Colour	Designer	Page
1991	E 250 T	Espresso Master	3062	white, matte black	L. Littmann	
	E 400 T	Espresso Master professional	3060	black/chrome	L. Littmann	**444**
1994	**E 20**	Espresso Master	3058	black	L. Littmann	**445**
	E 40	Espresso Master plus	3057	black	L. Littmann	
	E 300	Espresso Cappuccino Pro	3063	black	L. Littmann	
1995	**KFE 300**	Caféquattro	3064	black	L. Littmann	**445**
1996	E 600	Espresso Cappuccino Pro	3063	black	L. Littmann	

Coffee grinders

Year	Type	Name	No.	Colour	Designer	Page
1965	**KMM 1/121**	Aromatic coffee grinder w/stone-mill system	4398	white/red, white/green	R. Weiss	**446**
1967	**KSM 1/11**	Aromatic coffee grinder w/hammer mech.	4024/26	white, orange, red, green yellow, chrome/black	R. Weiss	**382**, 447
1969	**KMM 2**	Aromatic coffee grinder w/stone-mill system	4023	white, red, yellow	D. Rams	**448**
1970	CR 1	Aromatic[1] coffee grinder		white, yellow, red	D. Rams	
	CR 2	Aromatic[1] coffee grinder		white, red, yellow	D. Rams	
1975	**KMM 10**	Aromatic coffee grinder w/stone-mill system	4036	white, yellow	R. Weiss/H. Kahlcke	**446**
1978	CR 31	Aromatic[1] coffee grinder		white, yellow		
1979	KMM 20	Aromatic coffee grinder w/stone-mill system	4045	white, yellow	R. Weiss/H. Kahlcke	
	KSM 2	Aromatic coffee grinder w/hammer mech.	4041	white, yellow	H. Kahlcke	**449**
1980	CR 3	Aromatic[1] coffee grinder		white, yellow, orange, red		
1994	**KMM 30**	CaféSelect coffee/espresso grinder	3045	white, black	L. Littmann/J. Greubel	**449**
1995	M 30	Aromatic[1] coffee grinder		white	L. Littmann	

Heaters

Year	Type	Name	No.	Colour	Designer	Page
1959	**H 1/11**	heater w/thermostat	4305	white/grey	D. Rams	**380**, 432
1960	H 2/21	heater w/thermostat	4510	white/grey	D. Rams	
1962	H 3/31	heater w/thermostat	4513	white/grey	D. Rams	**432**

Year	Type	Name	No.	Colour	Designer	Page
1965	**H 6**	convection heater	4386	grey	R. Fischer/D. Rams	**433**
	HZ 1	room thermostat	4630	light grey	D. Rams	
1966	H 4	heater[1]	4514			
1967	**H 7**	heater[1]	4517	grey, brown	R. Weiss/D. Rams	**434**
1970	H 9	heater[1]		light grey	L. Littmann	
1973	**H 5**	Novotherm	4302	white, olive green, orange/black	J. Greubel	**434**
1979	H 91	heater[1]		light grey	L. Littmann	
1983	H 10	air heating apparatus	4358	white/black	L. Littmann	
1984	H 20	axial[1] heater		white, black	D. Rams	
	H 92	heater[1]		grey	L. Littmann	
1985	H 102	heater[1]		light grey	L. Littmann	
1986	H 103	heater[1]		light grey	L. Littmann	
1989	**H 30**	heater[1]		black/grey	L. Littmann	**435**
1991	H 104	heater[1]		white/black	L. Littmann	
1992	**H 200**	heater[1]		black/grey	L. Littmann	**435**

Tabletop heaters/ air filter

Year	Type	Name	No.	Colour	Designer	Page
1961	**HL 1/11**	Multiwind	4530	light grey, graphite	R. Weiss	**436**
1962	HL 2/23	car fan	4382	dark grey, brown	R. Weiss	
1971	**HL 70**	tabletop heater	4550–4552	white, brown, yell.	R. Weiss/J. Greubel	**436**
1973	ELF 1	Air-Control	4451	white, black	J. Greubel	**437**

Irons

Year	Type	Name	No.	Colour	Designer	Page
1979	PV 2	dry iron[1]		white/blue	L. Littmann	
1984	**PV 4 series**	vario 200/plus/special/de luxe	4374	white	L. Littmann	**438**
1986	PV 5 series	vario 5000/plus/special/ de luxe/protector	4374	white, green, blue	L. Littmann	
1987	PV 6 series	vario 6000/standard/plus/special/ protector electro	4332/4334/ 4378/4381	white, blue	L. Littmann	
1989	**PV 3 series**		4323–4325/4347	white/black	L. Littmann	**439**
1992	PV 7 series	saphir 7000/ultra/sensor/protector	4388/4389/4399	white	L. Littmann	
	PV 5 series	5000/standard/super/special/ protector saphir 5000/standard/super	4322/4333/4262–4365	white/grey	L. Littmann	
1995	PV 1000	Turbo-jet	4316	white/grey	J. Greubel/L. Littmann	
	PV 1002	Turbo-jet	4318	white/grey	J. Greubel/L. Littmann	
	PV 1005	Turbo-jet	4313	white/grey	J. Greubel/L. Littmann	
	PV 1010	Turbo-jet	4314	white/grey	J. Greubel/L. Littmann	
	PV 1200	Ceramic-jet	4319	white/mint	J. Greubel/L. Littmann	
	PV 1205	Ceramic-jet	4394	white/green	J. Greubel/L. Littmann	**440**
	PV 1202	Ceramic-jet	4300	white/mint	J. Greubel/L. Littmann	
	PV 1210	Ceramic-jet	4683	white/green	J. Greubel/L. Littmann	
	PV 1212	Ceramic-jet	4682	white/mint	J. Greubel/L. Littmann	
	PV 1500	steam iron[1]		white	J. Greubel/L. Littmann	
	PV 1505	Saphir-jet	4315	white/blue	J. Greubel/L. Littmann	
	PV 1510	Saphir-jet	4684	white/blue	J. Greubel/L. Littmann	
	PV 1512	Saphir-jet	4687	white/blue	J. Greubel/L. Littmann	
	PV 1550	Saphir-jet	4686	white/blue	J. Greubel/L. Littmann	
	PV 2200	steam iron[1]		white	J. Greubel/L. Littmann	
1996	PV 1502	Saphir-jet	4685	white/blue	J. Greubel/L. Littmann	
	PV 2500	steam iron[1]		white	J. Greubel/L. Littmann	
1997	PV 2000	steam iron[1]		white	J. Greubel/L. Littmann	

Year	Type	Name	No.	Colour	Designer	Page
1997	PV 2002	Combi-jet	4691	white/grey	J. Greubel/L. Littmann	
	PV 2005	Combi-jet	4691	white/grey	J. Greubel/L. Littmann	
	PV 2202	ProGlide-jet	4692	white/mint	J. Greubel/L. Littmann	
	PV 2205	ProGlide-jet	4692	white/green	J. Greubel/L. Littmann	
	PV 2210	ProGlide-jet	4692	white/green	J. Greubel/L. Littmann	
	PV 2502	Saphir-jet	4689	white/blue	J. Greubel/L. Littmann	
	PV 2505	Saphir-jet	4689	white/blue	J. Greubel/L. Littmann	
	PV 2510	Saphir-jet	4689	white/blue	J. Greubel/L. Littmann	
	PV 2512	Saphir-jet	4689	white/blue	J. Greubel/L. Littmann	
	PV 2550	Saphir-jet	4693	white/blue	J. Greubel/L. Littmann	
1999	PV 3102	OptiGlide-jet	4695	vanilla	J. Greubel/L. Littmann	
	PV 3110	OptiGlide-jet	4695	vanilla	J. Greubel/L. Littmann	
	PV 3205	ProGlide-jet	4696	dark green	J. Greubel/L. Littmann	
	PV 3210	ProGlide-jet	4696	light green	J. Greubel/L. Littmann	
	PV 3505	Saphir-jet	4697	light blue	J. Greubel/L. Littmann	
	PV 3512	Saphir-jet	4697	blue	J. Greubel/L. Littmann	
	PV 3570	Saphir-jet	4697	light blue	J. Greubel/L. Littmann	
	PV 3580	Saphir-jet	4698	light blue	J. Greubel/L. Littmann	
2000	SI 6210	steam iron[1]		pastel grey, pastel blue, white	L. Littmann/J. Greubel	
	SI 6220	FreeStyle SI 6220	4696	light blue	L. Littmann/J. Greubel	
	SI 6230	steam iron[1]		white	L. Littmann/J. Greubel	
	SI 6510	FreeStyle SI 6510	4696	lilac	L. Littmann/J. Greubel	**398**
	SI 6530	FreeStyle Saphir	4694	green	L. Littmann/J. Greubel	
	SI 8510	ProStyle SI 8510	4697	light blue	J. Greubel/L. Littmann	
	SI 8570	ProStyle SI 8570	4697	light blue	J. Greubel/L. Littmann	
	SI 8580	ProStyle SI 8580	4698	light blue	J. Greubel/L. Littmann	
	PV 8512	steam iron[1]		white	J. Greubel/L. Littmann	
2001	**SI 6575**	FreeStyle Saphir	4694	silver-metallic	L. Littmann/J. Greubel	**440**
2002	SI 6585	steam iron[1]		w./green, blue/green, pastel blue, white/grey, blue	L. Littmann/J. Greubel	
	SI 4000	Easy Style SI 4000	4670	blue	L. Littmann	
2003	SI 3120	OptiStyle SI 3120	4695	light green	J. Greubel/L. Littmann	
	SI 3230	OptiStyle SI 3230	4671	light blue	J. Greubel/L. Littmann	
	SI 6120	steam iron[1]		white	L. Littmann/J. Greubel	
	SI 6250	steam iron[1]		blue, lilac	L. Littmann/J. Greubel	
	SI 6260	steam iron[1]		lilac	L. Littmann/J. Greubel	
	SI 6550	steam iron[1]		green	L. Littmann/J. Greubel	
	SI 6560	Freestyle SI 6560	4674	light lilac	L. Littmann/J. Greubel	
	SI 6590	Freestyle SI 6590	4675	silver-metallic	L. Littmann/J. Greubel	
	SI 6595	steam iron[1]		white/met., dark blue	L. Littmann/J. Greubel	
	SI 8520	ProStyle SI 8520	4672	blue-metallic	J. Greubel/L. Littmann	
	SI 8520	steam iron[1]		white/blue-metallic	J. Greubel/L. Littmann	
	SI 8590	ProStyle SI 8590	4672	blue-metallic	J. Greubel/L. Littmann	
	SI 8595	ProStyle SI 8595	4673	blue-metallic	J. Greubel/L. Littmann	
	SI 8590	steam iron[1]		white/blue-metallic	J. Greubel/L. Littmann	
2004	SI 9200	FreeStyle Excel SI 9200	4678	green	L. Littmann/M. Orthey	
	SI 9500	FreeStyle Excel SI 9500	4677	blue	L. Littmann/M. Orthey	**441**

Year	Type	Name	No.	Colour	Designer	Page

Other Appliances

Year	Type	Name	No.	Colour	Designer	Page
1961	**HGS 10/20**	tabletop dishwasher		white	manufactured in USA	**429**
1964	**HMT 1**	Multitherm electric skillet	4921	chrome/black	R. Weiss/D. Lubs	**422**
	HTK 5	freezer		white	D. Rams	**431**
	KZ 1/11	kitchen waste grinder	4950	white/green	manufactured in USA	
1970	H 0 750	oil radiator[1]		white	D. Rams	
	AM 2	hand-held vacuum cleaner[1]		white/blue	H. Kahlcke	
	AT 1	vacuum cleaner[1]		white/blue	D. Rams	
1971	CO 1	Abrematic[1] can opener		white	J. Greubel	
1972	DS 1	Sesamat can opener	4922	white	D. Rams/J. Greubel	
1973	**US 10**	universal slicer electric	4933	white	K. Dittert	**426**
	US 20	universal slicer electronic	4926	white	J. Greubel	**427**
1974	AM 6	hand-held vacuum cleaner[1]		white/blue	H. Kahlcke	
	WT 10	drymatic clothes dryer	4990	white	J. Greubel	**430**
1975	AM 4	hand-held vacuum cleaner[1]		white/blue, orange	H. Kahlcke	
	AT 4	vacuum cleaner[1]		white/blue	D. Rams	
1976	AT 2	vacuum cleaner[1]		white/blue	H. Kahlcke	
	AT 5	vacuum cleaner[1]		white/blue	H. Kahlcke	
	AM 5	hand-held vacuum cleaner[1]		white/blue, brown	H. Kahlcke	
	AM 7	hand-held vacuum cleaner[1]		white/blue	H. Kahlcke	
	FP 1	floor polisher[1]		white/grey	D. Rams	
1977	AT 3	vacuum cleaner[1]		white/blue	D. Rams	
	YG 1	yoghurt maker[1]		white	D. Rams	
1978	**EK 1**	electric knife[1]		white	L. Littmann	**428**
	LM 1	electric carpet cleaner[1]		white	D. Rams	
	LM 2	electric carpet cleaner[1]		white	D. Rams	
	PS 2	radiator[1]		white	H. Kahlcke	
	PS 3	radiator[1]		white	H. Kahlcke	
1980	FP 2	floor polisher[1]		white/grey	D. Rams	
	WF1	water filter[1]		white	H. Kahlcke	
1982	AT 7	vacuum cleaner[1]		grey	D. Rams	
	AT 8	vacuum cleaner[1]		orange	D. Rams	
1983	H 10	radiator[1]		white/black	L. Littmann	
1984	YG 2	yoghurt maker[1]		white	L. Littmann	
1985	AT 6	vacuum cleaner[1]		white, green, grey	D. Rams	
	FR 2	deep fryer[1]		black	L. Littmann	
1996	**FS 10**	MultiGourmet steamer	3216	white	L. Littmann	**428**
	FS 20	MultiGourmet plus steamer	3216	white	L. Littmann	

1 Manufactured in Barcelona, without further details

Registered trademarks: 3D Excel, Activator, Allstyle, AquaExpress, AromaPassion, AromaSelect, Aromaster, Aromatic, Braun exact, Flex control, Braun linear, Braun reflex, Braun silencio, Braun universelle, Braun voice control, CaféSelect, Ceramic-jet, citromatic, Combi-jet, Combimax, cosmo, cruZer[3], E.Razor, Flex, Flex Integral, Flex XP, FreeGlider, FreeStyle, Impression, Independent, Interclean, InterFace, Lady Braun, micron, Minipimer, MultiGourmet, Multimix, Multi-practic, Multipress, Multiquick, OptiStyle, OxyJet, Plak Control, Plak Control 3D, Pocket Twist, PowerBlend, PowerMax, ProGlide-jet, Professional Care, PrecisionSensor, Protector, Silencio, Silk-épil, Saphir, Shave & Shape, Silk&Soft, sixtant, Smart Logic, Straight & Shape, supervolume, supervolume twist, Swing, synchron, Syncro, ThermoScan, TriControl, VitalScan, volume shaper, control shaper, style shaper, Turbo-jet.

Braun Design. Biographies

Otl Aicher, 1922–1991. Graphic artist, designer and writer. He was a co-founder and for a time director of the Ulm Academy of Design and a lecturer there in Visual Communication starting in 1954. Pioneer of Corporate Design (designed the corporate identity of the Olympics in Munich in 1972). At Braun from 1955 to 1958. Along with →Hans Gugelot, designed the company's new coherent, rational corporate image, which was then implemented by →Wolfgang Schmittel

Artur Braun, born 1925. Son of Max Braun. Entrepreneur, technician and inventor. Learned electrical engineering in his father's company after completing his schooling. Co-director of the company with his brother, Erwin, from 1951 to 1967, supporting him with restructuring; in charge of technical development and production. Product design of milestone *SK 1* radio with Fritz Eichler (page 74).

Erwin Braun, 1921–1992. Son of Max Braun. Entrepreneur, art connoisseur and jazz fan; described by contemporaries as a sensitive and ambitious man. 1946–1949 studied business administration. Co-directed the company after his father's death with his brother, Artur, from 1951 to 1967. Was the driving force behind the Braun Design project, which, like his friend and advisor →Fritz Eichler, he regarded as part of a comprehensive, integrated concept involving not only innovative technology but also the creation of a distinctive corporate identity (→Wolfgang Schmittel) as well as product design (→Dieter Rams). His friends included artists such as Arnold Bode, designers such as →Otl Aicher, Hans T. Baumann, →Hans Gugelot, →Herbert Hirche and Peter Raacke as well as the entrepreneur Philip Rosenthal. Founded the Braun Prize. After leaving the company he devoted himself to medicine, his true passion, earning the title "Dr. med." in 1988.

Max Braun, 1890–1951. Entrepreneur and inventor. Grew up in the East Prussian countryside. Worked before the First World War in Berlin (including at AEG and Siemens), acquiring knowledge in mechanical and electrical engineering, and founded his own workshop for appliances in 1921; in 1928 the first factory building in Frankfurt; in 1929 the first radio. Already adopted an international orientation in the 1930s as "Braun Radio". Produced a dynamo flashlight in the 1940s, household appliances and electric shavers beginning in 1950.

Rido Busse, Industrial designer and entrepreneur. Designed products for Braun in the 1970s, including the *duo* pocket lighter (1977).

Claus C. Cobarg, born 1921. Physicist; studied under Werner Heisenberg and others. Worked at Braun from 1957 to 1986.

Developer, director of central laboratory and director of engineering for the New Products department. Set up a documentation system for the Engineering Department, devoting time to compiling a product history even after leaving the company; since 1968 scientific-technical advisor to Braun Prize jury.

Karl Dittert, born 1915. Furniture and industrial designer. *US 10* universal slicer for Braun (1958).

Fritz Eichler, 1911–1991. Art historian, painter, film director and design organizer. 1935 doctorate in theatre studies. Freelance starting in 1953, 1955–1978 employed at Braun; on Supervisory Board until 1990. Close friend and advisor of →Erwin Braun. "Dr. Ei" quickly became the top advisor in aesthetic matters. Responsible for contacts with the Ulm Academy of Design (→Otl Aicher, →Hans Gugelot). As guiding spirit of Braun Design, saw it as an interdisciplinary project embedded in a cultural framework and situated between technology, advertising and marketing – himself acting as mediator, especially between communication (→Wolfgang Schmittel) and product design (→Dieter Rams). In the beginning he also designed products and made sure colour schemes were consistent, e.g. in the *SK 4* and *sixtant* shaver. Milestone: *SK 1* radio with Artur Braun (page 74).

Richard Fischer, born 1935. Industrial designer. Studied at the Ulm Academy of Design. At Braun from 1960 to 1968; designed numerous electric shavers (from 1963), household appliances and photographic devices, including the *hobby professional* flash (1961).

Jürgen Greubel, born 1938. Industrial designer. Studied at the University of Applied Sciences in Wiesbaden. At Braun from 1967 to 1973. Worked 1973–1975 at DRU, Design Research Unit, London. Design work for London Transport. Designed products in the areas of body care and household appliances, including grills and heaters. Was involved in the development of the *Lectron* learning system. Stood for a softer flow of line at Braun, featured in the *Multipress MP 50, MPZ 2* citrus press, *DS 1* can opener and *HLD 6/61* hair dryer. Independent designer for Braun and others since 1976.

Hans Gugelot, 1920–1965. Architect, engineer, product and furniture designer. Of Dutch origin, grew up in Switzerland. Taught at the Ulm Academy of Design and was contact there for →Erwin Braun (who called him the "actual creator of Braun Design, with the help of →Otl Aicher"). With Aicher and →Herbert Lindinger, shaped the new corporate identity. Systematic approach; designs for phono devices, shavers and a flashlight. Milestones: *SK 4* with Dieter Rams (page 76) and *sixtant* shaver with Gerd Alfred Müller (page 268).

Heinz Ullrich Haase, born 1949. Industrial designer. Studied at University of Wuppertal; planner at various architecture offices. At Braun from 1973 to 1978; designed curling irons and hair dryers, including the milestone *PGC 1000* (page 304).

Peter Hartwein, born 1942. After apprenticing as a carpenter and studying interior design at a school of applied arts, structural engineering planning at various architecture offices. 1967–1970 industrial architecture in Peter C. von Seidlein's office, Munich. Since 1970 industrial designer at Braun. Designed especially projects in photography (slide and film projectors), phonographs (from 1977), oral care and blood pressure monitors, from 1990 also worked on various corporate identity projects, such as the new administrative building in Kronberg. Milestones: *atelier* hi-fi system (page 98), *OC 3 dental center* (page 348) and *D 7022 Plak Control* electric toothbrush (page 352).

Herbert Hirche, 1910–2002. Architect, furniture and industrial designer. Studied at the Bauhaus and worked with Ludwig Mies van der Rohe. Following Second World War, high-profile representative of Modernism. Organized exhibitions such as *Die Gute Industrieform* (1952). At Braun from 1958 to 1963, responsible for designing radios, television sets and a home for →Erwin Braun. Milestone: *HF 1* television (page 80).

Arne Jacobsen, 1902–1971. Danish architect, furniture and industrial designer. Combined industrial production with organic form. *L 460* round speaker for Braun (1967).

Hartwig Kahlcke, born 1942. Industrial designer. At Braun from 1970 to 1988 (thereafter design studio with →Florian Seiffert). Analytical approach; continued clear line from Braun's early days. Household appliance designs. Milestones: *KGZ 3* meat grinder (page 392) and *KF 40* coffee machine (page 390).

Björn Kling, born 1965. Industrial designer. Studied at University of Fine Arts in Hamburg, under →Dieter Rams. Second place in 1992 Braun Prize. At Braun since 1993. In addition to product design, also in charge of colour and trend research. Designs primarily in the fields of oral and body care, household appliances and shavers. Milestones: *PRSC 1800 Professional* hair dryer (page 306) and *ThermoScan IRT Pro 3000* with Dietrich Lubs (page 310).

Herbert Lindinger, born 1933. Graphic artist and industrial designer. At Braun from 1955 to 1958 as part of Gugelot working group at the Ulm Academy of Design; designed *studio 1* hi-fi system (with Hans Gugelot); in his dissertation, developed – encouraged by Gugelot – the basic ideas behind the phono "building

block system". Milestone: *SK 4* compact radio-phonograph system with Hans Gugelot and Dieter Rams (page 76).

Ludwig Littmann, born 1946. Industrial designer. Studied at the Folkwang School of Design in Essen. Winner of 1972 Braun Prize. At Braun since 1973; designs primarily in the household appliances area. Analytical, ergonomic approach; recent designs increasingly feature free-form surfaces and almost always hard-and-soft technology; development of a sculptural and emotional formal repertoire. Milestones: *MR 500* (page 394) and *MR 5000* (page 400) handblenders and *FreeStyle* iron (page 398).

Dietrich Lubs, born 1938. Industrial designer. Learned ship-building; at Braun from 1962 to 2001; deputy director of the Design Department from 1995. From 1971 in charge of product graphics; designs mainly in the areas of clocks and pocket calculators. Milestones: *functional* (page 210) and *voice control* (page 218) alarm clocks, *DB 10* (page 220) and *DW 30* (page 212) wristwatches, *ABW 41* wall clock (page 216), *ABR 21* radio alarm clock with Dieter Rams (page 214) and *ThermoScan* thermometer (page 310).

Rory McGarry, born 1979 in Cambridge, Ontario, Canada. Industrial designer. Studied at Ontario College of Art and Design, Toronto (Canada). Participant in Braun Prize exhibition in 2003. At Braun since 2004. Works mainly in oral care field.

Gerd Alfred Müller, 1932–1991. Industrial designer. Studied at School of Applied Arts in Wiesbaden, where he met →Dieter Rams. At Braun from 1955 to 1960 as permanently employed industrial designer; designed shavers and household appliances. With his analytical, organic approach, represented an important line in early Braun Design. Milestones: *KM 3* food processor (page 376) and *sixtant* shaver with →Hans Gugelot (page 268).

Robert Oberheim, born 1938. Industrial designer. Studied at School of Applied Arts in Wiesbaden. At Braun from 1960 to 1994. Worked mostly in the film and photography field and in hair care; from 1973 deputy director of the Design Department. Analytical approach with organic, ergonomic elements. Designed some of the early black products. Milestones: *Nizo S 8* cine film camera (page 176), *D 300* slide projector (page 178) and *F 022* flash (page 180).

Markus Orthey, born 1973. Industrial designer. Design studies at University of Applied Sciences in Mainz, including under →Florian Seiffert, and at Swinburne University, Melbourne, Australia; freelancer in various design offices, some in Japan. At Braun since 2001. Focus on computer-assisted design. Designs for household appliances (*FreeStyle Excel* steam iron station), clocks (*AW 200 F* radio-controlled wristwatch with →Peter Hartwein) and oral care (*D 18* with →Björn Kling).

Dieter Rams, born 1932. Product and furniture designer. Architecture studies at School of Applied Arts in Wiesbaden. At Braun from 1955 to 1997. 1961–1995 director of the Design Department; representative of "good design" vis-à-vis the Executive Board, engineering, marketing and public. 1981 professor at University of Fine Arts in Hamburg. 1988–1998 president of Rat für Formgebung (Design Council). Numerous designs in radio and phonograph field, as well as for lighters, clocks and household appliances. Analytical approach with references to classical Modernism. Milestones: *SK 4* compact radio-phonograph system with Hans Gugelot and Herbert Lindinger (page 76), *TP 1* phono combination (page 82), *studio 2* hi-fi system (page 84), *T 1000* short-wave radio (page 86), *PS 1000* record player (page 90), *TG 60* tape recorder (page 92), *L710* speaker (page 94), *audio 308* compact phonograph system (page 96), *manulux NC* flashlight with Reinhold Weiss (page 252), *T 2* and *T 3* flashlights (pages 248 and 250), *ABR 21* radio alarm clock with Dietrich Lubs (page 214) and *H 1* heater (page 380).

Wolfgang Schmittel, born 1930. Graphic artist, advertising specialist and photographer. At Braun 1952–1980. Designed the Braun logo in 1952 based on a grid. Made key contribution to a consistent corporate identity, designed according to the rational principles promulgated by →Otl Aicher. From 1958 manager of the newly founded Advertising Department (director from 1962), which at times employed a staff of over 50 and had its own film and animation studio. Has been photographing jazz musicians since the 1950s (some of these motifs were used in Braun ads). Developed the Gillette logo around 1970, which is still in use in slightly modified form; responsible for choosing agencies in the 1970s that today work for Braun worldwide; later professor of Visual Communication in Columbus, Ohio, USA, and Schwäbisch Gmünd.

Peter Schneider, born 1945. Industrial designer. Grew up in South America. Studied design at Folkwang School of Design in Essen. At Braun since 1973 (winner of Braun Prize). Since the 1980s also in charge of external contracts (Deutsche Bank, Hoechst AG, Lufthansa, etc.); created a new CI and product look for Jafra Cosmetics; developed the cooperation with Gillette subsidiary Oral-B that led to the new Braun field of toothbrushes. Director of the Design Department since 1995; had the Braun logo redesigned. Since 1996 chairman of Braun Prize jury. Designs in all areas, mainly film and photography, along with oral and body care. Future-oriented, analytical approach taking into account emotional aspects. Milestones: *integral* cine film camera

(page 182), *Silk-épil eversoft* epilation device (page 308), *Oral-B Plus* (page 350) and *Cross Action* (page 354) toothbrushes, both with Jürgen Greubel.

Cornelia Seifert, born 1961. Industrial designer. Design studies at University of Design in Pforzheim; assistant there until 1991; 1991–2003 at Braun; designs in the field of body care, including *supervolume* hair dryer.

Florian Seiffert, born 1943. Industrial designer. Design studies at Folkwang School of Design in Essen; professor at University of Applied Sciences in Mainz. Winner of first Braun Prize, in 1968. At Braun 1968–1973. Thereafter independent designer (studio with →Hartwig Kahlcke in Wiesbaden); works for Braun and others. Designs primarily in the areas of household appliances and shavers. Analytical approach, taking into account emotional aspects. Milestone: *KF 20* coffee machine (page 386).

Roland Ullmann, born 1948. Industrial designer. Technical training at Siemens in Frankfurt; studies at University of Design in Offenbach. At Braun since 1972; designs mainly shavers (since 1977); had major role in shaping the look of the modern electric razor; patented improvements in shaving technology; one of the main developers of hard-and-soft technology. Analytical approach incorporating organic forms and references to classical Modernism. Also coordinates Advanced Design; numerous contributions to this field in various product areas. Designed the top-selling coffee machine *Aromaselect*. Milestones: *micron plus* (page 272), *micron vario* (page 274), *Flex Integral 5550* (page 276) and *Activator* (page 278) shavers.

Duy Phong Vu, born 1972 in Vietnam. Industrial designer; dissertation under →Peter Schneider. Trained as model builder and studied design at University of Design in Darmstadt. At Braun since 1998. The Vietnamese designer works mainly in the areas of body and oral care, including cooperation with external manufacturers; designs include Oral-B *sonic complete* electric toothbrush

Wilhelm Wagenfeld, 1900–1990. Industrial designer. Studied at the Bauhaus. Worked for various glassmakers in the 1930s; personified the link between classical Modernism and the "good form" propagated in the 1950s. 1954–1958 designs for Braun (according to Erwin Braun, the "mentor" of Braun Design). His designs, including the *combi* portable phonograph, a shaver plug and the *PC-3* record player, exhibited organic forms.

Benjamin Wilson, born 1979 in Melbourne, Australia. Industrial designer. Studied at Swinburne National School of Design (Australia). 2001–2002 Swinburne Design Center, 1999–2003

international internships. Participant in Braun Prize exhibition in 2003. At Braun since 2003. Mainly active in oral care and Trends & Research (*Future Lab*) areas.

Till Winkler, born 1965. Industrial designer. Design studies at University of Kassel; 1995 grant from the International Forum for Design in Ulm; at Braun since 1996; since 1998 assistant to Braun Prize jury; responsible for the design of numerous tooth-brushes for Oral-B, including *New Indicator.*

Reinhold Weiss, born 1934. Industrial designer. Graduated from Ulm Academy of Design; 1959–1967 at Braun; from 1962 deputy director of the Design Department. Introduced model building to the company. Designs primarily in the household appliance area. Was responsible for introducing many new prod-ucts to the range. Analytical approach with close interplay between technical structure and design. Milestone: *KSM 1/11* coffee grinder (page 382).

Sven Wuttig, born 1970. Industrial designer. Trained as industrial clerk and studied design at University of Applied Sciences in Darmstadt. 1998–2004 ran design office vierdeedesign with Ingo Heyn. Winner of 2001 Braun Prize. At Braun since 2004. Designs and concepts in the area of corporate identity and the Braun Prize.

Klaus Zimmermann, born 1945. Master model builder. Training as model builder in Frankfurt; at Braun since 1968. Graduated from Master School for Model Building in Bielefeld in 1974; direc-tor of design model building at Braun since 1987. Developed this field crucial to visualization from simple beginnings into a high-tech discipline able to realize even complex designs with a high degree of perfection; played a key role in the development of sur-faces, especially with respect to hard-and-soft technology and the creation of a colour database.

Bibliography

Sigfried Giedion, *Mechanization takes Command*, Oxford 1948

Alexander Mitscherlich, *Die Unwirtlichkeit unserer Städte. Anstiftung zum Unfrieden*, Frankfurt am Main 1965

Leo Kofler, *Geschichte und Dialektik*, Darmstadt 1972

Earl Lifshey, *The Housewares Story. A History of the American Housewares Industry*, Chicago 1973

Wolfgang Schmittel, *design concept realisation*, Zurich 1975

Herbert Hirche and Dieter Godel, *herbert hirche. architektur innenraum design 1945–1978*, Stuttgart 1978

Wolfgang Schmittel, *process visual. Entwicklung eines Firmen-profils*, Zurich 1978

François Burkhardt and Inez Franksen (eds.), *Design. Dieter Rams &*, Berlin 1981

Heinz Hirdina, *Neues Bauen. Neues Gestalten. Das Neue Frankfurt / die neue stadt. Eine Zeitschrift zwischen 1926 und 1933*, Dresden 1984

Kenneth Frampton, *Die Architektur der Moderne*, Stuttgart 1987

Hans Wichmann (ed.), *System-Design Bahnbrecher: Hans Gugelot 1920–65*, Basel 1987

Bernd Polster (ed.), *Swing Heil! Jazz im Nationalsozialismus*, Berlin 1989

Michael Erlhoff, *Designed in Germany. Since 1949*, Munich 1990

Jo Klatt and Günter Staeffler, *Braun + Design Collection*, Ham-burg 1990 and 1995

Rudolf Schönwandt, *German Design. Neue Dimensionen für Form und Funktion*, Dortmund 1990

Christian Marquart, *Industrial Culture – Industrial Design*, Berlin 1991

Phil Patton, *Made in USA. The Secret History of the Things that Made America*, New York 1993

Maribel Königer, *Küchengerät des 20. Jahrhunderts. Kochen mit Stil und Styling*, Munich 1994

Jochen Wiesinger, *Die Geschichte der Unterhaltungselektronik*, Frankfurt am Main 1994

Frank Gnegel, *Bart ab. Zur Geschichte der Selbstrasur*, Cologne 1995

Eric Hobsbawm, *Das Zeitalter der Extreme. Weltgeschichte des 20. Jahrhunderts*, Munich 1995

Dieter Rams, *Weniger, aber besser*, Hamburg 1995

Artur Braun, *Max Brauns Rasierer*, Hamburg 1996

Hans Wichmann, *Mut zum Aufbruch. Erwin Braun 1921–1992*, Munich 1998

Matthias Götz (ed.), *Der Tabasco-Effekt. Wirkung der Form, Formen der Wirkung*, Basel and Halle 1999

Claudia Neumann, *Designlexikon Italien*, Cologne 1999

Bernd Polster, *Designlexikon Skandinavien*, Cologne 1999

Bernd Polster and Marion Godau, *Designlexikon Deutschland*, Cologne 2000

Nicola Stattmann, *Handbuch Materialtechnologie*, Ludwigsburg 2000

Kai Buchholz et al. (eds.), *Die Lebensreform. Entwürfe zur Neu-gestaltung von Leben und Kunst um 1900*, Darmstadt 2001 (2 volumes)

Andreas Dorschel, *Gestaltung. Zur Ästhetik des Brauchbaren*, Heidelberg 2002

Heine et al. (eds.), *Ansichten von und zu Dieter Rams*, August 2002

Bernd Polster and Tim Elsner, *Designlexikon USA*, Cologne 2002

HfG-Archiv (ed.), *ulmer modelle – modelle nach ulm. Hochschule für Gestaltung Ulm 1953–1968*, Ulm 2003

IF International (ed.), *50 Jahre IF*, Hanover 2003

Volker Gebhard, *Das Deutsche in der deutschen Kunst*, Cologne 2004

Bernd Polster (ed.), *Handbuch Design International*, Cologne 2004

Braun Materials

- Braun phonograph catalogues, 1955–1990
- Standards for the visual presentation of information and advertising, Braun, ca. 1960
- Annual reports, 1961–2002
- Braun photo and film catalogues, 1961–1979
- Unsere Haltung. Brauns Unternehmensphilosophie (German/English), Braun 1979
- Braun typography standards, Braun 1979–2004
- Ansichten zum Design [Views on Design]; Braun Design – the realization of a business plan; Guidelines for correspondence, Guidelines for Braun packaging design; Braun retrospective 1921–79; Company history (pamphlets in slipcase), Braun 1979/1980
- Braun catalogues, 1955–2005
- Braun beispielsweise, Sonderdruck Kunst. Design, Wirtschaft, 1983
- Ansichten zum Design [Views on Design], 1988
- Braun Design. Principles and standards, Braun communications department, 1989
- Braun Design, Braun GmbH / Peter Schneider 2002
- Interview transcripts, 2002–2005, including all current Braun designers and the designers Herbert Lindinger, Hartwig Kahlcke and Florian Seiffert, as well as Claus C. Cobarg, Dieter Rams, Wolfgang Schmittel, Dieter Skerutsch and Bernhard Wild (Supervisory Board Chairman of Braun GmbH)
- Design models, presentation in 2003

  www.braun.com

  www.braunpreis.de

  www.braun-sammlung.info

Thanks

We wish to thank the Braun company for its support and intensive cooperation, without which this project would not have been possible. Our special thanks go to Peter Schneider, who worked with us to develop the idea for this book, Bernhard Wild and Dieter Rams, Gerlinde Kress, Horst Kaupp (CCS), Claus C. Cobarg and Josefa Gonzalez, as well as all the current and former Braun designers who so willingly provided us with information about their work and designs.